# Wellington's
# Worst Scrape

# Wellington's Worst Scrape

## The Burgos Campaign 1812

*To Fiona,*
*With best wishes,*

Carole Divall

Pen & Sword
**MILITARY**

First published in Great Britain in 2012 by
**PEN & SWORD MILITARY**
An imprint of
Pen & Sword Books Ltd
47 Church Street
Barnsley
South Yorkshire
S70 2AS

ISBN 978-1-84884-842-9

Typeset by Concept, Huddersfield, West Yorkshire.
Printed and bound in England by the MPG Books Group, Ltd.

Pen & Sword Books Ltd incorporates the imprints of Pen & Sword Aviation,
Pen & Sword Family History, Pen & Sword Maritime, Pen & Sword Military,
Pen & Sword Discovery, Wharncliffe Local History, Wharncliffe True Crime,
Wharncliffe Transport, Pen & Sword Select, Pen & Sword Military Classics,
Leo Cooper, The Praetorian Press, Remember When, Seaforth Publishing and
Frontline Publishing.

For a complete list of Pen & Sword titles please contact
PEN & SWORD BOOKS LIMITED
47 Church Street, Barnsley, South Yorkshire, S70 2AS, England
E-mail: enquiries@pen-and-sword.co.uk
Website: www.pen-and-sword.co.uk

# Contents

## Dedication

To John and Mary, good friends and fellow travellers
on the retreat from Burgos

# List of Maps

# List of Plates

# Preface

On 12 August an Anglo-Portuguese army under the command of Arthur Wellesley, Lord Wellington, marched in triumph through the streets of Madrid. The conquerors of the border fortresses of Ciudad Rodrigo and Badajoz, and the victors of Salamanca, had brought the war against the French to the very heart of Spain. Three months later, that same army under that same commander were once more on the Portuguese border, where their campaign had started eleven months before. They had not marched back in triumph. Instead they had slunk away from Salamanca and dragged themselves back through torrential rain and ankle-deep mud. Between the August triumph and what in November looked like defeat lay the fortress of Burgos, the only fortress that successfully resisted Wellington's attempt to take it, and the site of his worst scrape.

Both the failed siege and the retreat that followed, as well as the French campaign which chased the allied army back to Portugal, are stories of human endeavour which embrace all that is best and all that is worst in human nature. Deeds of great courage and humanity marched in tandem with cruelty, despair and all the excesses of indiscipline. For the nations involved – Britain, France, Spain and Portugal – there was much to admire and much to deplore.

There are many histories of these events, from the monumental works of Napier, Oman and Fortescue to modern reinterpretations, often with a specific national focus, which seek to reinterpret what happened at Burgos and afterwards. Military historians inevitably focus on strategy and tactics, on the objectives and achievements of a campaign and the mistakes made. They create what might be termed the big military picture. However, there are other stories to be told: the stories of the thousands of men who marched and fought and died in the autumn of 1812.

Interestingly, the first account of the retreat, which was published in 1814, was written by an assistant surgeon, George Frederick Burroughs, whose intention seems to have been not just to relate what happened, but also what it felt like to be part of the events he was describing. What I have tried to create, in this study of Wellington's worst scrape, as he himself termed it, is a similar focus on the experiences and perceptions of those involved, from the men in command to those in the ranks and even those who trailed behind the armies.

The Napoleonic Wars are notable for the wealth of written material they generated, either in the form of contemporaneous accounts in letters and journals or in later productions such as memoirs. Although Wellington himself refused to write a memoir, he wrote copious letters, official dispatches which nevertheless give clear glimpses both of his intentions and objectives and his state of mind. These letters and memoranda provide an invaluable structure for a study of Burgos and the retreat. They can then be amplified by the thoughts, feelings and opinions of others involved in the struggle for Spain. Among the different voices which inform this work and provide a commentary on the actual events are senior and junior officers, British and French, NCOs and soldiers from the ranks, non-combatants like surgeons and commissaries, and the occasional civilian who found himself caught up in an alien environment. Between them they create a multi-faceted view of their world, of what happened in it, and of the major players involved. They praise and they criticize; they are puzzled by things that appear to make no sense; or perhaps they just struggle to survive. Above all, though, they live on through their words.

Obviously, from a strictly historical perspective, letters and journals may be regarded as having more validity and authority than memoirs, which were often composed many years later. This is particularly true of those memoirs written after Napier produced his history of the Peninsular War, a brilliant literary effort which had an inevitable influence on those who subsequently wrote their own accounts. But such accounts should not be totally disregarded. What a man remembers, or is stimulated to remember by the writing of others, may reveal the relative significance of the events he experienced. Nor should every letter and journal be regarded as presenting an unvarnished version of the truth. Situations may easily be misunderstood. Opinions are often coloured by prejudice. What a man experiences may be only a small part of the whole. Consequently, it is the sum of the many parts, contemporaneous and retrospective, which enable us to recognize *through a glass darkly* the reality of experiences from two centuries ago.

# Acknowledgements

Once again I have every reason to be grateful to the staff of the National Archives at Kew and the National Army Museum in Chelsea for their help and expertise. Particular thanks are due to Richard Dabb at the NAM for his assistance in accessing images for this book.

As ever there have been many friends and associates who have helped me locate particular information, or have made suggestions about particular material that might prove useful. Such suggestions have proved invaluable as I have attempted to recreate the experience of Burgos and the retreat. Michael Crumplin FRCS has been particularly supportive in making available a wealth of medical information. He also enabled me to access the reports of Wellington's surgeon general, James McGrigor, which shed a fascinating light on the medical conditions of the British army in the Peninsula. McGrigor's findings also help to explain why there were so many casualties; wounded men who should have recovered but failed to do so, and hundreds who died of natural causes. (See Appendix III.) I am grateful to the Aberdeen Medico-Chirurgical Society for allowing me to make use of this unpublished material.

Thanks to the help of John Williams some seemingly intractable problems with translating French documents have been solved, allowing the French to have a voice in this work. Similarly, Mary Bomphrey's knowledge of Spanish proved invaluable when we were searching for some of the more obscure scenes of action.

I also owe thanks to Rupert Harding for his unfailing patience as deadlines came and went.

Finally, my husband has once again been stalwart in his support: as driver along the routes taken by the different armies, as photographer and cartographer, and as statistician when I struggled to process the casualty returns of all the battalions in Wellington's army. Without his constant encouragement this book would not have been written.

# PART I

# Madrid

## Chapter 1

# 'See the Conquering Hero Come'

On 12 August 1812 Madrid was ready to celebrate. The detested *soi-disant* king, Joseph Bonaparte, had abandoned his capital with his guard, the Army of the Centre and a train of men, women and children who had thrown in their lot with the French. The allied Anglo-Portuguese army was approaching the city gates. The whole population, young and old, rich and poor, had taken to the streets to welcome the conquering hero, Arthur Wellesley, Lord Wellington.

Wellington himself wrote laconically in an official dispatch to Earl Bathurst, Secretary of State for War, that 'It is impossible to describe the joy manifested by the inhabitants of Madrid upon our arrival,' before turning his attention to the wider implications of this welcome.

> I hope that the prevalence of the same sentiments of detestation of the French yoke, and of a strong desire to secure the independence of their country, which first induced them to set the example of resistance to the usurper, will induce them again to make exertion in the cause of this country, which being more wisely directed, will be more efficacious than those formerly made.[1]

What Wellington found impossible to describe was certainly not beyond the powers of the troops who accompanied him into the city. Words flowed freely from the pens of officers and men alike, in letters and journals, and for years to come in memoirs of this apotheosis of triumph.

Led by the 7th division, with the 51st at its head, the victors of the battle of Salamanca, fought three weeks before, drew near the Spanish capital. At the first sight of the city in the morning haze there were raucous cries of 'Madrid! Madrid!' Some, however, wondered how they would be received in a place that had enjoyed more than three years of relative peace as the rest of Spain was caught in the turmoil of war. These concerns were soon put to rest. Five miles from the city gates, the vanguard of the allied army encountered the first crowds: men, women and children bearing boughs of oak and laurel, symbols of victory. On every side they were greeted with enthusiasm and delight, as well as with flowers, bread, grapes, melons, wine, aquadente, lemonade, tobacco and sweetmeats.

*A map of the Iberian Peninsula showing principal towns and rivers.*

For one man nothing was more pleasing than the pretty, pale-faced and black-eyed maidens who modestly presented nosegays to the passing troops. For another, it was the generous offer of pigskins of wine, more generous than even the deepest-drinking soldier could manage to consume, that brought the greatest delight.

As they neared the city, colours flying, drums beating, bands playing, the excitement which greeted them was almost overwhelming. The people were mad with joy. All the bells of Madrid were ringing to the heavens. There was singing, dancing, guitars, tambourines, all adding to the cacophony of welcome. And joyous acclamations from all sides. They were hailed as liberators, deliverers, saviours. 'Viva los Ingleses! Viva los Ilandes! Viva los Colorades!' greeted these scarlet-jacketed fellows. God was called upon to save King George. King Ferdinand. England. Even Portugal, their Iberian rival and age-old enemy. As for Wellington, riding at the head of his troops, every other *viva* hailed the hero of the hour as he rode through the gate which had been turned into a triumphal arch decorated in his honour. The populace fell to their knees on the ground that bore the imprint of his horse's hooves. Even the children's caps were decorated with 'Wellington' and 'Salamanca'. It was, as a staff officer wrote home, the 'fondest idolatry'.

Tens of thousands of laughing, cheering, jubilant people were crammed into the streets, so that the troops could pass along only with the greatest difficulty. Indeed, some men fainted in the heat and the crush, to be succoured by the concerned citizens.

Everywhere eager hands reached out, to caress their deliverers, to touch the colours, to drag the soldiers into their houses and the ice and lemonade shops, where they were plied with free refreshments. Or even just to walk hand-in-hand with them. Not only the officers were embraced with a fervour which threatened to unseat them; even their horses received the same attention. The colours were kissed, and so were the ensigns carrying them. As was everyone else, by pretty girls and men with garlic-laden breath and moustaches so stiff and sweaty that one soldier was reminded of brooms that had been daubed in the gutter.

Every viewpoint, up to the very rooftops, was occupied. The balconies were crowded with fair and elegant ladies, waving their white handker-chiefs and showering flowers on the troops below. Velvet and silk hang-ings, richly embroidered with gold and silver thread, were suspended from every balcony as if it were a great feast day of the Church. Garlands of flowers festooned every door and window. As the sun set, wax candles in silver candlesticks, flaring torches and variegated lamps turned night into day. Shops were closed. Business was suspended. For three days and three nights Madrid was *en fête*.

It was a time of delirium: an ecstasy of the brain, shared by soldiers and citizens alike. To the sober mind it was like a dream, but a dream of confusion and rapture that everyone was experiencing.

Yet the war was never far away. Joseph had left, taking his guard and a train of *afrancesados* with him, but a garrison 2,000 strong remained in the fortified Retiro palace with enough pieces of cannon to raze Madrid to the ground, so the governor boasted. Even as the citizens continued to celebrate, and the troops were still marching in, Wellington turned his attention to the reduction of the Retiro. On the evening of the 13th, against a background of illuminated buildings, detachments from the 3rd and 7th divisions drove in the French outposts at the Prado, the Botanical Gardens and the works outside the walls of the Retiro park. They were then able to establish themselves in the park by breaking through the wall close to the La China building, which served as an arsenal.

The following morning preparations were soon underway for an attack on the interior lines. People were already packed in the nearby streets and houses, and perched on the housetops, ready for the show. Every move-ment of the troops was loudly applauded, the shouts of the people being echoed by the cheers of the men, so that no orders could be heard and disorder threatened. Then, without warning, the governor sent an aide to seek terms. Negotiations ensued, resulting in the garrison marching out with the honours of war, but escorted by Spanish guerrillas as a compliment to the Spanish nation.

As Wellington reported to Bathurst, the allied haul was considerable:

> 189 pieces of brass ordnance in excellent condition, 900 barrels of powder, 20,000 stand of arms, and considerable magazines of clothing and provisions, and ammunition. We have likewise found the eagles of the 13th and the 51st regiments, which I forward to England to be presented to His Royal Highness.[2]

This was the Prince Regent, whose birthday coincidentally was 12 August.

For the soldiers there were other rewards. Many of the men made an excellent breakfast of the fruit in the park, while the more enterprising spirits of the 68th helped themselves from the stockpile of clothing the French had left behind. William Wheeler of the 51st found more unexpected but equally desirable plunder.

> I strolled into a summer house and was agreeably surprized to find a quantity of books, Spanish, French and English. I secured all I could find in my own tongue but as I have not the means of carrying them I distributed them amongst my comrades who I know are fond of reading.[3]

He even found a guide to his home town, Bath.

With Madrid firmly in allied hands, officers and even some of the men were able to enjoy the pleasures of what many considered the most beautiful city they had ever visited. The clean, wide streets and spacious avenues, shaded by wide-spreading trees and cooled by refreshing fountains, were favourite places of resort, despite the constant importuning of beggars. Museums, palaces, theatres, all demanded the attention of the avid sightseer, as so many officers were, while the novelty of the bull-fight attracted men and officers alike. They were fascinated by this barbarous and ancient national amusement, recognising both the skill and the innate cruelty, which one officer considered as evidence of the effects of early habit on the character. The suffering of the horses provoked particular outcry.

As befitted the city's deliverer from the French yoke, Wellington gave dinners and balls, to which complements of officers were always invited. Here they encountered the Spanish generals and, probably of more interest, the guerrillas, who had made their names by waging an irregular war against the French.

There was only one disadvantage to this period of pleasure which, for some battalions, extended from weeks to months, and that was the chronic shortage of money. Pay was far in arrears, despite Wellington's frequent reminders to the government. Some officers were reduced to selling what valuables they possessed to purchase the necessities of life, while others confessed to pilfering the occasional shirt or boots. Nevertheless, for most officers their stay in Madrid was remembered as a time when they 'passed some of the happiest days of [their] life'; a time they would 'ever look back on with mixed sensations of pleasure and regret'[4] that they had to leave for the realities of war.

For the commander-in-chief, however, Madrid represented something more challenging: the need to make a decision on the future prosecution of the campaign which had brought him to the heart of Spain.

\* \* \*

1812 was the year when Wellington took the war into Spain on his own terms, rather than in concert with the Spanish, as had been the case with the Talavera campaign of 1809. Or, the previous year, Sir John Moore's doomed foray into the Spanish interior. Spanish help could, and did, play its part, whether through the activities of the guerrilla bands or when a general like Ballesteros provided a distraction to French manoeuvres, but even Napoleon, contemptuous as he was of British land forces, recognized that the 'English' would have to be beaten if French power was ever to establish itself unchallenged in Spain.

At the beginning of the year two major obstacles needed to be overcome before the Anglo-Portuguese army could operate in Spain, safe in the knowledge that their lines of communication with Portugal would remain secure. Ciudad Rodrigo and Badajoz guarded the northern and southern routes between Spain and Portugal. Ciudad Rodrigo was invested on 8 January in bitter cold weather and fell on the 20th before Marshal Marmont, in command of the Army of Portugal, could effect its relief. This triumph was followed on 15 March by the investment of Badajoz. This much stronger fortification had already resisted allied attempts to take it during the previous year, and indeed had only fallen into French hands under strong suspicion of treachery. Badajoz finally fell on 6 April, after a siege conducted in wet and miserable conditions, and with a bloodier outcome. The allies took nearly 5,000 killed and wounded, against about 550 at Ciudad Rodrigo.

Meanwhile, the French forces in Spain were weakened by Napoleon's need for troops for his Russian adventure. The emperor also placed his brother in overall command of the different French army commanders in an attempt to end the jealous bickering and lack of cooperation between the marshals. The latter decision did not have the desired effect. The former was obviously beneficial to the allies.

In the middle of June Wellington brought his troops from the border area and advanced on Salamanca, from where Marmont withdrew, leaving a garrison to hold some fortified convents. These needed to be taken before the allies could progress deeper into Spain. The 6th division was given the task. Inexperienced and with inadequate resources they made little progress; after five days and a failed assault it was the use of incendiary heated shells that decided the issue, forcing the garrison to capitulate on 27 June, just as another assault was launched. During these five days Wellington's dispatches reveal a marked degree of uncertainty. On the 25th he wrote to the prime minister, Lord Liverpool,

> Matters have not gone as I could wish at Salamanca; but the truth is that my attention has been so much and so constantly taken up with Marmont's movements and my own, that I have not been able to attend to the operations of the siege as I ought.[5]

The following day he confided to his brother, Henry, who was the British ambassador in Cadiz,

> The armies are about five miles distant from each other. Marmont will not attack us, and I doubt whether I can attack him, even when I shall have taken the Salamanca forts.[6]

Two days later, though, he was able to write to General Hill, on detached duty in Estremadura with his 2nd division,

> We took the forts of this place yesterday, two of them by storm, and the third by capitulation. It was stormed, however, at the very moment it capitulated. Marmont has retired and we march forward to-morrow.[7]

There followed a period of manoeuvring as Wellington and Marmont each tried to outwit the other. By 9 July, however, Wellington knew that Marmont had been reinforced by the troops of General Bonnet of the Army of the North. He was also aware that the latest French movement, towards Toro, could be intended to threaten his communications with Portugal. As this initial supposition became increasingly valid, a series of retrograde movements brought him back to Salamanca, pursued by Marmont, so closely that on the 19th the two armies were marching in parallel.

By this point it was clear that Marmont was seeking to turn the allied right. On the 22nd, however, he made a fatal mistake. Believing the Anglo-Portuguese to be in retreat, he attempted a wide flanking movement which sent his army across the allied front. This was a serious misreading both of the situation and of Wellington as a commander. As far as the French were concerned he was a defensive general. As Wellington later wrote to Bathurst,

> The extension of his [the enemy's] line to the left, however, and its advance upon our right, notwithstanding that his troops still occupied very strong ground, and his position was well defended by cannon, gave me the opportunity of attacking him, for which I had long been anxious.[8]

To Hill Wellington wrote, the day after the battle,

> we beat Marshal Marmont's army yesterday evening, near Salamanca, and they are now in full retreat, and we following them ... We have taken a good many prisoners and cannon, above 3,000 of the former, and I should think 20 of the latter, and I understand two eagles. All the troops behaved admirably.[9]

Perhaps the most interesting comment on the battle was written soon after the event by a French general, Maximilien Foy, who would play a significant part in the events to come.

> It raises Lord Wellington's reputation almost to the level of Marlborough. Hitherto, we had been aware of his prudence, his eye for choosing a position, and his skill in utilising it. At Salamanca he has shown himself a great and able master of manoeuvre.[10]

Victory at Salamanca presented Wellington with a choice of options, just as did the possession of Madrid three weeks later. To understand the decisions he made, however, it is necessary to consider the situation of the French.

# Chapter 2

# The Other Side of the Hill

When Marshal Jean Baptiste Jourdan was created King Joseph's chief of staff by Napoleon in March 1812 his first concern was to inform the emperor of the true situation in Spain. A memorandum dispatched to Paris in May made clear his view that the French forces must be regarded as an army of occupation, a point which a survey of the different forces and their specific responsibilities demonstrates. To summarize briefly, there were five armies of varying strength, each with its own sphere of interest, nominally under the overall command of the king, 'an irresolute leader, not made for the military life'.[1] As Foy later commented, 'If the profession of king does not agree with his character, one could say that the one of general in chief is against his nature.'[2]

The Army of the North, under General Jean Marie Dorsenne and then General Louis Marie Caffarelli, had a total strength of nearly 50,000 men, although in May 1812 only about 38,000 were present with the eagles, two infantry and one cavalry division (Bonnet's command) having been detached to the Army of Portugal. The territory ostensibly controlled by the Army of the North comprised Galicia, the Asturias and Navarre, south to Burgos. Its principal concern was to protect the Burgos to Bayonne road and the coastal harbours, thus ensuring communication with France. This was the area where some of the most effective guerrilla leaders operated, men like the older Mina and Longa. They were supported by British naval activities under Sir Home Popham, forcing the French into what was essentially a series of holding operations if their primary task was to be fulfilled. It was also this task which made both Dorsenne and Caffarelli reject Joseph's overall command, since they could argue that their purpose was more strongly connected to France than the rest of Spain.

The now misnamed Army of Portugal had been harried out of that country in April 1811. Its commander, Marshal André Masséna, was replaced by Marshal Auguste Marmont, Duke of Ragusa, who concentrated his activities on Leon, Old Castile and northern Estremadura, although the hope of reoccupying Portugal had not been abandoned. Notionally 52,000 strong, plus the detachment from the Army of the

North, this force was required to keep the Anglo-Portuguese army out of Spain via Ciudad Rodrigo and Salamanca, and to work with Marshal Soult in Estremadura. Its main practical problem stemmed from the French habit of living off the land. Troops had to be dispersed into garrisons, which held major towns such as Astorga, Valladolid and Palencia, while there were about 29,000 men in the vicinity of Salamanca. Marmont paid lip-service to Joseph as commander-in-chief, but this did not prevent him disobeying an order not to attack Wellington until Joseph had brought up reinforcements. The result of his disobedience was the debacle at Salamanca.

The Army of the South controlled southern Estremadura and Andalusia, over which Marshal Nicolas Soult, Duke of Dalmatia, ruled in almost vice-regal style. About 63,000 strong, this army had one of the most enterprising, if also one of the rashest, Spanish generals to deal with. When Soult marched west in a futile attempt to relieve Badajoz, General Ballesteros, aided by General Morillo, reacted immediately by threatening Seville, which inevitably brought Soult back to his sphere of interest. More symbolic was the failure to take Cadiz, now the seat of the Spanish government and which had been under siege since February 1810. Soult, like Marmont, paid only lip-service to Joseph's command. Nor was there any love lost between king and marshal.

The smallest of the French forces was the Army of the Centre, under the king's direct command. With less than 20,000 men it was too small to exercise effective control over New Castile. Nevertheless, in concert with another of the armies it could swing the numerical balance in favour of the French against the allied army, which would have been the situation at Salamanca if Marmont had deferred to the king's orders, in which case Wellington might not even have risked a battle.

Finally, Marshal Louis Gabriel Suchet, Duke of Albufera, was in command of the Army of Aragon, which also controlled Catalonia and the recently occupied Kingdom of Valencia. It was the strongest of the French armies with 66,000 men, all arms, and was the only one still engaged in conquest. As a coastal region, however, its territory was vulnerable to British naval activities. Although Suchet never explicitly refused to acknowledge Joseph's overall command, he was unwilling to cooperate either with the king or with his fellow marshals, as he demonstrated when he would not send troops to help in the relief of Badajoz. From his viewpoint, pacifying Valencia was more important.

Jourdan's memorandum, written by a man who was 'prudent and far-seeing' but who 'lacked the strength of character to enforce his own decisions'[3], made the valid point that it was impracticable for an army of occupation to live off the land in a country where food was scarce and requisition was bitterly resented. Instead, the army needed to be made more mobile, which required adequate means of transport and large magazines of stores on all the lines of communication. This would allow larger concentrations of troops and facilitate future operations. He also advocated that the French should occupy less territory. What he considered a deplorable habit of seizing as much territory as possible may have been intended to demonstrate to the rest of Europe that Spain was firmly held, but in reality it was both expensive and an inefficient use of resources.

For Jourdan the principal territorial problem was Andalusia, furthest detached from France and French interests. Soult, not surprisingly, saw things differently, and this difference of opinion was a source of friction between the king and the marshal. Furthermore, Soult was convinced that Wellington intended to attack Andalusia, Badajoz being a prelude to such an attack. Wellington certainly had considered this possibility, which had been reported in a Gibraltar newspaper seen by Soult, but by mid-May he had abandoned the idea. Nevertheless, it remained fixed in Soult's mind, reinforced by the activities of another player in the game of cat-and-mouse which followed the fall of Badajoz.

General Sir Rowland Hill was one of the very few of his subordinates that Wellington trusted with independent command. He had already proved his worth in October 1811 when he overwhelmed a French force under General Girard at Arroyo dos Molinos. Having been part of the covering force during the siege of Badajoz, Hill's second division remained in the area, keeping an eye on the activities of General Drouet, Comte d'Erlon, who commanded a third of the Army of the South. In May, however, Wellington entrusted Hill with a task which was essential to his strategic intentions. If he was to venture into Spain, whether against the Army of Portugal or the Army of the South, it was vital that Marmont and Soult should be kept apart. To facilitate communications between the two armies, the French had put a pontoon bridge in place across the Tagus at Almaraz, guarded at each end by two forts, Napoleon and Ragusa, the whole overlooked by the stronghold of Mirabete. Destroying the bridge would seriously hamper any supporting movement by either army because it would involve a long and difficult detour.

On 12 May, after the bridge at Merida had hastily been repaired, Hill took his three British brigades and Ashworth's Portuguese brigade, supported by the 13th light dragoons, across the Guadiana for a rapid march to Almaraz. On 18 May the three battalions of Howard's brigade, the 1/50th, 1/71st and 1/92nd, and the 6th line regiment of Ashworth's brigade, supported by twenty artillerymen, made a slow and hazardous descent to the Tagus, so difficult that the 30-foot ladders had to be cut in half. By six o'clock they were close to Fort Napoleon. Meanwhile, a false attack had been launched against Mirabete.

Anxious not to let the French see his exact position or his strength, Hill ordered an immediate escalade of Fort Napoleon. The French were quickly overwhelmed, although they managed to release the pontoon bridge. Hill's men now turned the French guns on Fort Ragusa, which was soon abandoned. When two men of the 92nd dived into the river and successfully brought the bridge back to the near shore, it became possible to destroy the forts and all their contents and then burn the pontoon boats, although Hill decided to leave the French alone in Mirabete, judging it too strong for an assault. In fact, the French themselves abandoned this stronghold soon afterwards.

Having decided that Marmont was to be his target, Wellington could now take the northern route into Spain secure in the knowledge that Soult, even if he were so inclined, would not be able to bring support to his fellow marshal with any rapidity.

Hill remained in Estremadura to pin down d'Erlon's force. At the same time Ballesteros was hovering in the vicinity of Seville. When Soult moved against one, the other would create a situation to draw him away. Thus Hill spent June and July manoeuvring against d'Erlon without ever coming to battle, although on several occasions action seemed inevitable. By early July he was able to outflank d'Erlon, despite the reinforcements the French general had received from Soult, and force him back to Berlanga and Azuaga in order to maintain his vital communication with Andalusia.

D'Erlon himself had earlier received a direct dispatch from the king ordering him to march to Toledo. Soult had also received a command to detach d'Erlon's force, but he had no intention of complying. Instead, he maintained that if he parted with a third of his army Andalusia would have to be abandoned, and for nothing because d'Erlon could not arrive in time to help the Army of Portugal. For his part, d'Erlon claimed that he was outnumbered by Hill, so that to move would be to endanger his troops.

Soult was not the only French commander to assist Wellington by refusing to help his fellow marshal. On 24 June Marmont wrote to Caffarelli: 'I am manoeuvring opposite Wellington. Your reinforcements are required *at once.*' Two weeks later he explained to Jourdan: 'I had to retreat to the Douro because Caffarelli sent no help.' At this stage of the campaign lack of mutual cooperation was a dangerous weakness in the French situation and a significant factor in the events which culminated in the Battle of Salamanca.

# Chapter 3

# Wellington's Gamble

Salamanca was not only a blow to Gallic pride; it was also the point in the war when the French had to reassess Wellington as a commander. The new Marlborough finally had the whip hand in the Peninsula and in the short term this disrupted French dispositions: the Armies of Portugal, the Centre and the South were all affected by Marmont's defeat.

When considering the choice Wellington made early in August, it would be facile to conclude that he chose to advance on Madrid simply because he believed the Army of Portugal too damaged to pose a threat, although this was certainly part of his thinking. Or that 'for once, British pride had sacrificed efficiency for ostentation.'[1]

In part Wellington's decision was influenced by Joseph's movements. As soon as the king received the news of Salamanca, during the night of 24 July and while still on his way to join Marmont with the Army of the Centre, he immediately retired towards Madrid. A dispatch from General Bertrand Clausel, in command for the wounded Marmont, made clear that the defeat had been a disaster. With less than 20,000 men fit for action, even the arrival of the Army of the Centre would not strengthen the Army of Portugal sufficiently to take a stand against Wellington. Instead, Clausel recommended that Joseph should demand help from Soult and Suchet. Furthermore, if Joseph moved north to join a seriously weakened army, he would lose contact with the Armies of the South and Aragon.

Wellington initially concentrated on Clausel and the wreck of the Army of Portugal because he did not see Joseph as a threat. Unlike the king, he knew from intercepted dispatches that Soult had no intention of obeying the royal order to detach d'Erlon. He advanced as far as Valladolid, therefore, where he received a hero's welcome from a city reputedly the most pro-French in Castile. By now Clausel had retired beyond the Arlanzon, and Wellington pursued him further.

Joseph, however, had changed direction and advanced to Segovia as the result of an over-optimistic letter from one of Marmont's aides-de-camp. He now intended to unite with Clausel in a stand against the Anglo-Portuguese army. However, Clausel had continued to retreat. At this point, though, Wellington believed the king would join Clausel. He wrote to Bathurst on 28 July from Olmedo:

> All accounts concur in regard to the great loss sustained by the army of Portugal; but I think probable that they will endeavour to join the King on the upper Duero, if the King should continue on this side of the mountains, unless I should previously have it in my power to strike a blow against his corps.[2]

The blow he chose to inflict was an advance on Madrid.

On 1 August, when Joseph realized he had been misled by the information from Marmont's aide-de-camp, he turned back to his capital, anxious as ever to protect his limited royal power. At this point he received a dispatch from Soult in response to orders sent on 6 July, which required the marshal to abandon part of Andalusia, as well as to send d'Erlon to Toledo. After using an exaggerated estimate of Hill's strength, Soult made clear that he would not abandon Andalusia, since to do so would be a disaster for French interests in the Peninsula.

> We could not find means to subsist either on the Tagus or in Estremadura, and from one position to another we should retreat as far as the Ebro. There is a way to avoid this; by taking the initiative we can save 6,000 sick and maimed men whom I shall probably have to abandon, as well as 200,000 Spaniards (who have declared for your Majesty, and will be lost without hope), also 2,000 guns, and the only artillery arsenal now existing in Spain. A single order by your Majesty can effect this, and shorten the Spanish war by six campaigns. Let your Majesty come to Andalusia in person, with every man that can be collected: if the number is large we can increase the expeditionary force in Estremadura to 25,000 or 30,000 men, and transfer the seat of war to the left bank of the Tagus ... I have the honour to repeat to your Majesty that I cannot send any detachments beyond the Sierra Morena or the Guadiana, save by evacuating all Andalusia and marching with my whole army. I must have a positive order from your Majesty to that effect.[3]

Joseph responded by commanding Soult to abandon Andalusia and bring the whole of the Army of the South to Toledo.

Wellington sent a cavalry reconnaissance to Segovia, which confirmed that Joseph was no longer there, and then spent three days in Cuellar before departing on 5 August for Madrid. He left Clinton's 6th division and five weak battalions (The 2/4th, 1/5th, 1/38th, 1/42nd, 1/82nd and all Walcheren battalions] to watch Clausel, while Anson's cavalry brigade took up forward positions beyond the Duero. Furthermore, he used the

Army of Galicia, General Santocildes at Valladolid and Captain-General Castaños at Astorga, to besiege the French garrisons in those towns while General Silveira blockaded Zamora with a Portuguese militia force.

Buoyed by the conviction that the Army of Portugal was out of the game for the foreseeable future, Wellington marched for Madrid. On 8 August Joseph abandoned his capital, leaving only a small force under General Lafon Blaniac to hold the Retiro.

*   *   *

Having entered Madrid in triumph on 12 August, Wellington did not leave until the end of the month. As had been the case after Salamanca, he needed to judge the French response before he formulated his own plans. The key to this was Soult. The marshal had three choices. He had already advocated that he should remain in Andalusia, where Joseph and the Army of the Centre should join him. He could, however, obey the king's command and unite their two armies in a combined operation against Wellington; but if Joseph went to Valencia, he could join him there.

If Soult held firm in his determination not to evacuate Andalusia, Wellington could take the war to him. As he wrote to Bathurst on 18 August, 'Any other but a modern French army would now leave the province, as they have absolutely no communication of any kind with France ...' With Joseph making his slow, encumbered way to Valencia, the Spanish still in possession of Murcia and the Army of Portugal out of contact with the Army of the South, Soult was indeed cut off. 'But I suspect that Soult will not stir till I force him out by a direct movement upon him; and I think of making that movement as soon as I can take the troops to the south without incurring the risk of injuring their health. In the meantime I must have possession of the whole course of the Duero.'[4]

Should Soult choose to obey Joseph, then Wellington in his central position would have a choice, depending upon who posed the greater threat, Soult or Clausel. The situation changed, however, when Clausel realised that Madrid was Wellington's objective. He immediately moved back towards the Duero, entering Valladolid on 14 August. This movement was made more dangerous to the allies by the enterprise of General Foy. Having obtained Clausel's rather reluctant permission, Foy marched with the 1st and 3rd divisions of the Army of Portugal to relieve the beleaguered French garrisons. On the 17th he took up the 200 men at Toro and two days later he attacked the Spanish rear guard at Castro Gonzalo. The next day he was at Baneza, but on the 21st he reported to Clausel that 'Astorga fell on the 18th, after a blockade of 62 days, during which it experienced all the horrors of famine; the garrison left on the 19th at 8a.m.; they are prisoners of war. I learnt this distressing news yesterday on arrival at La Baneza ... The army of Galicia has quickly retired to Villafranca; it appears that they will cross the mountains.' In fact, General Castaños, in command of the blockading force, had sent his guns away, under cover, as soon as he heard of Foy's approach. Ironically, the French surrendered the day before Foy could arrive to relieve them.

Foy's next objective was Zamora, but General Silveira was warned of his approach and took his Portuguese militia back across the border, although on the 24th there was a skirmish between the French advance guard and the Portuguese rear guard. This was not particularly satisfying, however. Foy had expected his cavalry to destroy the militia but 'I was deceived in my opinion. It was said that the horses were tired and that they could not meet with the enemy; the pursuit was almost halted, despite me; eventually Silveyra [sic], his troops and his artillery were made to flee and re-entered Portugal. They fled, abandoning shoes, baggage, wagons laden with tools and left us some prisoners.'[5] This is a somewhat disingenuous account which omits the fact that the Portuguese were already heading for Portugal.

It may have frustrated Foy that his French troops failed to crush a body of militia men, but on the 25th he had the satisfaction of entering Zamora.

Clausel's return to the Duero and Foy's activities had passed unchallenged by Clinton, who merely maintained a watching brief, another of those occasions which justified Wellington's conviction that most of his subordinates could not be trusted with independent command. Nevertheless, as he wrote to Henry Wellesley in Cadiz, on the 23rd, 'I hope the French will carry off the garrisons of Zamora and Astorga, as well as that of Toro. Any thing is better than that I should have to attack and carry those places.'[6]

Further south Soult finally accepted the inevitability of evacuating Andalusia. Although he had heard rumours of Marmont's disaster at Salamanca, he had chosen not to credit them for as long as possible. Eventually he received the first official confirmation in the form of a dispatch from Joseph written on 26 July. This reached him on 18 August, by which time he had reluctantly accepted the truth of the rumours. He had also accepted that Joseph would not join him in Andalusia. Consequently, on 12 August there were the first signs of an evacuation when the castle at Niebla was abandoned. By the 24th the Lines of Cadiz were being destroyed. In Estremadura d'Erlon had continued his manoeuvring. On the 20th, though, Captain Hippolyte d'Espinchal, a cavalry officer serving with General Pierre Soult, the marshal's brother, was dining with his commanding officer when 'The fatal news which we had been given some days before was confirmed; I was apprised of all the details ... the occupation of Madrid by the English, the king retiring on Burgos and the duke

of Dalmatia forced to abandon Andalucia.' D'Espinchal had no doubt
who was to blame. Not the king, whom the soldiers were inclined to hold
responsible. He was a principal victim. The disaster had occurred because
Marmont had refused to wait for the arrival of the Army of the Centre; he
'wanted to have the sole glory of winning, he has given battle at the
Arapiles, not far from Salamanca. Completely defeated, wounded by a
cannon ball, he has suffered 5,000 killed or wounded, more than 2,000
prisoners and he has lost 11 pieces of cannon.'

From d'Espinchal's viewpoint, however, 'what was painful was the
loss to Marshal Soult of the fruit of three years' combat and the millions
vainly employed up to this time in the siege of Cadiz, which had to be
abandoned at the moment when everything supported the belief that it
was coming to an end.'[7]

This last was a vain hope, perhaps, but d'Espinchal's comments, combined with the marshal's pleasure in independent command, explain why
Soult was so reluctant to leave Andalusia.

By 24 August French troops were arriving in Seville from all directions,
while a combined Anglo-Spanish force from Cadiz was threatening the
enemy outposts. Once Conroux and Villatte's divisions had come up from
Cadiz Seville was evacuated by all but a skeleton force on the night of
the 26th. The city then fell to the allies, who overwhelmed the remaining
defenders.

Also on the 24th, Wellington received news from Hill, sent on the
17th, that Soult was abandoning Andalusia. Yet with the adventurous
Ballesteros poised to disrupt Soult's advance to Granada and the
expectation that the autumn rains would fill the rivers, he believed he
had time to deal with Clausel before Soult could combine with Joseph and
Suchet. Furthermore, there were other players in the game ready to take
an active role.

Sir Home Popham had begun his cooperative operations with the
northern guerrillas in mid-June, so effectively that Caffarelli was unable to
spare any troops to help Marmont – or plausibly claimed he was. On the
night of 2 August the governor, General Dubreton, and his 1,200 strong
garrison, abandoned Santander, which had been under attack since
22 July. Since Santander was the largest and safest harbour between Ferrol
and the French border, this was a notable coup. Furthermore, Popham
saw the possibility of transporting six or eight heavy guns to take Burgos
and disrupt French communications. At the same time that Santander fell,
unrest spread across the northern provinces, even affecting previously
subdued Aragon.

As another diversion, an expedition launched from Sicily to attack the
east coast of Spain, Suchet's territory, had been postulated as early as

January 1812 by the commander of the British forces in Sicily, General Lord William Bentinck. Although Bentinck preferred the idea of operating either on the Italian mainland or in Corsica, the Spanish plan was picked up by Lord Liverpool, the prime minister, and by Wellington, who by mid-May was expecting a landing to be made in Catalonia. Bentinck, however, was temporarily distracted by Italian affairs. On 30 July Wellington acknowledged a letter from Bentinck which gave the details of an expedition to the east coast under the command of General Maitland. Bentinck himself was doubtful that anything would be achieved, but Wellington was confident that they could 'succeed in taking Tarragona, and in opening a communication between the fleet and the Spanish army of Tarragona – which is in itself a service of the greatest importance ...' Even if this proved unachievable, Wellington saw some advantage to his own operations.

> I have lately, on the 22nd, beaten Marshal Marmont in a general action, fought near Salamanca, and I have pursued him beyond the Duero; and our troops this day entered Valladolid. The King is at Segovia, with a corps of 12,000 or 15,000 men; and having driven Marmont from the lower Duero, my next object is to prevent him and Marmont, if possible, from joining, which I am about to attempt. But either the French must lose all their communications with their troops in the north of Spain, or they must oblige me to withdraw towards the frontier of Portugal. They cannot effect this object without bringing against me Suchet's army, or the army of the South, or both. I cannot but think it very important that the attention of Suchet should be diverted from his supposed operations against me by the operations of the Sicilian army, which will go to such important objects as Tarragona and Valencia.[8]

Maitland first made for Tarragona but, judging the French too strong, he sailed south and landed at Alicante on 7 August. The Spanish under General Joseph O'Donnell had suffered a crushing defeat at Castella on 21 July, losing troops from the Murcian army who would have been useful to Maitland, but General Roche managed to extricate the 3,700 men of his division in good order and was ready to cooperate with Maitland. The joint force now made a tentative advance but found no enemy in front of them.

In fact, according to a later commentator, the Sicilian expedition was fated never to achieve anything:

> besides that the strength of the corps never exceeded 6,000 men, the officer in command (General Maitland) committed the twofold

mistake of landing at a wrong place, and entering upon his work upon a spirit of despondency. Lord Wellington made haste to apply, as far as circumstances would allow, a correction to both grievances. He caused the troops to re-embark, and go round to the theatre of their operations; and he assured General Maitland that whatever the issues of the enterprise might be, he himself was prepared to assume the entire responsibility. But the loss of two precious weeks could not be atoned for, and the consequences in due course developed themselves.[9]

Nonetheless, the Anglo-Spanish force in Alicante, however impotent, was a threat that Suchet could not ignore and an excuse for not cooperating with the other French commanders.

Suchet had drawn back his own forces in response to Wellington's move on Madrid, which the marshal knew might well bring Joseph and the war to his territory. Maitland, unwell and unused to independent command, retired to Alicante when it became clear that Joseph was bringing the Army of the Centre to Valencia. He set about fortifying the city as the situation became one of stalemate. Neither side was prepared to take the offensive at this point. Everything depended upon Soult, and Soult was still firmly rooted in Andalusia.

This was the situation when Wellington set off for the lower Duero. He left behind him in Madrid the 3rd and light divisions, while the 4th division were at El Escurial. Carlos d'España's Spanish force was at Segovia, supported by d'Urban and Victor Alten's cavalry. Hill's 2nd division, reinforced by troops from Cadiz under Colonel Skerret, was marching for Madrid. These forces combined constituted 40,000 men. Yet it is notable that the three divisions Wellington left behind in Madrid, although they had suffered in the hard campaigning of 1812, were also the most experienced, particularly in siege warfare, while two of those he chose to take with him, the 1st and the 7th, were the least.

# PART II

# Burgos

*Chapter 4*

# Opening Gambit

Marmont, who went to Burgos with the remains of his army, has returned to the line of the Douro [sic] and re-occupied the country between Burgos and Valladolid, which latter place he has also entered – as he is not in a state to undertake any serious offensive operation this movement of Marmont's must have been made with a view to favour the garrison of El Retiro, but they having surrendered he will, I think, again retire, especially as General Clinton has been ordered to move against him.[1]

This expectation, which Lieutenant Aitchison of the 3rd foot guards included in a letter to his brother written on 22 August, proved mistaken. Eight days later he wrote in his diary while at El Escurial:

Four divisions of infantry, viz 1st, 4th, 5th, 7th, are now collected in this place and well-lodged in large buildings and barracks ... These troops, it is reported, are to march to join General Clinton, who with the 6th division was left at Cuellar to keep the enemy in check during our advance to the capital – he has since, it seems, found it necessary to retire all his posts to the left of the Douro in consequence of the advance of General Foy with the remains of the 'Army of Portugal'. He entered Valladolid on the 14th inst, having previously obliged the Galician army under Santocildes to retire; he has since continued to advance towards Astorga with about 12,000 Infantry and 1,200 Cavalry and he arrived with the latter at La Baneza within 5 leagues of Astorga on the 21st, but the garrison of that place had been obliged to capitulate on the 19th ...[2]

Aitchison even believed, as he revealed in a subsequent letter, that Wellington wanted to entice the Army of Portugal back to the Duero, and had given Clinton orders to retire before their advance. Certainly, it was in the allied interest to deal with the Army of Portugal before Soult in the south could make a move.

Wellington himself left Madrid on 1 September, the same day that the divisions at El Escurial, with the exception of the 4th, began their advance to join Clinton. For those coming north with Wellington there was some reluctance to leave the Spanish capital where 'we had been very comfortable, and had received marks of great kindness and attention'[3] for the uncertainty and discomfort of campaigning. Nevertheless, the situation on the Duero was becoming increasingly serious. Captain William Tomkinson of the 16th light dragoons, on a mission to the guerrilla leader El Principe, reported that the French were in force at Tordesillas and that another 1,000 men were preparing to blow up the bridge at Simancas.

By 2 September headquarters were at Villacastin, at the northern foot of the Guadarrama mountains. John Green of the 68th, Lincolnshire born,

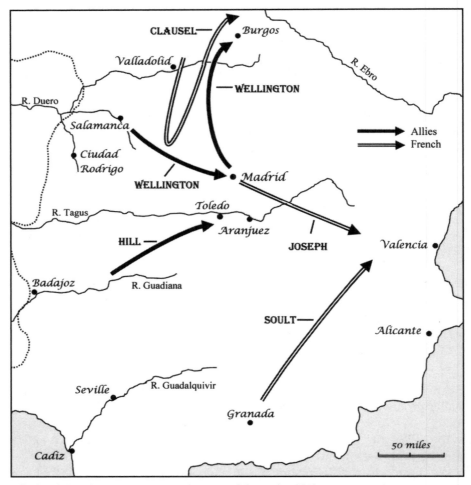

*Allied and French troop movements, August and September 1812.*

was impressed by 'this vast chain of mountains which can be distinctly seen for more than sixty miles.'[4] Daniell of the Commissariat, however, although equally impressed by the mountains, from the summit of which Madrid was clear in the distance, dismissed his quarters at Villacastin as wretched. Nor were they any better for Benjamin D'Urban, quartermaster general with the Portuguese Army. Suffering from the ague, he found himself in an old palace which was damp, depressing and full of owls and bats. The conditions of campaigning were all too quickly making themselves felt.

At Villacastin Wellington received the good news that the French had evacuated Zamora which, as he wrote to Maitland at Alicante, 'is a fortunate event, as it will enable me to rejoin troops to the south at a more early period.'[5]

The following day at Arevalo Wellington overtook the troops which had left El Escurial as he departed from Madrid. He now assumed command of an army which, when combined with Clinton's forces, would comprise the 1st, 5th, 6th and 7th infantry divisions, the 1st hussars King's German Legion and 14th light dragoons, Anson's light cavalry brigade, and Bock and Ponsonby's heavy cavalry, about 28,000 men. At this point General Castaños was at Astorga and the Army of Galicia on the Esla, while the French were now at Valladolid and on the Duero in strength. Wellington wrote to Castaños, explaining why he had returned to the Duero. Essentially, this matched Aitchison's supposition.

> I believe that Soult has the intention of leaving the south of Spain, but whether or not he has this intention, it is absolutely necessary to hunt down Marmont's troops without waste of time, to leave me at liberty to oppose Soult with all my forces. I shall take advantage of the moment that the King's departure has given me to come to this side and I shall push matters as far as I can. But I have great need of your assistance. I have some large guns, and I have the idea of undertaking the siege of Burgos.

Although this is the first mention of such an objective in the Dispatches, Wellington's intention seems to have been known in the army by this point. Aitchison reported in a letter home 'and (they say) in less than three weeks he will have left *us* in *Burgos* and returned to Madrid.'[7]

According to Lieutenant Colonel George Bingham of the 34th, the 6th division had been enjoying a restful month in Arevalo. 'General Clinton has been very quiet since the battle, so that our time passes pleasantly enough.' The arrival of the three divisions from Madrid, however, suggested that 'if we do not move tomorrow, we certainly shall the following day, and perhaps shall not halt until we arrive at Burgos, for I do not think the French will make any stand short of that place; what may take place afterwards I cannot foresee.'[8]

According to John Mills of the 2nd (Coldstream) guards the situation in Arevalo was chaotic. 'We found the 5th and 6th Divisions in the town and we were consequently very much crowded. By great good luck I got in to a house' with a fellow officer. The next day, however, 'Headquarters came in . . . from St Chidrian and the Divisions were moved out and bivouacked to make room for them. There is more confusion and fuss about quarters with these gentry than with the whole army besides. I remained, and by these means got a day's halt.'[9]

On the 4th the El Escurial divisions came up and the whole army marched to Olmedo, where news arrived by a mail from England that the commander-in-chief was now Marquis of Wellington. Anson's brigade, familiar with the area, were acting as the army's eyes and ears. Tomkinson discovered from the local peasants that the French appeared ready to leave Valladolid, although they were seemingly unaware of the allied advance. Corporal John Douglas of the first Royal Scots, however, was more interested in this land of milk and honey than military matters.

> The harvest was now in its prime. Wheat, grapes, &c were more than abundant. In Arevalo we started to grind the wheat, and succeeded amazingly well. Large flagstones were plentiful here. These served as the nether millstone, while a piece as large as a man could conveniently work formed the upper one. It must not be expected that we produced meal of the best quality, but to men having good appetites, and the tenor of the Commissariat far in the rear, you may depend upon it, not to be despised.[10]

There followed a day's rest for some of the troops, although the French outposts were reconnoitred and Wellington rode to Valdestillas to look for fords across the Duero. For the 1st division problems soon developed, however. Having bivouacked in a wood near Fresma, they suffered a three-hour delay when they attempted to move off, which Aitchison blamed on the ignorance or neglect of the quartermaster general's department. '. . . nobody could conduct the columns to the proper road – and it was ludicrous and melancholy to see three different Divisions attempting to get out of the wood – their leaders becoming so confused – changing the direction of march and returning to wherever they had set out from – till at length it was thought best to halt till a guide could be procured.'[11] Routes for troops and supplies were the responsibility of the quartermaster general who, according to Douglas and Aitchison, was already failing in the movement of both.

Rumours that the French had abandoned Valladolid proved premature. On the 6th the allies marched five leagues to Boecilla and then crossed the river by fords above Puente de Duero, at Herera and El Abrojo. The French had taken up a strong position on the far bank, a few miles beyond the river on the heights of La Cisterniga. Their right wing was at Valladolid, apparently posted to extricate their baggage train, which matched Tomkinson's information that they were preparing to abandon the town. Anson and Ponsonby's brigades, at the head of the allied force, drove in the French cavalry vedettes after some skirmishing.

At this point, according to Aitchison, the purpose of the campaign, which was to render the Army of Portugal *hors de combat* before Soult could pose a threat,

> was nearly being crowned by the most complete success. The enemy we had every reason to expect had no notice of our approach. Indeed, we took them so completely by surprise that their cavalry and artillery were out of camp foraging, and several were taken prisoner by our advanced guards. I spoke to these men and they represented the number of their troops encamped on the heights of La Cisterniga and its neighbourhood at about 6,000 men with 6 pieces in position. They certainly did not seem more, and notwithstanding the nature of their position, which was strong, we had no doubt of success – three strong divisions of Infantry and two brigades of Cavalry were up but from some mistake the guns of the 5th Division, which was to have led, missed their way and the attack in consequence was delayed – before they arrived and the other divisions had taken their stations, the enemy had assembled and encircled themselves with vedettes – they also had strong bodies of Infantry on the heights flanking the roads to their position. It was then so late, nearly 5 in the evening, and Wellington then judged it advisable not to attack – we returned to the river and began cooking.[12]

His fellow guards officer, Mills, recorded in his diary that the 6th proved

> a long and tedious day from four in the morning till five in the evening. At Boecilla the 1st, 5th and 7th Divisions were formed behind the hill. The enemy did not appear to have the smallest idea of our approach. The cavalry went forward and crossed the river without opposition. They advanced skirmishing and took a few prisoners. The three divisions crossed the river and advanced to within a mile of the village of Cisterniga where the enemy showed symptoms of resistance. They had constructed a fort on the left and their men were

very advantageously posted on some hills and strong ground. Their videttes [sic] and ours were close to one another. I was glad to see my old friends and all the show of war. The 1st Division was ordered to attack the hills, to be supported by the 5th who had not come up, and before they did the enemy moved off, the greatest part of his force not leaving sufficient to make it worth our while to attack. We should on our way up there have been very much exposed to their guns which were on a commanding situation … At five o'clock things remained quiet and we moved off and bivouacked in a fir wood in our rear.[13]

\*   \*   \*

The French withdrew during the night, and the following morning the allies took up the position the enemy had abandoned on the heights of La Cisterniga in time to see the French cavalry retire through Valladolid. The gates were closed to the pursuers and a body of light infantry was stationed near the Puente de Toro. Once the gates had been forced open the 12th light dragoons and a party of guerrillas skirmished with a French cavalry squadron in the town. As the French crossed the bridge over the Pisuerga it was obvious that it would then be blown up. Wellington ordered the 12th light dragoons to charge the bridge, but too late to prevent its destruction. The French then blew up the bridge at Berecal. Again the pursuing cavalry were too late to prevent this happening, or to inflict any casualties.

This frustrating conclusion to a promising situation provoked the comment from Aitchison that

> This unhappy result to our expedition, which had every prospect of succeeding, has caused great disappointment in the whole army and an inquiry, it is said, has been ordered into the cause of it, at present it appears to have been originated with Maj.-Gen. Pringle, who commanded the 5th division in the absence through illness of General Hulse in not sending *explicit orders* and a guide to the Artillery attached to it.[14]

Gomm, who was on the staff of the 5th division, made his own judgement on Pringle. 'In the meantime [Leith's absence], we are commanded by a man who is liked by all the world in private life, and respected by no one in public.'[15] Pringle, it would seem, was an effective brigadier, as he had demonstrated at Salamanca, who now found divisional command beyond him.

The Pisuerga, although narrow at this point, was deep, rapid and difficult to cross. As the French retired upstream towards Dueñas, Anson's cavalry could do no more than move parallel with them on the opposite bank.

Headquarters were now established at Valladolid, which meant that a Commissariat officer like Daniell could obtain a good billet. He was well pleased with the reception the allies received. 'It has been remarked, that [the] inhabitants are attached to the French interests: this may arise from its situation upon the right bank of the Douro [sic], and in the great military road from France ... however, be this as it may, the people received the British with much cheerfulness and apparent good will.'[16]

The dispatches written by Wellington on 7 September serve as a useful reminder that, unlike his French opponent, Clausel, he had more than one situation that required his attention. To Castaños, for instance, he sent an account of crossing the Duero, and his failure to attack at La Cisterniga, explaining that 'as I saw that I could only take the post of La Cisterniga yesterday afternoon and would not have time to manoeuvre in order to make the [French] forces leave the town, I put the affair back until this morning'[17] – by which time the enemy had slipped away, of course. He then described the French evacuation of Valladolid, including the destruction of the bridges there and at Simancas. He estimated the French strength at that point as between 16,000 and 18,000, but added 'I believe Foy re-joined them this morning.' This led into an urgent request that Castaños send his latest news, including where he was and what he was doing.

General Carlos de España had been left as Governor of Madrid and for him there was a specific instruction not to reveal where Wellington was at this point, as well as general guidance on how he should act.

To Major General Murray, his recently departed quartermaster-general, he was more specific about his strategic intentions.

I hear that the siege of Cadiz is raised; and there is a storm brewing up from the south, for which I am preparing by driving the detachments of the army of Portugal away from the Duero; and I propose, if I have time, to take Burgos from them. In the meantime I have ordered Hill to cross the Tagus by Almaraz, when he shall find that Soult moves out of Andalusia ... I have, I hope, relieved General Maitland of all anxiety at Alicante, by taking upon myself all responsibility, and giving him positive orders for his conduct, so that he will only have to fight in a good position, his supplies being secured to him from the sea ... Matters go on well, and I hope before Christmas, if affairs turn out as they ought, and Boney requires all the reinforcements in the North, to have all the gentlemen safe on the other side of the Ebro.[18]

Significantly, this last hope was shared by some of Wellington's officers. Major Edward Charles Cocks of the 79th wrote to his brother the following day:

It is probable we shall push our operations as far as Burgos or the Ebro and then turn by Aranda de Duero and meet Hill at Madrid in time to strike a blow against Soult ... If we meet with no reverse and you send us *Dollars* mind, not bills but coins, I think the enemy will be behind the Ebro before Christmas, perhaps then an opportunity may occur for my coming home ...[19]

Others who received communications from Wellington on the 7th were Lieutenant General Sir Stapleton Cotton, his cavalry commander, who was still recovering from the wounds he had received at Salamanca, Sir Home Popham in the north, Colonel Torrens, secretary to the Duke of York, commander-in-chief of the army, York himself, and Lieutenant General Sir John Murray. Lord Liverpool, the prime minister, received two letters and Bathurst three. The next day there were another seven, including one to the Commissioners of the Transport Office to arrange the exchange by cartel of three French officers for two Portuguese and a British officer.

So far the advance had been conducted at a fair pace, but at this point progress slowed down, giving Wellington time to have the new constitution proclaimed. This had been framed by the Spanish government in Cadiz, and was a strange mixture of traditional Spanish, American and British political practices. Wellington had taken it upon himself to have it proclaimed in every major town he passed through. Tomkinson heard this proclamation from the town hall and commented on the illuminations which celebrated the event. He also noticed that few people of any respectability attended, a possible indication of future dissension in Spain between radicals and reactionaries once the war was over.

For some the delay in Valladolid could be explained by the need to repair the bridges across the Pisuerga, but a staff officer like Browne recognized that a major contributory factor was the dilatory movement of Castaños. Not surprisingly, therefore, Wellington wrote to Bathurst, 'I have halted here this day to give rest to the troops which have marched for several days, and to receive intelligence from General Castaños.'[20] But although Castaños was willing to serve with Wellington, he lacked any sense of urgency.

This apparent dilatoriness was open to criticism. Mills complained that

We halted here and have not marched on today though we expect it tomorrow. It is quite impossible to judge of the Marquis's intentions. On the 6th he might have got upon them or at all events might have hurried them out of Valladolid. They were employed during the whole night in conveying stores out, which would have fallen into our hands, and even yesterday we could by running for it have cut off their retreat to Burgos, as the nearest road is on this side of the river. However, today's halt has given them a start which we cannot make up.[21]

Wellington had sent the 6th division, Pack and Bradford's Portuguese and the light dragoons forward in a gesture of pursuit, which took them across the Pisuerga at Cabezon on the 9th, where they 'rather unexpectedly found the French at Dueñas, four leagues from Valladolid, to which place they had return'd finding we did not immediately follow them, and having been reinforced by a Division under Caffarelli, they occupied very strong ground ...'.[22] Wellington himself remained in Valladolid and sent another dispatch to Castaños which stressed the necessity for speed. Whatever the frustrations for the commander, however, there were compensations for the men. William Wheeler of the 51st wrote home that they were now passing through 'a country abounding in vineyards, every night we encamped in some vineyard, and as the grapes were ripe for the harvest we had our fill.'[23]

Douglas was more specific in his memoirs.

From here we passed through a delightful country. At the time the grapes were at the height of perfection, and in the fields (or rather the plains) we were under the necessity of encamping. At all times we were as far removed from these tempting articles as possible, but in the instance it was out of their power to avoid our eating them.[24]

As for Green, he and his comrades found a simple means of thwarting authority.

At this time grapes were ripe, but they were on the opposite side of the river; this, however, did not prevent us from obtaining a supply. For some of the men, taking off their clothes, swam over, ran a mile or two, filled their haversacks, and returned with their valuable cargo. Grapes and bread make an excellent meal, wholesome, affording considerable nourishment.[25]

\* \* \*

The main allied advance continued on the 10th when Wellington decided to move forward in easy stages rather than wait any longer for Castaños and his Galicians. The remaining divisions now left Valladolid. By the end of the day's march headquarters were at Cigales, the troops having crossed the Pisuerga at the fords of Santa Maria and the bridge at

Cabezon. That evening, though, the French rear guard left Dueñas, which Wellington reached the following day. The enemy, meanwhile, marched on to Torquemada. Tomkinson was amused that when he rode two leagues beyond Dueñas to take a look at Palencia 'Lord Wellington was in at the same time, and received in the usual flattering manner, as in other places, a thing he does not object to, though he effects to despise such things. (Circumstance of guerilla going on before him to apprize them in Palencia of his approach.)'[26]

Green also enjoyed a moment's amusement on the march. As the 7th division passed through a small market-town the inhabitants came out to cheer them. 'One poor woman came out of her house in a great hurry, and began to shout "Vive los Francoses!" or "Long live the French!" From this it appears, that the Spanish used to cheer the French army, as well as ours; but the woman had forgotten which army it was, and perhaps to her it was of little importance.'[27]

Although there was further progress on the 12th, with headquarters now at Magaz, two leagues on from Dueñas, Wellington's dispatches make clear his increasing impatience. He wrote to Bathurst: 'I cannot get the Spaniards to make an exertion for themselves; and they are really more backward in the military art than I had thought it possible. Of 30,000 men who are fed as soldiers in Galicia, Santocildes has brought into Castile only 11,000 ragged infantry and 350 cavalry, and I cannot prevail on these to make a direct movement to join me. The object of our operation in the north is therefore making but slow progress, and I fear that I shall have to return to Madrid without having accomplished it ...'[28] At the same time he instructed Santocildes, who had continued to march to Valladolid after the allied army had left the town, to redirect his movements on Palencia, which he was to reach by the 14th.

To his brother Henry Wellington reported that Castaños claimed not to have received his letter of 30 August, while that of 3 September had apparently taken four days to reach him. Furthermore, Santocildes was still marching in the wrong direction.

Thomas Sydenham, a politician attached to the army who had previously been with Henry Wellesley in Cadiz, was blunter in his criticisms of the Spanish generals.

There is Castaños cracking his stale jokes at Leon, and writing humorous letters to Alava, instead of joining Lord Wellington and consulting upon the ulterior operations of the Galician army. He writes that Santocildes will march towards us by a certain route: Lord Wellington sends his aide-de-camp to meet him on that route, to hasten his progress and to direct his movements; but Santocildes changes his route, and the aide-de-camp of course misses him. Santocildes was directed to move on to Valladolid, but his progress is so slow that we are nearly half way to Burgos; yet Santocildes will still move towards Valladolid, and yesterday actually made a retrograde movement instead of a forward one. Instead of being on our flank, he is in our rear, and Lord Wellington must wait two days to enable Santocildes to join us ... If the Galician army had been properly brought forward, we might have been at Burgos the day after to-morrow, and in a few days more Lord Wellington might have been at liberty to return to Madrid after accomplishing the objects for which he left that capital.[29]

There was also frustration for the light dragoons of Anson's brigade, on the heights of Torquemada, where two squadrons, from the 11th and 16th dragoons were on duty.

We remained watching the enemy until 12 a.m., when their infantry marched over the bridge on the Pisuagre for Burgos, leaving six squadrons of cavalry on this side of the water, in front of the town. The brigade was a mile in the rear, and when too late General Anson sent for one gun; two were brought, but before these arrived, the enemy had passed, and we could only come within range of their rear.

It was the most evident thing before it happened that could be, and we lost a chance that may never again occur.

The two squadrons on duty followed their rear close to Quintana, on the Arlanzon, and the enemy at dark, finding we had only so small a force up, attempted to drive us back. The road up as far as this is the finest I ever saw, and from Torquemada to Quintana raised two feet above the level of the ground. The country is covered with vineyards, and intersected with ditches. Cavalry can only act on the road, which made our small numbers equal to theirs. They came down the road at a trot, trumpeting to charge. We stood still, and they halted within thirty yards, firing volleys at us. When they moved forward, we retired, and we kept our ground till dark. Colonel Ponsonby spoke highly of our squadron, and we can with equal justice bear testimony to his conduct. The enemy's rear occupied Quintana; the two squadrons bivouacked a league in front of Torquemada, which place was occupied by the brigade.[30]

Finally, this day of mixed fortunes ended in a wet, stormy night during which the French retired three leagues to Pampliega. The following morning 'General Anson, with the two squadrons coming off duty, occupied

Villajera, a little to the left of the main road, to which place he ordered the brigade; but this was not allowed by Colonel Gordon, the new quartermaster-general, just come *from England*. (He will not stay long with the army.)'[31]

The weather was definitely proving a trying challenge to the allied army. As Mills wrote to his sister, 'The weather is now so bad that campaigning is more than a joke. We are never under cover even of a shrub for this country is not favoured with anything bigger than a vine. The rain comes down in torrents. Headquarters and the staff are always snug in houses, and do not care about the weather and you must know that our Noble Marquis is not gifted with much feeling – ambition hardens the heart. He only regards the comforts of his men as far as it is actually necessary to his purpose; all have their faults and this is his.'[32] However justified this opinion of Wellington, these comments suggest the degree to which the weather would become a factor in the campaign, both as a physical problem and as a depressant of men's spirits.

\* \* \*

Headquarters were now at Torquemada, where Wellington wrote to Bathurst: 'I have continued to follow the movements of the army of Portugal since I last addressed you, but I have not pressed them as hard as I might, as I wished to be joined by the army of Galicia. These troops, to the number of 11,000 infantry, 350 cavalry and 6 pieces of artillery, will be at Palencia, about three leagues from hence tomorrow.'[33]

A hopeful sign that Wellington's expectations would be realized was the arrival of General Castaños, bringing an assurance that the Galician troops were close at hand. On the other hand, not everyone shared Wellington's impatience. Daniell took pleasure in the opportunity to pitch his tent under some willow trees while Green's battalion camped in an extensive 'grape-field', while all around 'The valleys produce wheat, barley, beans, and other grain. We had also good pasture for our horses and mules, and a plentiful supply of water; but wood was very scarce, there being little to be found, except poplar, which will not burn without a great deal of trouble.'[34]

While the man in the ranks could concern himself with such mundane matters, Wellington had more serious issues to deal with. On the east coast General Elio wanted to withdraw the troops of General Roche from Alicante, despite their function as a garrison for that city, a duty which Elio believed could be performed by Maitland's troops. Wellington made clear that if Elio withdrew Roche, he would order Maitland to embark and abandon Alicante, a threat which had the desired effect. He also insisted that General Joseph O'Donnell must stay in communication with the

Anglo-Portuguese army 'lest the troops under his command should be destroyed by those of Soult, on the expected march of the latter from Andalusia into the Kingdom of Valencia; and I recommend the same to you.'[35] The warning was apposite. As already noted, O'Donnell had suffered a crushing defeat at Castella when he launched a foolhardy attack against part of Suchet's army.

On the 15th headquarters had advanced to Villajera, while the army camped before Valleverde and Villodrigo. The French were 'a long league' from Venta de Pozo, with Anson's brigade watching them until nightfall. When the French finally retired from this position the light dragoons occupied Los Valbases to the left of the road. They alone were under cover during a night of continuous rain, which again depressed the spirits of officers and men alike. However, there was a general understanding of the situation. 'The Galician army is said to be in Palencia, and that we are waiting for them. As yet we have not advanced above two leagues each day.'[36]

The next day the Galicians finally arrived. 'They were about 10,000 men badly clothed and equipped & still worse in discipline. The men themselves were in general, fine stout looking fellows, but had the appearance of not being more than half fed.'[37] Another view saw them as very indifferent troops who were no better organized than they had been at the beginning of the war. More outspoken was the suggestion that in appearance the men were like scarecrows and would be considered a disgrace even to the English hulks. Mills, however, was somewhat more complimentary. 'They are in general, soldierly-looking men and tolerably clothed. They have about four hundred cavalry which are bad. I saw one troop of hussars that looked well, and his artillery looks well appointed.'[38] Whatever the true quality of these troops, now that Wellington had the long-awaited Spanish reinforcements, he decided he was strong enough to attack the French the following day.

The French also seemed ready for battle.

In a position about a league from Pampliega, the French army was seen drawn up in three lines, their flanks & centre covered by Artillery. Their Cavalry in Squadrons. On the right bank of a stream falling into Pesuerga [sic], called the Adaja, where the country was flat & well adapted to Cavalry manoeuvres. The numbers of the French were about 30,000 men, as Clausel had been joined by General Souham, who brought up with him 10,000, and being the senior Officer took chief Command. Up to a late hour at night, the enemy showed no disposition to abandon his position & Ld. Wellington resolved to attack them at day-break. The plan of attack was given out, baggage was sent to the rear, & every arrangement made for a general action.[39]

In the meantime, there was some communication between the opposing vedettes. Initially, this took the form of skirmishing, but 'at dark two officers from the 22nd Chasseurs rode up to us. Since Salamanca their tone is a good deal altered, they talk of nothing but joining the grand army in the north, and say the Emperor is at St Petersburg.'[40] This was an optimistic interpretation of Napoleon's Russian expedition.

During the night the rain fell steadily, an aberration in the normal conditions in this part of Spain, but there was 'a brilliant show [of fires] which covered tall the mountain.'[41]

Expectation of action spread through the army as orders for the attack were received. 'The 6th Division, with Pack and two Squadrons of Cavalry and one Spanish Dragoons, to get into the valley of the Tamaron before day-light and turn the Enemy's right by Hormaza the 1st, 5th, 7th; and Cavalry Divisions to advance in front upon Celada del Camino, Bradford and Don Julian with two Squadrons of Cavalry and one Spanish Dragoons to move by the left bank of the Arlanzon upon Cavia, to show upon the Enemy's left, and to be a real attack in case of necessity and occasion offering.'[42]

Captain Thomas Browne of the 23rd, but serving with the Adjutant General's Department, was disturbed during the night when he was ordered to the quartermaster general's office and charged with delivering a letter to

the General Officer commanding a Division of Spaniards on our left. I also had verbal instructions as to the part which this Spanish Division was to take in the attack, & enjoined to see that the orders contained in the letter to the Spanish General were punctually obeyed. The night was so dark that I had some difficulty in finding him & his division. When I had made them out, I proceeded to the General's quarters & gave him the dispatch. He and his Aid de Camp [sic] were sitting smoaking [sic] together in the cottage of a wretched village, which had been completely destroyed by the Spanish Soldiery. Doors, windows, & furniture had been used as fire-wood, & the confusion & noise around the General's quarters were such as to be hardly described, which seemed to give the General no sort of concern. He read his letter which had been written in Spanish by General Alava a distinguished Spanish Officer attached to Head Quarters; immediately shook me by the hand, said he was very glad to see me, & assured me that his division whilst employed in the contemplated attack would implicitly obey any orders that I might be charged with.

He then gave me some cigars & put before me some spirits & water, & as I spoke Spanish pretty fluently we were soon excellent friends ... This General's name was St Pol. He was a fat goodnatured man who looked much more like a monk than a General Officer. I must however do him the justice to say that he had his division under arms an hour before day-break ...[43]

\*   \*   \*

Despite all these preparations there was no battle. The allied troops were formed up and under arms by 4.00am, but the French had retired under cover of darkness, leaving their camp fires burning. The allies advanced as planned, however, and came across the French cavalry rear guard at Estapar, while the main force was sighted on the heights above Arcos, with its left on Pardajos. This was a strong position, but it was surrendered without a fight when the position was turned by the 6th division. The rest of the army advanced up the main road: 'It was a beautiful day, and to see the two armies marching along, each having a line of skirmishers in its front, was grand; but to observe our cavalry scouting their rear, and how the enemy scampered off, was very diverting, especially as few lives were lost on the occasion.'[44]

Browne, still with St Pol's division, had tried without success to persuade the Spaniards to form up in a quiet, military manner.

> They marched off, however, in tolerable silence but when it was made known that the French had decamped ... nothing could exceed the tumult of these Spaniards. They swore & called the French every name of reproach that was possible, using every term of opprobrium to which they felt that they themselves could possibly lay claim. Liars, Thieves & Cowards they were who dared not face brave Spaniards. One would have supposed they had been fighting a desperate battle & gained a complete victory. St Pol proposed to halt his division & that they should pile arms & go to sleep. I pointed out to him that the troops on his right were moving forwards & that he would be expected to accompany their movements, which he ordered his division to do. The whole army halted about mid-day.[45]

It would seem that his

> favourable ground, and the immediate vicinity of Burgos induced Clausel to remain in position till the allied army was nearly formed for the attack. All his battalions could be distinctly numbered, and the force drawn out was calculated at 22,000: they did not, however, risk the shock, but quickly retired at the approach of the Allies, forming

a sad contrast to the imposing appearance and bold conduct they maintained prior to their defeat [at Salamanca].[46]

Headquarters were now established at Frandoviñez, while the main army camped before Villa Buniel and the left column occupied ground near Tarjados, on the other side of the Arlanzon.

Several days later Wellington described the events of the 16th and 17th to Bathurst.

> The enemy had on the 16th taken up a strong position on the heights behind Celada del Camino, and arrangements were made to attack them on the morning of the 17th; but the enemy retired in the night; and they were driven on the 17th to the heights close to Burgos. They retired through the town in the night, leaving behind them some clothing and other stores, and a large quantity of wheat and barley; and have since continued their retreat to Briviesca, there it is reported that the Prince of Essling has been ordered by the local government in France to come and take command of the army.

In fact, Marshal Masséna had declined a return to the Peninsula on the grounds of ill health and, as has been noted, General Souham had arrived in his place with about 10,000 conscripts.

The way was now clear for Wellington to focus his attention on Burgos, which the French abandoned on the 18th, leaving a garrison of 2,000 men in the castle under General Dubreton, the general who had successfully evacuated Santander in August. Wellington, with his staff, reconnoitred the defences at midday and seems not to have been deterred by what he found. However, Lieutenant Colonel Robe R.A. commented to Alexander Dickson, in command of the Portuguese Artillery, but who was absent sick, 'we have had a view of the castle which appears a more tough job than we might have supposed.'[47] It was to prove a prophetic judgement.

## Chapter 5

# Taking the Castle

Having reconnoitred the castle, Wellington set about placing his troops, some to besiege it and others to cover the siege. The first division and Pack's Portuguese were chosen to invest the castle; the 6th division, with one Galician brigade attached, was posted south of the Arlanzon in the suburbs of Burgos; and the 5th and 7th divisions, Bradford's Portuguese and the rest of the Galicians were cantoned in villages to the north-west of Burgos, covering the route taken by the French. Anson's brigade took up positions a league in front of these covering troops to watch the French piquets at Quintanapala. At the same time, Clausel had joined Caffarelli, who had been at Burgos on the 17th, when he had placed the garrison in the castle. At Briviesca Clausel was to find the new commander of the Army of Portugal; not Masséna, who had declined on grounds of ill health, but General Joseph Souham, who had brought reinforcements with him from France. Souham, when he arrived, was in no hurry to make his presence felt, however, preferring to wait upon events further south.

The castle of Burgos had been identified by Napoleon as crucial to French communications and he had given orders that its defences should be strengthened to protect the town, which constituted a major depot for the French army. However, according to Jacques Vidal Belmas, in his narrative of the sieges of Spain and Portugal, there was never enough money or workmen or means of transport to effect these improvements. Nevertheless, the castle, situated on a height above the river, was well placed to cover the bridges which crossed the Arlanzon, as well as the roads leading into the town. It was protected by three lines. The first or outer line was the old escarp wall of the town or the castle. It was revetted and surrounded by a shot-proof parapet, while a ten-metre ditch constituted a further obstacle for an attacking force. The second and third lines took the form of field retrenchments and were strongly palisaded. The third line incorporated an old donjon and the church of La Blanca, which served as a redoubt.

On a level with the keep and 250 metres to the north was the outwork of San Miguel. The two branches, or horns, of the work were imperfect, neither the front nor the branches being palisaded or fraised. Work had

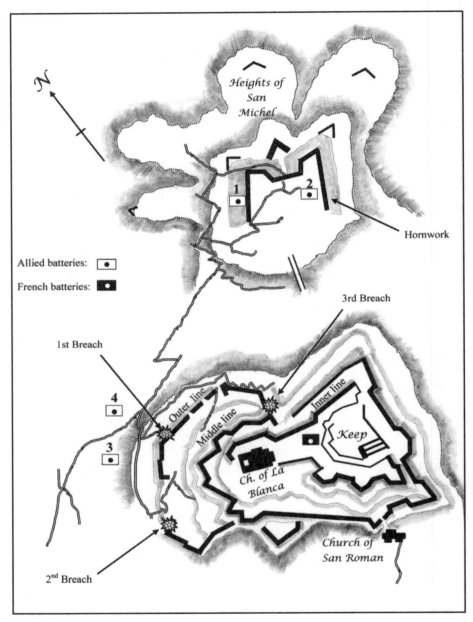

*The siege of Burgos*

begun on a redoubt above the ravine which separated the height of San Miguel from the castle, and a communication to cross the ravine, but these had barely taken shape. The front scarp of the hornwork, though, was twenty-five feet high, steeply inclined, and protected by a counter-scarp ten feet deep, while the rear had been closed by strong palisading. The interior was in range of the defenders' principal battery, called Napoleon, and the branches, of the guns mounted on the castle. According to John Jones RE, who was at the siege, the defenders had nine heavy guns, eleven field pieces and six mortars or howitzers in battery.

The fortification was vulnerable in several ways. An attack from the southern end of La Blanca would present a small front, while the defenders' guns could not be sufficiently depressed. Also, this was the side of the castle where the lines were weakest. The outer line was susceptible to attack to the front and the left flank, while the middle line had little defence against frontal fire, and the inner line gave the defenders little room for manoeuvre because of the position of La Blanca. Furthermore, the parapet and scarp could be cannonaded from San Miguel.

Wellington drew an inevitable conclusion from his initial reconnaissance that the limitations of allied artillery meant each line would have to be taken in turn. In other words, the middle line could not be attacked until a secure lodgement and safe communications had been secured on the outer line; and any attack on the inner line could only take place when the middle line had been secured. Furthermore, before any assault could take place, the target line would have to come under sustained fire from batteries on San Miguel, which meant that taking the hornwork had to be the first objective.

As a result, a surprise attack on the front of the hornwork was planned for 8.00pm on the 18th. A detachment of 300 men of the 1/42nd were to line the counterscarp and provide covering fire for 200 men of Pack's Portuguese brigade, who would escalade the demi-bastions of the work, having been preceded by a ladder party and forlorn hope, also from the 1/42nd. The light companies of this battalion, along with those of the 1/24th and 1/79th, were to force an entry from the rear.

Jones kept a journal of the sieges at which he served, thus creating a narrative which effectively conveys an engineer's view of events as they developed. This makes clear that the attack did not evolve as planned.

The firing party, on being put in movement, were discovered by the garrison of the hornwork, and instantly a heavy discharge of musketry was directed on them from the whole front. This fire induced the British line, contrary to orders, to open fire also, although 120 yards distant from the hornwork; and the men continuing to fire whilst advancing to the edge of the counterscarp, by the time they reached that alignment, such numbers had been killed or wounded, that the few remaining, able to move, dispersed.

The Portuguese troops allotted for the escalade of the left demi-bastion were preceded by a party of Highlanders under Lieutenant Pitts, Royal Engineers, carrying the scaling ladders. The Highlanders coolly raised the ladders against the escarp, and the attention of the garrison being much occupied by the firing party, they mounted to the upper staves of the ladders almost without opposition; but the assaulting party, notwithstanding this stimulating example, could not be prevailed upon to enter the ditch.

The escalade of the right demi-bastion was also unsuccessful.[1]

Events developed rather differently at the rear of the hornwork. Although under heavy fire from the castle, Major Cocks, in command, brought his men up to the palisade, which was successfully escaladed. 'We tumbled the garrison out, bayoneting 70, taking 70, and wounding from 2 to 300,' Cocks wrote to his brother, while he told his father, 'It pleased God I should receive only a slight wound in the arm which, as it did not disable me, I have not returned.'[2]

Tomkinson, a close friend of Cocks from their days together in the 16th dragoons, expanded on this achievement.

Cocks never thought of a false attack, and moved with the intention of a real one. The castle opened a heavy fire on him as he advanced. He ran up a slope of fourteen feet, at the top of which palisades of seven feet were to be passed. These he got over without the help of ladders, and under a heavy fire from the troops stationed to protect the gorge, gaining the body of the work with about 140 men. Those troops of the enemy employed in repulsing the attack made by General Pack were all in the ditch, and Cocks, by gaining the work, drove the remainder of the garrison to them.

With his 140 he took possession of the right demi-bastion, as the most commanding point he could find, and from it kept up a heavy fire on the ditch. He had so few men that he could not spare sufficient numbers to guard the sally-port into the ditch, and he could not go there with his whole force, not knowing how many passages they might have out of the ditch; and had there been another and they had come into the work, he being at that point, all would have again been lost.

The people in the ditch found their case desperate, made a rush at the entrance, drove back the men there placed, and gained the body of the place. They had no sooner entered than he charged them, drove them out of the gorge, bayoneting fifty, and making as many more prisoners, leaving him, with his handful of men, in possession of the place.

Tomkinson added a humanizing detail: 'Cocks made sure his men got their dinner before the attack'.[3]

The French perspective on the loss of the hornwork can be found in Dubreton's report, which focused on the determined defence offered by the 34th regiment, who

> made every effort possible to push the enemy back; but the large extent of the fortifications did not allow them to guard all the accessible points, and as the palisading at the gorge was not finished, it was not possible to prevent the English penetrating as far as the platform, under the sustained fire of all parts of the main fort. The defenders, overwhelmed by numbers, managed however to make their way out with the bayonet, and get back to the fort, but not without heavy losses ...[4]

Jones gave French losses as six officers and 137 men killed or wounded. The French also lost seven field pieces.

Wellington, however, was more pessimistic when on the 20th he wrote to General Sir Edward Paget, who was on his way to join the army. 'Although we succeeded, the operation was not well carried on, and I am afraid that our loss is not less than 300 men. After all, I am a little apprehensive that I have the means to take this castle, which the French have strengthened to the utmost in their power. I shall be able to judge better in a day or two.'[5] He made the same point to Bathurst the following day, but added that he had received information suggesting the garrison had limited supplies of water, while their provisions were stored in a building which could be set on fire. 'I think it possible, therefore, that I may have it in my power to force them to surrender, although I may not be able to lay the place open to assault.'[6] His figures for the losses suffered on the night of the 18th, which he added to the dispatch, were seventy-one officers and men killed, 333 wounded and fourteen missing.

\* \* \*

Work now began on a lodgement to the front of the hornwork and a connecting communication from the rear of the hill. The working party of 300 men came under heavy fire from the castle, but it was felt necessary to persevere because the same vulnerability which had enabled the allies to take the hornwork would still apply if the French attempted a sortie to regain it. Good progress was made on the lodgement during the night of the 19th, so that on the 20th a further 150 men could work during the day to improve it and establish a secure communication. Furthermore, such was the security of the working party that it was considered unnecessary to return the garrison's fire, although as a precaution the trench guard was kept under cover.

During the night a party of 600 men was employed to start work on No. 1 battery to the front right of the hornwork. Although the garrison fired shot and shell, causing some casualties, the battery itself was protected by the uneven ground. At this early stage of the siege there was an optimistic expectation that Burgos would fall within a week, which was in clear contrast to Wellington's more cautious expectations.

Work on the lodgement continued throughout the 21st, helped by some inaccurate French fire, while fifty men were specifically engaged on No. 1 battery. At night another working party of 600 men opened a trench which was designed to support the battery and enable communication from the lodgement to the hornwork. This last was on higher ground and more exposed. The grape, shot and shell which fell on the working area meant that not everything had been completed by daylight. Also, guards had to be placed in the approaches or under cover of the hill in expectation of a sortie by the enemy, while a strong detachment was ready to stand at arms in the lodgement. The French, however, stayed within their defences.

Wellington also took the opportunity to confine the French more closely in the castle, instructing General Clinton to direct Colonel Brown, commanding the 9th caçadores,

> to make arrangements for placing the troops under his command in the houses close to the walls, and for keeping possession as soon as we shall be prepared to lodge ourselves in the exterior lines.
>
> I shall also be much obliged to you if you will look at the posts occupied by the Spaniards, and see whether, by a better connection of their posts with ours, or by a better arrangement of them, we could confine the enemy more effectively than we have hitherto.[7]

He also sent the covering force further forward. The 5th and 7th divisions were now to the rear of Quintanapala, where they expected to fight should the French attempt to relieve Burgos.

No. 1 battery was operational by the morning of the 22nd. This allowed two 18-pounders and three howitzers to be put in place to support an assault on the outer line. A second battery was then started in the gorge in front of the hornwork. This would have a clear view of the keep and could be used when the time arrived to breach the keep.

At this point Wellington took the decision to escalade the outer wall and establish a lodgement as a means of counteracting his shortage of artillery.

The point chosen was the north face of the outer wall where the scarp was twenty-four feet high, but the ditch was shallow and the counterscarp was not revetted. This point could be approached by the sunken road from the suburb of San Pedro. The storming party comprised 400 men from the 1st division with five ladders. When they came up from San Pedro, 200 of the men were to take post on the bank to prevent the garrison mounting the parapet and bayoneting the escaladers. The other 200 were to climb the ladders in parties of twenty, each party to wait for the previous party to complete its ascent. As soon as the whole 200 had successfully escaladed, the firing party would demolish the masonry scarp to create a practicable ramp. A working party, under the command of engineer officers, would be standing by with gabions and fascines. As diversion, Colonel Brown's caçadores were to assault the outer line at a point directly opposite the escalade, where the defences were particularly weak.

The attack began at midnight, but once again things did not go to plan.

> The attack of the flank defences by the Portuguese battalion never came to anything like a serious attempt. They were checked while advancing by a fire from a guard-house on the line, and did not enter the ditch. The escalade in front, therefore, even if correctly executed, would not, probably, have had more than a momentary success. As it was, the men with the five ladders reached the wall, and reared them almost unopposed; but the main body, although the ground was perfectly open, advancing on a front of only four men, had lengthened out so considerably before they reached the point of contention, that, on the garrison opening their fire, much confusion was created by the efforts made to close up the ranks, and, in consequence, the firing party never took post on the bank, but the whole pushed together into the ditch. Several gallant attempts were made to ascend the ladders, and some of the assailants each time gained a momentary footing, but were as often bayoneted down; after which the garrison mounted on top of the parapet, and in addition to a fire of musketry, threw over a great number of 4-pound shot and much burning composition, which caused many of the men's pouches to explode.[8]

Mills was scathing in his account.

> Our men got the ladders up with some difficulty under a heavy fire from the top of the wall, but were unable to get to the top. Hall of the 3rd Regiment [3rd Foot Guards] who mounted first was knocked down. Frazer tried and was shot in the knee. During the whole of this time [the French] kept up a constant fire from the top of the wall and threw down bags of gunpowder and large stones. At last, having

been twenty-five minutes in the ditch and not seeing anything of the other parties they retired having lost half their numbers in killed and wounded. 3 officers were wounded. The Portuguese failed in their attempts. Thus ended the attack which was almost madness to attempt.[9]

In the confusion which followed the death of the officer in command, Major Laurie of the 79th, fifteen minutes passed before the decision was taken to retire, by which time there were 158 casualties, including at least forty men killed. Injuries could be horrific. George Bingham, in command of the first brigade of the 6th division, instanced the misfortune of one of the officers of his brigade.

Lieutenant Stewart of the 61st, who had volunteered his services as acting Engineer, and had only arrived from Salamanca (where he had been left in the hospital wounded) had half his face carried away by round shot; of all his features one eye only is left.[10]

Presumably, some of the damage was actually superficial because Lieutenant Gilbert Stewart survived and was reported in the *London Gazette* as having been 'slightly wounded' at Burgos. He subsequently received a pension of £100 per annum for loss of an eye and a further £100 for other wounds.

Dubreton justifiably congratulated himself that the assault had been

received with vigour by five companies of the second battalion of the 34th of the line. A few of the assailants reached as far as the parapet, but they were knocked over, and the rest were put to flight by our fusillade and by the loaded shells which we rolled into the ditch ... The enemy suffered greatly in this action, and left in the ditches the shells which they had brought, and about forty dead, including three officers. There were a great number of wounded, if one judges by the wreckage abandoned at the point of attack.[11]

French losses were nine killed and thirteen wounded.

Among the allies, whose only consolation was the kindness with which the French cared for the wounded, recriminations began almost immediately. Lieutenant Colonel Burgoyne, the senior engineer officer, blamed the Portuguese. Wellington blamed Major Laurie for rushing on like a common soldier. As he later explained to Lord Liverpool, the prime minister,

the field officer who commanded, did that which is too common in our army. He paid no attention to his orders, notwithstanding the pains I took in writing them, and in reading and explaining them to him twice over. He made none of the dispositions ordered; and instead of regulating the attack as he ought, he rushed on as if he had been the leader of a forlorn hope, and fell, together with many of those who went with him.[12]

Jones, taking a different view, questioned the wisdom of using detachments from different regiments, a measure which he believed to be particularly dangerous when used for night movements or in hazardous situations. Five days after the failed escalade, though, Wellington presented Bathurst with a more sanitized account than Liverpool was to receive, in which 'the Portuguese troops were so strongly opposed that they could not make any progress on the enemy's flank; and the escalade could not take place ...' He praised the efforts of Laurie and Captain Frazer, whose leg had to be amputated. 'Both these officers, and indeed all those employed on this occasion, exerted themselves to the upmost; but the attack on the enemy's flank having failed, the success of the escalade was impracticable.'[13]

*   *   *

On the morning of the 23rd the garrison opened an unusually fierce cannonade and succeeded in seriously damaging the parapet of the communication trench which ran through to the rear of the hornwork. This was despite the gabions which had been put in place. The batteries, however, were almost ready. Yet this progress was balanced by another factor very much to the allies' disadvantage. At 9.00pm it began to rain heavily. On the 21st Captain Thomas Dyneley RA had written to his sister, 'The cold weather has set in, and I shall now do very well. We have had a vast deal of rain lately, but I manage to keep it out remarkably well by a tolerable proportion of blankets, and Mr Lyon's umbrella fastened to the head of my bed. I do not expect we shall have much wet this winter.'[14] Dyneley's hopes were to be sadly disappointed.

With the failure of the escalade it was evident that different tactics were needed. Mining was the obvious alternative, but there were two basic problems: lack of specialist sappers and miners, and lack of appropriate tools for work underground. Despite these problems, initial progress was promising. The sunken road from San Pedro was converted into a parallel, which was formed by cutting steps along the summit of the bank. The working party of 250 men was then able to open the ground undetected by the garrison. As work continued on the trench, which was necessarily deep and narrow to safeguard the workmen, a firing party was posted to add further protection. By this means head-on fire was prevented, but Dubreton had posted three marksmen behind a projecting palisade which overlooked the trench at an angle, and two of them in particular were able to cause a considerable number of casualties.

The following night work began on a diagonal flying sap, from the new parallel towards the outer line, coming to within twenty yards of the scarp wall. The French responded by rolling shells down onto the workmen as well as engaging in some well-aimed musketry fire, which killed Captain Williams RE, shot through the heart while directing operations in the sap.

The positioning of the guns had also been reorganized. Two 18-pounders were transferred from No. 1 battery to No. 2, while two 24-pounders were put in their place. Early on the morning of the 25th the 24-pounders opened fire on the strong palisade which was sheltering the French marksmen, but failed to destroy it. This was due to the lack of precise firing from the howitzers, which meant that they would need a great deal more ammunition than they had available. The implications of undertaking the siege with inadequate resources were becoming increasingly clear.

No. 2 battery was now ready for action, being both protected and disguised by earth-filled embrasures, and ground was chosen for 'a Battery of five Howitzers to throw Spherical Case upon the top of the Castle to annoy the Enemy at his seven-gun Battery of 18-pounders when our Batteries open.'[15] In fact, the French guns were 16-pounders. There had also been an early start on the mine, while at night a series of zig-zag trenches were dug downhill from No. 1 battery to open a second musketry trench about a hundred yards from the outer wall. The garrison reacted quickly to this development and

> the showers of grape-shot which fell without intermission all round the spot, causing an incessant whizzing and rattling amongst the stones, appeared at the moment to be carrying destruction through the ranks; but, except the necessity of instantly carrying off the wounded, on account of their sufferings, it caused little interruption to the workmen. It was remarked here, as it had been on former occasions, that a wound from a grape-shot is less quietly borne than a wound from a round-shot or musketry. The latter is seldom known in the night, except from the falling of the individual; whereas the former, not infrequently, draws forth loud lamentations.[16]

Among the wounded on the 25th was 2nd Captain Charles Dansey of the artillery. As he wrote to his mother the following day,

> you must know then, that being yesterday morning on a battery, leaning against the merlon, a round shot took it on the outside, and

laid me sprawling on the platform, under the weight of about ½ a ton of sandbags, first for half an instant I thought I was killed, then for about a minute I did not think at all, & at last, when I began to think again I made an uncommon good guess of what had happened, for concluding I was wounded I politely begged a stretcher, and was carried out of the trenches, then being lifted on a horse I rode home to my tent, and here I am now lying on my back with my elbows into my sides like the pinions of a goose, my shoulders are both contused so that I cannot lift my arms, and I have only the use of them as far as the elbows, but there is no blood drawn and no bone broke and the doctors tell me it will be merely an *appledildode* affair, as long as I lay still I am easy and tolerably free from pain, but I expect to be confined to my tent for about three days longer, I thank God, I have every comfort and attention that a sick man can wish for, sick indeed I ought not to say (but sore as you please) for independent of a twitch now & then when I begin to be restless (and you know I was never given to be over quiet) I am just as well as I ever was, I have an excellent appetite, but they keep me to chicken broth, sago and the like, which makes me very much inclined to be mutinous.[17]

Work continued on the mine on the 26th and progress was so good that by the end of the day the gallery extended eighteen feet, at a height of four feet and a width of three feet. The soil stood well without supports. Above ground, however, French marksmen continued to inflict casualties. Allied sharpshooters had some success in limiting the effect of this musketry, but 'The fire of musketry from behind the palisaded tambour continued to be very destructive to the workmen in the sap whenever they became exposed to it. A gabion having been knocked down by a shell this morning, Captain Kenny, 9th regiment, assistant engineer, was shot through the head in the endeavour to replace it.'[18] Kenny was one of several volunteer officers who supplemented the engineers, just as volunteer detachments from the covering battalions were engaged in sapping and mining.

Despite the efforts of the garrison, the zig-zags were extended and a musketry trench was opened, although French fire meant that gabions had to be carried forward, two men at a time, to protect it. After dark the original parallel was extended southwards to within twenty-three yards of the outer wall, and a second mine was planned. Mines, however, were an allied tactic that Dubreton had already anticipated. On the 25th he reported that 'Always presuming that the enemy will make a breach with a mine, we have prepared several means of obstacles to push back the assault.'[19] These obstacles lay in wait for the allies.

Although the siege was proving more protracted than had been expected, the wider picture was satisfactory. The suggestion of an advance by the Army of Portugal a few days before had proved unfounded. Instead, Clausel now dispersed his forces, some on the left bank of the Ebro and some as far as Domijos de la Callada. Despite this French inactivity, Wellington had other reasons to be concerned. On the 26th he wrote to Sir Home Popham: 'I am very much in want of 40 barrels of gunpowder, each containing 90 pounds, for the attack of this place; and I should be very much obliged to you if you could let me have this quantity from the ships under your command.'[20] The next day, when the request was for biscuit, he added, 'We are not getting on very rapidly, and I do not feel certain that I shall succeed, as I have very little artillery and stores for my object; but I hope I may succeed.'[21]

When day broke on the 27th it was observed that the French had been strengthening the middle line by directing a covered way towards it, while a strong stockade had been erected in front of the gateway, as if to secure communication with the covered way. This suggested that the defenders had abandoned the outer line. At the same time they were still attacking the sap (the new musketry trench) with stones and other missiles, as well as directing artillery fire which destroyed the gabions and made the trench untenable. The unfinished parapet offered inadequate protection and the working party was withdrawn.

On the allied side work now began on the gallery for the second mine, and on a trench to accommodate a firing party. The gallery for the first mine already extended to twenty-eight feet, despite the picks and shovels being inappropriate for working in a confined space. The men, however, were increasingly resentful of the situation in which they now found themselves and when the working party assembled at night to work on a communication trench from No. 1 battery towards San Pedro only 350 men reported for duty instead of the 500 required. Those who did report worked well, but once again the garrison resorted to grape-shot, not well-directed, but sufficient to require a double-height parapet to protect the trench. With the advantage of daylight and the gradient, French fire became more accurate. Also, 'it was found that the reverse of the trench, being much higher than the front, the enemy's shells either stuck into it and burst there, or, when pitched beyond it, rolled back from the hill into the trench, which rendered the work so perilous, that it was deferred till night',[22] when the parapet was raised and strengthened, although the trench remained vulnerable to shells.

During the night the musketry trench below the hornwork was repaired, allowing counter-fire against the garrison. Work also continued on the galleries. By daybreak on the 29th the first gallery was forty-two feet long and the second thirty-two feet. At noon the first gallery hit solid masonry, which was assumed to be the foundations of the scarp wall. A powder chamber was now dug out, five feet long, and filled with twelve barrels, each containing ninety pounds of powder requisitioned from the artillery. A fuse was laid in a wooden channel and the tunnel was packed with bags of earth for fifteen feet to force the explosion upwards. By 10.00pm the mine was ready to be fired.

An attempt was made to extend the musketry trench below the horn-work to the allies' right in order to bring a greater force of fire on the space above the outer line. Without gabions to protect the men, though, the number of casualties quickly mounted and the attempt had to be abandoned.

Everything was now in place for an assault, dependent only upon the successful springing of the mine.

> At midnight a storming party of 300 men, having been paraded in the lower town, and a working party, with the necessary tools and materials, being in their rear to form a lodgement, the mine was sprung. The explosion made very little report, but brought the wall down. The earth of the rampart behind the ruined scarp remained very steep, but next the broken parts of the wall, on both sides, the ascent was easy.[23]

Unfortunately, the breach was not as extensive as might have been expected after such an explosion, because the masonry which the miners had encountered was actually the foundations of an older wall rather than of the outer line.

The breach was initially mounted by a sergeant and four men who found the defenders so panic-stricken that they offered no opposition. This shock was momentary, however; the French quickly recovered and drove the assailants back, bayoneting them in the process. This was the total success of the assault.

> The night being dark, and the circumstances of the case novel, the officer commanding the first division of the storming party erred in the direction of the breach, and reached the escarp wall too much to his right; where, finding the masonry uninjured, he returned with his party into the parallel, reporting that the mine had produced no effect, and in consequence the storming party was ordered to retire.
>
> Soon afterwards the sergeant and three men returned [the fourth had been maimed], and being examined, proved the existence of the breach by their burns and bayonet wounds; but, as during the interval, the garrison had formed under arms, and a considerable

force had marched to the breach, so as to preclude all hopes of success in a second attempt, no further effort was made.[24]

It would seem that this debacle was a direct consequence of the shortage of engineer officers. At this point in the siege none of the three surviving officers, excluding Colonel Burgoyne in command, was fit for duty. As a result, for the first time in a siege the men were sent into action without an engineer to direct them.

Without artillery or musketry fire to protect the breach, the allies were unable to prevent the French from forming a parapet behind it during the rest of the night.

Ensign Aitchison had a clear view on this failure. 'Thus again has another failure taken place – I shall not say from deploying detachments of different regiments, but in this as in the former instance [on the 22nd] such were deployed.'[25] This was to be a recurrent theme in his letters and diary entries. He also criticized the decision not to inform the men of the service required of them until just before they were sent into action, with the result that they did not have time to work themselves into an appropriate frame of mind.

\* \* \*

The morning of the 30th revealed just how limited had been the effects of the explosion and how effectively the French had repaired the damage. Consequently, no further assault at this point in the defences was possible. It was no surprise that the troops were losing confidence in the engineers, and the commander-in-chief himself. They had been working for twelve days under fierce and well-directed enemy fire, while their own batteries had yet to fire a useful shot. Not surprisingly, the working parties were disinclined to exert themselves as their discouragement grew.

One cause of this discouragement was the accuracy of the French marksmen. Any man who made himself visible was likely to be hit. The only solution was to destroy the stockade which sheltered the sharpshooters. A French 6-pounder, found at the hornwork, was taken into No. 1 battery. The battery then opened fire on the stockade, which was totally destroyed within three hours.

At dusk a third battery, positioned below the outer line to destroy the scarp wall, was marked out sixty-five yards from the wall. Its position, so close to the outer defences, meant that it would be screened from French artillery fire. A musket-proof parapet was quickly constructed to make it doubly safe. Then 200 infantrymen were employed in removing three 18-pounders from the trench near No. 2 battery and hauling them to No. 3. By 9.00am on 1 October, as the carpenters laid the platforms, the new battery was declared ready. The guns were run out and the embrasures were about to be unmasked to reveal 'Thunder', 'Lightning' and 'Nelson'. The sense of achievement was short-lived, however. As Dickson, who was now on the scene, reported,

> the enemy at the same time commenced a fire of 6 inch shells over the parapet, apparently from a howitzer or mortar with small charges, which rolling down upon the battery did some injury to it, and in a very short time afterwards, having made an opening in an outer wall, they brought a light gun to bear on the battery which fired through the parapet every round, and with the addition of a brisk fire of Musketry on the battery, rendered it so hot, that Lord Wellington ordered the Artillery men to evacuate it without the guns having ever been unmasked. In the course of the morning the fire of the enemy was increased to three guns, assisted by two or three mortars or howitzers, which nearly demolished the parapet, disabled two of the gun carriages, and knocked a trunnion off one of the 18 Prs.[26]

A determined effort was now made to take out the French gunners.

> The best marksmen were selected from the guard of the trenches, and posted in different situations, from 30 to 100 yards distant, to fire in at the embrasures.
> Some officers, good shots, who had frequently shown their skill in picking off individuals, attempted to play the same game on this occasion; but the French marksmen speedily drove them out of the field. – Ensign N[eville], assistant engineer, lost part of an ear in this personal contention.[27]

Parke Percy Neville of the 2/30th had already volunteered for engineering duties at Ciudad Rodrigo and at Badajoz, where he was wounded.

After the destruction of No.3 battery, the decision was taken to site a fourth battery to its left rather than try to effect repairs. During the night the guns were withdrawn from No. 3 and placed close to No. 4, under cover of a steep bank. Also during the night 150 men were engaged in placing woolpacks, which had been collected during the day in San Pedro, to form strong revetments and protect the embrasures.

At daybreak on 2 October, however, No. 4 battery was destroyed by the French guns before the allied guns could even be brought into position and the besiegers' activities were effectively curtailed. The two surviving 18-pounders were moved to No. 2 battery after dark.

> The night being tempestuous with very heavy rain, the greatest difficulty was experienced in the movement, and all the Infantry

working party (with the exception of a detachment of the Brigade of Guards) having absented themselves, the two guns could not be got further than the top of the hill in front of the left salient of the Hornwork, when day light put an end to the labour.[28]

The engineers were more successful in recovering the woolpacks and other materials from No. 4 battery, despite the excessively wet and stormy weather. Underground, too, there was pleasing progress as the miners extended the gallery of the second mine to seventy-two feet, only three feet from the target wall.

The French, meanwhile, were able to raise the parapet behind the first breach, undeterred by sustained allied musketry.

Wellington was still keeping a careful watch on the Army of Portugal, despite its apparent inactivity behind the Ebro. He was also anxious that it should not receive reinforcements from the Army of the North. Thus he wrote to Popham:

> The great object for me is that you should draw the attention of the enemy, by your operations, from those which we are carrying on on this side, and that you should prevent Caffarelli from detaching troops to aid Marmont's army. It would be desirable for many reasons that you should get possession of Santoña, and also of Guetraria; but I confess that I entertain so bad an opinion of the Spanish troops that I do not think you can rely on them; and the body of marines that you have with you is not sufficiently large to do much of themselves, or to be a very efficient example to the Spanish troops.

Turning to his own affairs, Wellington was realistic about his chances of taking Burgos.

> I am very afraid that I shall not take this castle. It is very strong, well-garrisoned and well provided with artillery. I had only three pieces of cannon, of which one was destroyed last night, and not much ammunition; and I have not been able to get on as I ought. I have, however, got a mine under one of the works, which I hope will enable me to carry the exterior line; and when that shall be carried I hope I shall get on better. But time is wearing apace, and Soult is moving from the South; and I shall not be surprised if I were obliged to discontinue this operation in order to collect the army.[29]

He recognised the irony that Popham had the guns and ammunition but lacked the men for his operations, while Wellington had the men but lacked the guns for his. However, he was convinced that without adequate transport to convey guns from either Santander or Madrid he could not alter the situation, a view he maintained until too late.

Although the progress of the second mine had so far gone well, on 3 October problems developed. The miners hit rock at seventy-four feet, and the gallery had to be carried over it. Lack of ventilation was also an increasing problem. The air was bad and put the miners' candles out. It became necessary to bring the miners out for thirty-minute periods. Inevitably, this slowed down the progress of the gallery, which it was decided should be extended a further four feet beyond the wall, a decision based on the failure of the first mine. To make doubly sure that the gallery was long enough, eleven officers were separately employed after dusk to measure the distance from the mouth of the mine to the scarp wall. The external measurement was agreed to be between seventy-three and seventy-four feet, while the length of the gallery was seventy-nine feet. It was therefore certain that even if the gallery had not followed the shortest line, the miners had arrived under the wall. To make sure they had arrived behind it, they were ordered to tunnel yet another four feet, making the total length eighty-three feet.

The damaged guns and carriages were now being repaired, but only one was initially made serviceable. No. 1 battery opened fire to improve the partial breach made by the first mine, to allow two assaults when the second mine was fired. It seemed, though, that the French suspected the existence of this second mine because they began work on a second retrenchment behind the first.

Further afield there was even more cause for concern. 'As we were turning out at Fresno a report came in that the enemy was advancing, which caused us to move as quick as we could to the main road in rear of Monasterio.' French cavalry had driven the allied advance piquet from Castel Peones, but

> It fortunately happened that as the troops were that morning to be relieved, the squadron of the 11th remaining in Monasterio, was turned out to relieve the one of the 12th on duty, and on hearing the fire moved down the road and came up in time to charge at the bridge over the small river half a league in front of Monasterio, over which the 12th had retired in some confusion. The 11th charged them at the bridge, drove them back; the enemy turned again, and they were obliged to retire, formed again, and so advanced a second time. The enemy's intention was to surprise the advanced squadron, in which they failed, and retired again to their former posts. Had it not so happened that the 11th were turned out to relieve them, I have

little doubt they would have taken greater number of the 12th, and gained Monasterio before the troops there could have turned out.[30]

Although the French cavalry had obviously been probing the allied covering line, this advance was disturbing. Coupled with the news that General Souham was now in command of the Army of Portugal, it suggested that the French were ready to take the offensive. The following day a battalion of the 7th division was brought up to strengthen the allied position at Monasterio. This did not impress Tomkinson. The chosen battalion was the Brunswick Oels light infantry. To Tomkinson, this meant a flood of desertions would now take place. The ranks of the Black Brunswickers had been steadily filled with German prisoners of war who preferred (often temporary) service with the allies rather than confinement in England. Indeed, with the similarly constituted Chasseurs Britanniques also in the 7th, this division was peculiarly prone to desertion.

Back at Burgos Bingham wrote to his mother,

I did not expect to have addressed you from this place again but I am sorry to tell you we are as far off as ever from obtaining possession of the castle; our means are so miserably inadequate, and we have not talent enough amongst our engineers to compensate for the want of means. I see no end of the siege, which has already cost us very dear, and it is likely to be more expensive yet, in the articles of men and time, both precious in War.

At least Bingham had found dry quarters in a mill, 'although it swarms with fleas to that degree, that at first it was quite terrible.[31]

When on the morning of the 4 October No. 1 battery opened fire, the gun with the split muzzle was initially used cautiously. Later the full six-pound charge was used, and this gun, along with the only undamaged gun and the three 24-pounder howitzers, had created a sixty-foot breach by 4.00pm. Underground, the mine was charged with over 1,000 pounds of powder deposited in sandbags and the gallery was tamped for twelve feet.

The assault was planned for 5.00pm in the last of the daylight. It was to be undertaken by the 2/24th, with detachments from other battalions in support. Having formed up in the hollow way, undetected by the French, the 24th moved forward to attack the two breaches. Each half-battalion was preceded by a forlorn hope under the command of a subaltern, lieutenants Holmes and Fraser. Captain Hedderwick was in overall command. At 5.00pm, or half an hour later according to the French sources, the mine was fired. The explosion opened up a 100-foot breach and killed many of the defenders. The forlorn hopes were in the breaches even before the dust had settled. The rest of the battalion came up and managed to drive the surviving defenders back to their rear entrenchments after some fierce fighting which cost the 24th sixty-eight casualties.

From the French perspective, the fighting spirit of the assailants was difficult to gainsay.

> The enemy, despite our fire directed at them point-blank, forced us to draw back behind our coupures. Their attempts to evict us were in vain, but they remained masters of the two breaches and the entrenched camp.
>
> We had begun an entrenchment behind the position which we assumed the new breach would occupy, but this entrenchment was so little advanced that it could not save us.[32]

The reserve now came up and a working party, 500 strong, began to make the breaches defensible. Heavy French fire caused 122 casualties. There was also expectation of a French sortie and the workmen were ordered to arms, but despite the enemy bombardment and heavy musketry fire a lodgement was secured. Its front was narrower than might have been wished, but this foothold was the first success of the siege since the taking of the hornwork. Nevertheless, the wound that Captain Jones received during the action, in the ankle but serious enough for amputation to have been considered, meant that the complement of trained engineers was now reduced to Colonel Burgoyne and two lieutenants. As for the volunteers, their numbers nearly dropped by one when Ensign Neville, eighteen years old, engaged with two French soldiers after the explosion of the mine. Losing his balance, he fell and was immediately covered with earth. He only managed to save himself by grasping the foot of Lieutenant Pitts of the engineers.

Mills was a spectator, having taken up a position with many others on the hill which overlooked the position of the mine, and was impressed by what he saw.

> The explosion of the mine and the storming were so instantaneous that [the French] had not time to do anything before the men were in and then it was too late. The 6th Division got in at their breach without any sort of difficulty. The French now opened a most tremendous fire from every part of their works – musketry, shells, round shot and grape. Every musket and gun seemed to be at work. Our men returned the fire, and as it was getting dusk the sight was truly magnificent. As it got dark the fire slackened. I reckoned myself fortunate in having had so good an opportunity of seeing it – it is a chance if ever I may have another.[33]

Bingham's experiences were much closer to the action than Mills's view as a spectator, and he wrote a full account to his mother on 6 October.

I was on duty on Sunday in the trenches; and although we had hot work of it, escaped unhurt, and I hope gained some credit for my exertions. I was quite knocked up when I came off duty, not having sat down except just to eat my dinner, for twenty-four hours. At five o'clock in the afternoon the mine was sprung, and the breach made by the former mine, render'd practicable, and both these points were carried in a very gallant manner by the 24th Regiment, supported by the covering party in the trenches, under my command; the supporting and covering ourselves on the wall, after we had gained it, was a point of great difficulty. It was however effected notwithstanding a sortie, made in the night to interrupt the work, and the incessant fire of the musketry, and of shell which the enemy kept up; frequently five or six in the air at the same time, besides others that they roll'd down the glacis, at the foot of which our work began. These on a dark night together with the fire balls constantly thrown to discover our workmen, was a truly sublime sight. I pray'd heartily for a stout heart, that I might do nothing that any of you might be ashamed of, and it pleased God to grant me presence of mind to enable me coolly to direct what was necessary ... Much more might have been done had some pains been taken about the previous arrangements. I did not know the storm was to take place until the commanding officer of the 24th, reported to me that he had march'd his regiment into the trenches for that purpose; nor had I any orders till just about half an hour before the mine was sprung; when Lord Fitz Roy Somerset rode down from Lord Wellington, to say I was to support the 24th ...[34]

\* \* \*

Even at this moment of apparent success, Bingham was not alone in commenting on the conduct of the siege. D'Urban, for example, wrote in his diary that the assault was

remarkably well done. Great gallantry and excellent management. Confirms my opinion that *Corps* and not *detachments of Corps* should always be used for services of difficulty or more than ordinary danger. In the former there is a common feeling of honour and shame. The Officers know the men, the Men obey the officers. In the latter the very contrary of all this is the case, and the effects correspond with their causes.

On this occasion,

> the actual Storming Party lost comparatively few Men, but the supports, who were positively ordered not to go to the Breaches, unless their presence was necessary, by the assaulting regiment being pressed, and who yet did go there, although the necessity did not exist, lost 50 or 60 men. These were Detachments and less under control. Mem. – Support assaults with a *second Corps*, and not with the Duty of the Trenches.[35]

Furthermore, casualties were mounting. Lieutenant Harry Ross-Lewin of the 32nd, coming up to Burgos with a detachment of 250 men, met a great number of wounded returning to Salamanca.

Significantly, Wellington also had reservations about the conduct of his troops, who were not behaving well, while the Portuguese had behaved very badly.

Now a lodgement had been obtained on the outer line, it was possible to contemplate an attack on the second line. During the night of the 4th two 18-pounders and a 24-pounder howitzer were moved into No. 2 battery and an additional 24-pounder into No. 1. The aim was that No. 1 battery would destroy La Blanca church with hot shot, while the guns in No. 2 would mount a flank attack when the main assault was made on the middle line. The arrival of forty ninety-pound barrels of gunpowder from Popham on the 5th proved timely.

By daybreak on the same day the entrenchments at the breaches had been completed and were defensible, but although the guns were in position there was little firing, only the howitzers in No. 1 being employed to break down the palisades in the ditch of the middle line. Dubreton, however, was not a man to sit back and take what the enemy threw at him. At dusk he launched an attack by 300 voltigeurs from the covered way of the second line, thirty yards from the allied position. They charged the first breach, scattering the defenders and causing 150 casualties. They also destroyed the protective gabions and carried away the entrenching tools. Although they failed to gain the second breach, the situation was only restored when Wellington arrived from his headquarters at Villa Toro to take control;

> the Queen's Regiment [the 2nd] was moved up to support and the Breach was recovered. The work of the last night and today very trifling. Indeed upon many occasions in this Siege, the work done has not answered expectations or the time given. The Engineers blame the Troops for this. The Troops the Engineers. Great precautions

necessary to make all secure in this regard. Much valuable time has been lost by the want of this.[36]

D'Urban's comments indicate all too clearly what was going wrong.

Wellington had his own suspicions about the cause of the problems he was experiencing with his troops, which he shared with Marshal Beresford.

> Something or other has made a terrible alteration in the troops for the worse. They have lately, in several instances, behaved very ill; and whether it be owing to the nature of the service, or their want of pay, I cannot tell; but they are not at all in the style they were. I am rather inclined to attribute their misbehaviour to the misery and consequent indifference of both officers and soldiers, on account of their want of pay.[37]

Money to pay the troops was an issue which Wellington frequently raised with Bathurst. Another misery, equally demoralising, was the weather. Heavy rain made progress difficult and life uncomfortable. And the conditions of siege warfare were definitely unpopular with the men at the best of times. Now there was the rain to contend with, as well as an enterprising enemy in command of the defence. Workmen and covering parties alike felt themselves vulnerable to sudden French attack or sustained fire from the castle. Mills certainly experienced the uneasiness this caused.

> The covering party is now to be found by entire regiments to furnish 450 men to be relieved every twelve hours. Our party marched off at seven but the rains had made the trenches so bad, that the party did not get to the breach till ten o'clock. I was sent with twenty men as an advance party to give alarm on a sortie. My post was under the pile of shot, on any appearance of a sortie I was to advance, charge, and keep them off till the tools could be got away or in other words be a dead man for the sake of a few pickaxes.

To make the situation more uncomfortable for Mills,

> I discovered that our firing parties fired just over my head and several times hit the shot I was under ... Had a sortie been made I should have been between two fires, and between one and the other stood but a bad chance. The enemy threw a vast number of fireballs during the night for the double purpose of seeing where we were, and setting the gabions on fire. The distance is now so very short that a great many men are lost and killed every day.[38]

Ensign John Rous, like Mills in the Coldstreams, wrote to his father at the beginning of November, recalling his experiences at Burgos.

Part of the 1st and 6th Divisions were always in the trenches and my turn used to come round once in three days, twelve hours at a time where we had the pleasure of being shot at from the Castle without being able to return the compliment ... Our parties were in some places within 20 yards of the French, and almost every man that was hit was shot through the head, besides which, they rolled shells into our trenches which burst close to us.[39]

The sortie of the 4th was a reminder that the French were determined opponents. The damage, however, was soon repaired and work also began on a parallel along the glacis of the middle line to prevent further incursions by the garrison. Also, the fact that a lodgement had been made and the sortie had been beaten off seemed to breed some cautious optimism. Aitchison wrote in his diary,

This success has improved the spirits of the army, though those likely to know are not yet sanguine of taking the place – the garrison however are said to be suffering much from a scarcity of water and the enemy are reported to have made a movement to their left towards Logroño in the design, it is said, of bringing off the garrison. This perhaps would be the best thing that could happen to us, though they hold different language at H.Q. – there they talk only of preventing the *escape* of the garrison.[40]

On the 6th the howitzers in No. 1 battery resumed their attack on the palisades in the ditch of the middle line, as well as on the line itself, while No. 2 battery targeted the point where the outer line joined the middle line. In response to this bombardment, the garrison maintained a heavy fire from their own guns, although it was inability to depress the guns sufficiently rather than the accuracy of enemy fire that caused the guns in No. 2 to stop firing. The French had the same problem with their guns when they tried to destroy the lodgement. Instead, they resorted to musketry and rolling shells down the glacis.

The following day the two allied batteries were more successful. When the two howitzers in No. 1 battery were replaced with a French 4-pounder and an 8-pounder, taken at the hornwork, fire became more effective. Modifications at No. 2 battery also led to more accurate fire and between forty and fifty feet of parapet, where the outer and middle lines joined, was demolished. The 18-pounder damaged on the 1st was now brought into No. 3 battery, mounted on a block carriage, and a similar solution was used for a gun that had been knocked off its trunnion. On the other hand, the weather continued to cause problems. The rains now became exceedingly heavy, and much time was daily occupied with draining the trenches, and keeping the communications practicable up the steep banks and breaches. It also made sapping impossible. Two saps had already been abandoned, and a third was making minimal progress. Even though a deserter claimed that the garrison wanted to surrender and only the governor's determination prevented it, there was still a feeling that the siege had reached some kind of stalemate.

*    *    *

Suspecting that the allies were planning a subterranean attack, Dubreton now decided to take the initiative. At 2.00am:

> Two companies of grenadiers, two sections of voltigeurs, and a detachment of pioneers and workers came out rapidly and marched so precisely to the enemy's communication trenches with the parallel that everyone in the entrenched camp, with the exception of two English officers and thirty-six soldiers made prisoner, was bayoneted by the voltigeurs and buried in the trenches. Our troops, after having filled in the enemy's works, made their retreat in good order. During this sortie we lost an officer and six men killed, two officers and twenty men wounded.[41]

On the allied side 200 officers and men were killed or wounded. The greatest loss was Major Cocks of the 79th, famed for his zeal and intrepidity, and who had distinguished himself at the taking of the hornwork. On this occasion, as officer of the trenches, he had rallied the troops and led a counter-attack. Wellington later commented at his funeral that if Cocks had outlived the campaigns, although that seemed impossible when he exposed himself so readily to danger, he would have become one of England's greatest generals.

Noone was more distressed by Cocks's death than his close friend, Tomkinson, who received the news by letter during the afternoon of the 8th. The following day he went to the camp ground of the 79th and learnt the distressing details.

> He fell by a ball which entered between the fourth and fifth rib on the right side, passing through the main artery immediately above the heart, and so out at the left side, breaking his arm: the man was close to him. In Cocks, the army has lost one of its best officers, society a worthy member, and I a sincere friend.

He had always been so lucky in the heat of fire that I fancied he would be preserved to the army. He was killed in the act of rallying his men to regain the outer wall, which the enemy had carried, and was at the top of the breach when he fell. The man that did the fatal deed could not have been more than five yards from him. We buried him in the camp ground of the 79th, close to Bellima. Lord Wellington, Sir Stapleton Cotton, Generals Pack and Anson, with the whole of their staff, and the officers of the 16th Light Dragoons [Cocks's former regiment] and 79th Regiment, attended him to his grave. He is regretted by the whole army, and in those regiments in which he has been not a man can lament a brother more than they do him.[42]

Wellington made his feelings clear in the letters he wrote during the following days. To Beresford: 'I am sorry to say that we lost poor Cocks in the *sortie* yesterday morning. His is on every ground the greatest loss we have yet sustained.' To Hill: 'I am sorry to say, we lost poor Cocks, which grieves me much.' To Bathurst: 'I have frequently had occasion to draw your Lordship's attention to the conduct of Major Cocks, and in one instance recently, in the attack on the horn work of the castle of Burgos, and I consider his loss as one of the greatest importance to this army and to His Majesty's service.' Finally there was the letter of condolence that had to be sent to Cocks's father, Lord Somers.

Your son fell as he had lived, in the zealous and gallant discharge of his duty ... and I assure your Lordship that if Providence had spared him to you, he possessed acquirements, and was endowed with qualities, to become one of the greatest ornaments of his profession, and to continue an honor [sic] to his family, and an advantage to his country.[45]

Cocks's funeral was one of the rare occasions when Wellington was observed to shed tears.

*   *   *

As a result of the French sortie, there was no further attempt to push the works forward at this point in the defences. The guns continued to fire, however; No. 2 battery created a practical breach, twenty to twenty-five feet wide, where the outer and middle lines joined, while No.1 targeted the keep of the castle. After dark, as the guns fell silent, a zig-zag communication trench was brought to within thirty yards of the new breach and a musketry trench was dug at right angles with the objective of bringing fire on the new breach so that it could not be cleared by the defenders. The next day, the 9th, the first hot shot was aimed at La Blanca

church, but although the roof was soon smoking there was no conflagration. It was also decided to mine the church of San Roman, just
outside the defences. The miners started fifty yards away, and made good
progress.

Small arms ammunition was running so low that it had to be rationed,
but when the French tried to repair the breach during the night there was
still enough fire power, from the 3rd foot guards in the new musketry
trench, to drive them off.

Wellington explained his intentions at this point in a letter to Beresford.

> We have a practicable breach in the second line, notwithstanding that
> all our guns and carriages are what is called destroyed; and I am now
> endeavoring [sic] to set on fire the magazine of provisions. I cannot
> venture to storm the breach. We have used such an unconscionable
> amount of musket ammunition, particularly in two *sorties* made by
> the enemy, one on the 5th, and the other yesterday morning, that I
> cannot venture to storm until I am certain of the arrival of a supply.
>
> I have sent to the rear and to Santander; and we are making some.
> But I have not yet heard of any approaching. I fear, therefore, that we
> must turn our siege into a blockade.[44]

To make matters worse, there were persistent rumours that the Army of
Portugal had received reinforcements of 10,000 infantry and 1,500 cavalry
from the Army of the North and were now concentrating on Pancorvo. It
is no wonder, therefore, that Gomm wrote to his sister:

> I cannot give you a favourable account of our proceedings hitherto.
> Our loss is considerable; and if we succeed in the end, it will be
> because we do not intend to fail in anything we undertake, for I
> cannot help thinking we have set to work idly, and without half the
> means we might have commanded. Begging my Lord Wellington's
> pardon, I think we have not respected the castle of Burgos suffici-
> ently.[45]

And yet, even when things seemed to be going from bad to worse, and
the mood was generally pessimistic, there were still sources of amusement. Ross-Lewin related the case of a staff surgeon who moved his bed
into a hospital waggon, which he regarded as more comfortable than his
own billet. Here he would play cards with his friends. One night, when
they were all comfortably ensconced in the surgeon's new quarters,

> A lieutenant of the corps of drivers, whose spleen very probably was
> out of order, suffered himself to be nettled by what he considered
> the unceremonious occupation of his waggon; the doctor not having

thought proper to ask his consent; and he therefore resolved upon playing the gamblers a slippery trick in the midst of their enjoyment. Full of his uncharitable purpose, he ordered out a pair of horses, had them harnessed to the waggon with the least possible noise, and whispered to the driver to proceed as hard as he could to head-quarters – a drive of two miles over a very rugged road. The order was faithfully obeyed ... and head over heels went the tenants of the vehicle, all losing their equilibrium by the sudden jerk at starting ... nor could they recover from their uneasy and prostrate postures, before they had jolted over ruts and stones every foot of the way to headquarters. There they arrived with a pleasing confusion of ideas, but without injury, if we except a few slight scalds, cuts, and contusions, which, indeed, were hardly worth mentioning, as the travellers carried their surgeon with them.[46]

The attempt to set fire to La Blanca continued the next day, but as soon as there was any sign of a conflagration the garrison put out the flames. This they were able to do because of the time it took the allies to heat the shot. Dubreton, however, was prepared to abandon the church, which was being used as an armoury, and to burn the weapons, as there was nowhere else to store them. Nevertheless, the French made, or pretended to make, preparations for a vigorous defence. Dubreton, in his reports, also commented on the excessively wet weather, which was as miserable for the garrison as for the besiegers, the defenders having been constantly on duty, without shelter, since the siege began. Indeed, Tom Sydenham wrote optimistically to Henry Wellesley that all might yet be well because of the garrison's predicament.

> If we can take and establish ourselves in the second line, it is probable that the garrison must surrender, and at all events we can carry a mine under the third line. I examined a deserter this morning, who says that the garrison consisted of about 2100 men, from whom 500 to 600 are 'hors de combat'. Caffarelli promised to relieve them in eight days at the head of a reinforcement of 30,000 men, but as 23 days have passed since the promise was made, the garrison have abandoned all hope of being relieved, and are desirous of capitulating.[47]

Not that the situation was any better for the allies. The dangerously depleted stock of ammunition, combined with the need to concentrate on drainage and maintaining batteries and communication trenches, meant that no new work could be undertaken. Although the attack on La Blanca continued the next day, it achieved so little that it was then abandoned. The guns from No. 2 battery were withdrawn to the hornwork to protect them from French fire and the only progress was made by the miners, who were extending the gallery towards San Roman through soil that was easy to work. At least they were unaffected by the violent rain storms which continued throughout the next day, soaking assailants and defenders alike. As Aitchison wrote in his diary,

> Our hopes of taking this place are very low – indeed, it is quite evident that our means are inadequate and it is now said that our operations are to be suspended until the guns arrive from Santander. The sailors have run them up to Reinosa and an engineer and horses of the reserve are gone from here to bring them.[48]

Wellington had finally conceded that it was possible to transport the heavy naval guns from Santander to Burgos.

On the 13th Wellington sent a summary of the situation beyond Burgos to the newly arrived General Paget, who had officially replaced General Graham in command of the 1st division and was unofficially Wellington's second-in-command.

> I have just received a report that the enemy are in motion in our front. About 1,500 infantry and 600 cavalry drove in our piquets at Monasterio this morning. I am going out to the front at Riobena immediately, and shall send word if it be necessary that any troops should move.[49]

Within the defences of Burgos the garrison managed to clear eight feet from the top of the second breach and form a small trench at the back of the rubble so that they could work under canvas. On the part of the assailants it was decided that the guns should be turned on the wall with the Napoleon battery. This wall was to be brought down, but the weather made it impossible to run out the guns. At this point, with the threat from the Army of Portugal increasing and the siege achieving very little, Wellington committed himself to a further week, after which he would abandon Burgos. Not that much changed. There was no artillery fire on the 14th, although the intended destruction of the Napoleon battery took a step towards realisation when three 18-pounders and a howitzer were moved into No. 2 battery during the night.

There was more activity twenty miles from Burgos, though. Initially, life for the covering troops had been reasonably comfortable. According to Douglas, the Spanish in this area baked the best bread in the world and there was plenty of it. Also rations were regularly provided. But conditions soon deteriorated. Green described the discomfort.

> There were not more than three huts [made of boughs] that would turn the rain, so that for twenty-four days or more we were exposed

to the constant dribbling rains, which were now set in. Some days, indeed, it rained all day without intermission. What made our situation most uncomfortable and unpleasant was, we were almost naked; for we were nearly out of all the necessaries essential to our comfort; such as stockings, shoes, shirts, blankets, watchcoats, and trowsers [sic]; and, what was worse than all, it now began to be very cold, for when the rain ceased, there was a frost almost every night, so that we were nearly perished.[50]

On the 14th, in response to the previous day's French probing, the 51st and 68th advanced to Upper and Lower Monasterio, where they were engaged in building a breastwork across the valley to check a French advance. By this means Wellington hoped to buy some time for the continuation of the siege, although again events promised more than they delivered. On the 15th No. 2 battery opened up early on the castle to try to breach the wall, but the Napoleon battery and a further four-gun battery with two mortars situated in the second line returned fire so fiercely that the allied merlons were destroyed, and after only three quarters of an hour the allied battery fell silent. Wellington then ordered the angle of the embrasures to be adjusted so that the guns could target the new breach. When a French six-inch howitzer, taken at the hornwork, and two 24-pounders were put into No. 1 battery, they seriously damaged the second line, ruining the parapet and making the bank more practicable. Even limited fire against the earth scarp of the second line under La Blanca did so much damage that an extensive breach could have been created with more ammunition to hand. Supplies were coming up, however; 300 rounds of 18-pound ammunition from Ciudad Rodrigo and small arms from the rear depots. But then the rain intensified, damaging the batteries and making the guns unworkable.

The situation overall was not promising. But, as Mills somewhat sarcastically commented, 'His Lordship has been strongly advised to give up all idea of taking the place but he is still obstinate. I believe he is determined to wait for the mines which may perhaps frighten them into surrender.'[51]

As ever, Dubreton was ready to counter-attack. On the 16th, while the allies were repairing the batteries, the defenders began work on a cavalier-de-tranchée, a small raised bastion, constructed within the angle of the second line, to drive the guard out of the allied sap which ran back from the second breach. The governor's understanding of human psychology was admirable. With a garrison thinking in terms of surrender (if the deserters were to be believed), water running low, and meat so scarce that only a quarter ration a man was being distributed, to say nothing of the appalling weather and minimal cover, he kept his men too busy to dwell on their miseries, while the activities themselves were all obstacles that demonstrably hindered the enemy's progress.

The rain, however, meant that in this instance the French were not entirely successful. They were unable to complete the cavalier during the night of the 16th, although they were able to palisade the end of the sap. But the same rain ruined the sandbag revetments at No. 1 and No. 2 batteries and they had to be replaced with gabions.

The miners working on the San Roman gallery were more successful. As they could now hear the French talking in the church, it was decided that the gallery should be extended only a few more feet and then a return made to serve as a chamber for the mine. This was packed with 900 pounds of powder and left ready to be sprung. Two miners remained on guard with orders to fire the mine if the French started to counter-mine.

Depression was now becoming almost universal in 'this accursed place' as Sydenham described Burgos. Yet neither side was prepared to give up the struggle, either by abandoning the siege or surrendering. On the allied side the batteries reopened fire on the second breach and the wall of the keep. Despite brisk counter-fire from the castle, by 3.30pm the second breach was declared practicable, although Wellington cautiously ordered another day's fire. The French successfully completed the cavalier and killed nine men in the sap, whereupon the allies constructed a fougasse of two barrels of powder, which was sprung from the end of the sap to breach the angle of the garrison's palisades and the cavalier. The damage was not as extensive as anticipated, but it persuaded the French to abandon the position. They returned, though, when the allies started to build a lodgement at the same point, and this too had to be abandoned.

Despite this setback, everything was now ready for a final assault after one more morning session of artillery fire on the 18th which, among other objectives, targeted a cheveau-de-frise which the French had erected as an extra defensive measure. An afternoon attack on the second line was to be synchronized with the firing of the San Roman mine. The breach caused by the mine would be taken by Portuguese troops under the command of Colonel Browne, with Spanish support, while the main attack on the original breaches was the responsibility of men from the Guards and the King's German Legion line battalions in the 1st division. Once the breaches had been secured, both attacking forces would escalade the second wall.

The attack began as planned at 4.00pm when a party of 200 men of the KGL, under Major Wurmb,

advanced in a most gallant style, and carried the breach with very trifling loss. Some of the men even pushed into the third or upper line; but, being immediately attacked by very superior numbers, the assailants were in a few minutes driven back through the breach, with the loss of Major Wurmb and most of the other officers killed or wounded.

This setback meant the garrison could not be driven from the palisades, and the survivors could only join the assailants on their right, 200 men of the Guards who

advanced in an equally gallant style through the breach, to the part of the second line opposite the shot piles, where the palisades in the ditch had been beaten down by the fire of the batteries, and readily gained the summit of the parapet. In this position they formed, opposed by a fire of musketry from a strong body of troops, which assembled on the terreplein of the second line. After about ten minutes' sharp fighting, another body of the garrison joined the defenders from their left, when the whole defensive force advanced in overpowering numbers, and drove the assailants completely back from the line.[52]

Mills, who was with the Guards detachment, described the experience from a participant's perspective.

Burgess ran forward with 30 men, Walpole and myself followed with 50 each and ladders. Burgess got up without much difficulty, Walpole and myself followed. The place we stood on was a ledge in the wall about three feet from the top. A most tremendous fire opened upon us from every part which took us in front and rear. They poured down fresh men and ours kept falling down into the ditch, dragging and knocking down others. We were so close that they fairly put their muskets into our faces, and we pulled one of their men through an embrasure. Burgess was killed and Walpole severely wounded. We had hardly any men left on the top and at last we gave way. How we got over the palisade I know not. They increased their fire as we retreated, and we came off with the loss of more than half our party and all the badly wounded were left in the ditch.

Mills explained this failure quite simply – 'our want of men. Had we but double the number we could have maintained ourselves but they dropped off so fast and none coming to supply their place, we failed from sheer weakness.'[53]

Jones ascribed the failure to the overwhelming superiority of the defenders, which is merely to reverse Mills's opinion. When the French appeared the whole place seemed to be swarming with men.

When the mine at San Roman was fired, it created a large breach in the terrace in front of the church, but did little damage to the church itself. However, the explosion, combined with the advance of the Portuguese and Spanish, caused the garrison to abandon the position after exploding their own mines, which destroyed much of the building. The allies now took possession of the ruins. But the failure of the attack on the second line meant that nothing could be done from this new position.

Wellington did not communicate to Bathurst details of this further failure until 26 October, when he finally wrote:

> It is impossible to represent in adequate terms my sense of the conduct of the Guards and German Legion upon this occasion; and I am quite satisfied, that if it had been possible to maintain the posts which they had gained with so much gallantry, those troops would have maintained them. Some of the men stormed even the third line, and one was killed in one of the embrasures of that line; and I had the satisfaction of seeing, that if I could breach the wall of the castle, we should carry the place.[54]

Jones believed this failure prompted the decision to abandon the siege, despite the expected arrival of the guns from Santander. In fact, events elsewhere determined the decision.

* * *

The Army of Portugal was now 38,000 strong, slightly outnumbering the allied forces in Burgos and covering the siege. A large detachment from the Army of the North brought the French force occupying the area between Pancorbo and Briviesca to just under 50,000 men. Souham was ready to advance on Burgos. On the same evening as what proved to be the final allied assault a brigade from Maucune's division advanced

> in considerable force against the post of Monasterio ... Lieut. Liznelsky, of the Brunswick Legion, who commanded a piquet at Sta Olalla, disobeyed his orders in remaining in that village upon the approach of the enemy, and he was taken with his piquet. The enemy consequently obtained possession of the heights which commanded the town of Monasterio, and our outpost was obliged to retire, on the morning of the 19th, to the Burgos side of the town.[55]

The allied outposts were now brought back to Quintanapala and Olmos. Apart from Pack's Portuguese brigade, one brigade of the 6th division and three weak battalions of the 1st division, all the allied troops were in order of battle and holding a line from Ibeas on the

Arlanzon to Riobena and Soto Palacios. Although there was some activity around San Roman, which was briefly taken back by the French, Burgos was now of secondary importance as even the working parties were ready to march at short notice. Nor was the sense of crisis eased by a dispatch from General Hill, who intimated that the French forces further south were drawing together and threatening his position on the Tagus.

Wellington was so certain of an attack on his own covering position that he ordered Pack to set up a blockade of Burgos and Colonel Robe RA to remove the guns. Souham, however, had received a dispatch from the king the previous day which informed him that the troops in Valencia were about to march on Madrid. This would force Wellington to abandon Burgos, so Souham was not to risk a battle. Upon receipt of this dispatch, Souham sent Maucune and Chauvel's divisions and his light cavalry to test the allied position at Quintana, which was held by the Chasseurs Britanniques. These troops, from the length and breadth of Europe, promptly made a stand which Wellington approvingly described as rough handling of the enemy. Wellington responded to the threat by bringing up the 1st and 5th divisions under Paget to attack Maucune on his flank. Maucune immediately withdrew, saved by darkness from what could have been a disaster.

Wheeler later wrote to his family that 'there was some sharp skirmishing, at night we fell back on Almos, followed by their advance. Here was another sharp skirmish in which the enemy were worsted and fell back now, our brigade were put into a large church for the night.' He then described the problems that might arise in a division popularly known as The Mongrels.

> About midnight when all were fast asleep some one called out 'The enemy, the enemy, Fall in.' You can easily conceive what a confused scene followed, the place as dark as possible, as full as it would hold of soldiers laying down fully accoutred with their firelocks between their legs. All were up in a moment, shouting out 'Where are they, where is the door, fix your bayonets' some were cursing and swearing. The C. Britanique [sic] Regt., composed of men from every country in Europe, were each calling out in their native tongue. Add to this the noise occasioned by fixing bayonets. Everyone of course were [sic] seeking the door but no one could find it, at length some got out and discovered it was a false alarm. The word was soon passed and after some time the panic subsided.[56]

In Burgos all the guns and stores were being removed from the batteries, except for the French howitzer and gun in No. 1, which fired occasionally to deceive the garrison. At the same time staff officers like

Gomm received orders from the quartermaster-general to prepare for withdrawal. Gomm was specifically informed that

> The 5th division with their guns are to march by their left this evening as soon as it becomes so dark that the movements cannot be seen by the enemy. The above mentioned troops are to proceed by Quintana Dueñas to Villalon – thence by Badajos [Tardajos] across the Urbel river, there they are to halt. Lieutenant-Colonel Gomm is to conduct the column. The two Spanish divisions to follow the 5th division with their artillery.
>
> Lieutenant-Colonel Gomm to place the above troops in column of battalions as soon as they arrive on their ground; he will take care that these orders are duly communicated to the Spanish division. Care must be taken to make fires previously to their march.[57]

Possibly Wellington might have been inclined to linger but, as he explained to Pack in a letter written at 1.00pm:

> I am sorry to say that I am afraid I shall be obliged to give up our position here, in consequence of the intelligence which I have received from General Hill of the movement of the enemy in the South; and unless I should receive a contradiction of the intelligence, I propose to march this night.[58]

Pack was ordered to send the baggage still at Burgos to Frandoviñez, and move or destroy any remaining stores. He was then to wait for word from Wellington informing him that the army was in retreat, whereupon he was to march into the town when the moon rose, while keeping possession of the trenches until 5.00am. He would then bring the troops under his command to Frandoviñez. A further letter, written about the same time, informed Popham that the heavy guns would no longer be needed.

As Gomm's instructions indicated, the troops opposite Souham lit camp fires before marching. Then they retired in two columns on either side of the Arlanzon. The northern column, which skirted north of Burgos before marching for Tardajos, comprised the 5th division, most of the Galicians, Ponsonby's heavy dragoons and some Spanish regular cavalry. The southern column, made up of the 1st, 6th and 7th divisions, Bradford's Portuguese and the remainder of the Galicians, retired via Villa Fria and then crossed the Burgos town bridge in silence before marching to Frandoviñez and Villa de Buniel, two miles from Tardajos. Anson's light cavalry covered the rear of the southern column, holding their piquet line until 3.00am, while Bock's KGL dragoons and Valian Sanchez's irregular cavalry constituted a flank guard for this column.

The withdrawal of the covering forces was achieved with only minimal alarm when some guerrillas,

who, unused to such coolness, put their horses to their speed, and made such a clatter, that the garrison took the alarm, and opened a fire from the artillery directed on the bridge; the first discharge was, as might be expected, very effectual; but the gunners immediately afterwards lost the range and direction, and their fire only served to make the carriages file over the bridge with more speed than usual.[59]

Nevertheless, the rear of the southern column had to follow a side path. Within the environs of Burgos Pack supervised an efficient destruction of everything that could not be carried off. The French guns were buried. Carriages were burnt. At 11.00pm the artillery commenced their retreat, but the road was so deep in mud and the horses so weak that the 18-pounders had to be abandoned. The five howitzers and a French 4-pounder were finally brought into Frandoviñez early in the morning.

Burroughs, assistant surgeon in the 24th, was woken by his servant at 11.00pm and informed that the regiment was ready to march. Even as he dressed himself he could hear

the thunder of the artillery of the castle vibrating in my ears. My tent was instantly struck, and the baggage thrown upon the mule. The night was fine, the moon shone with that unvarying light an unclouded sky affords, and the neighbouring naked mountains, gilded by her beams, materially added to the solemnity of the scene. The distant sounds of the artillery rattling on the roads, the buzzing murmurs of the passing soldiery, and the angry lightning from the cannon of the besieged castle, could not fail of inspiring sublimity even in the most vacant mind.

Following the narrow road to Villa Toro, which had served as head-quarters during the siege, Burroughs came upon a scene of confusion.

The throng presently became so great, that the cargoes of the mules were overturned, and in proportion to the opposition, did the desire of pushing forward increase. Every thing was at a stand and in dis-order. In one place were two or three sick soldiers bolstered up by their comrades' knapsacks lying on a bullock cart, and surrounded by some less sick companions; in another, bags of biscuit trodden under foot, and casks of rum stove in: - here an artillery waggon had sunk axle-tree high in mud, the leading horses of which, having exhausted their strength to drag it out, were lying prostrate and panting in the road, so that it was with much difficulty I could proceed, and then only by striking out a path over the mountain.[60]

Ross-Lewin, like several others, was struck by the strange sensations he experienced during this night march; a disturbing mixture of a great number of men, cautious silence, the hour, and the constant awareness that any moment the guns of the castle might fire and strike them dead. Not surprisingly, the mood was not good.

After so many signal triumphs, the present failure was very morti-fying; but the army consoled itself with the persuasion that either in the environs of Valladolid or the plains of Salamanca, they should be allowed to face the enemy, or that if we were doomed to pass our winter again in Portugal, it would only be a kind of second retreat to the lines.[61]

The consolation which Daniell offered himself was to be disappointed in the weeks ahead.

*   *   *

Inevitably, questions were asked as to why the siege had failed. On the 19th Ensign Aitchison committed his opinions to his diary. He reasoned that

to ensure success men should have confidence in themselves, which in all desperate cases is only to be acquired by numerical superiority ... I am persuaded from what I have seen that a soldier knowing that whatever may happen *his party is the stronger* will go on to attack a large body with a confidence which will ensure success, whereas when his own party is inferior to that which opposes him both in numbers and situation, he is, in a measure, beaten before he begins ...

Aitchison had no doubt where the blame lay:

after a long month has this victorious army been defeated by a petty *fortress* with the loss of 2,500 men – merely I may say from self-sufficiency in its Commander – for it is the most lenient term which my imagination suggests in its excuse for him. As it is now beyond correction it will be of little use to vent reproach on the author of this defeat, but it may be an instructive lesson to examine the causes of it. It will show that the most noble minds and greatest heroes are liable to over-rate their own talents or by being intoxicated with success to commit themselves from nicer consideration.

Aitchison was convinced that the problems started on 6 September when the chance to engage Clausel was missed. Had there been a successful attack, Clausel would not subsequently have risked taking the offensive. Nor could Wellington be excused for pursuing the siege with inadequate means: at the outset he should either have brought up an adequate siege train or sent to Santander for the heavy naval guns.

> In every point of view this failure is most unfortunate – it has undeceived the French of our invincibility – it has dampened the ardour of our men – it has diminished their confidence in our Chief – as he betrayed unsteadiness in frequently changing his plan of attack and in resolution of carrying it into execution when fixed upon, and lastly it has excited apprehension in the Spaniards and in some places matured their passiveness into indirect hostility.
>
> In short it has blasted our prospects in the present campaign and damaged our plans for the next.[62]

These passionate sentiments, probably the feelings of a young man used to victory whose hopes for further success had been disappointed, were echoed to some extent by the more measured assessment of Jones, who saw the situation with an engineer's eye. He too recognised the inadequacy of the artillery, three 18-pounders and five howitzers, although he quarrelled with the further suggestion, made by many besides Aitchison, that even these inadequate resources were not effectively utilized. 'Other modes and other points of attack were suggested, and even submitted to Lord Wellington, but they were all found to be visionary schemes of men unacquainted with the details – beautiful as a whole, but falling to pieces on the slightest touch.'

In a footnote to his *Account of the War in Spain and Portugal* he argued that

> The plan of the attack of Burgos, had considerable professional merit as well as boldness, and, notwithstanding its failure, added much, in the opinion of the army, to the previously high reputation of Lieutenant Colonel Burgoyne, the Engineer in command.[63]

For Jones, every siege so far undertaken had courted misfortune because of

> the defective state of the siege establishments of the army, which were seldom equal to draw the full benefit from even the smallest supplies that were brought up. But on this occasion even such as those did not exist: there was not the semblance of an establishment of that nature; not even a half-instructed miner, or half-instructed sapper – barely an artificer: hence the deviations from the original project, and the delay in the execution of such parts of it as were

followed, which combined with accident, served to render the project unavailing.

Jones then listed the consequences of this deficiency. The attempted escalade of 22 September without a breach occurred because the lack of miners with the appropriate tools gave 'just cause to doubt the capability of the engineers to mine under the outer enceinte'. The subsequent failure then 'dispirited the besiegers whilst it in the same degree, raised the confidence of the garrison.' When volunteer miners, equipped only with common pick and shovel, were then set to work, it took them 108 hours to dig sixty feet, thirty-six hours longer than trained miners would have taken. The assault on 4 October was also less successful than it should have been because of 'the extreme ignorance of the workmen in sapping [which] caused the lodgement to be very imperfect, and a further advance by sap impracticable.'

As a result of these failures, 'The feelings of the two parties had undergone a complete change. Repeated failure had rendered the British cautious, whilst brilliant success had rendered the enemy confident.'[64]

Jones had no doubt that with even a moderately efficient siege establishment Burgos would have fallen within ten days.

Others agreed that inadequacy of means was the main cause of failure.

Everything was done which under such circumstances courage and skill could effect, but to no purpose. Having no corps of practical engineers to help him, [Wellington] drove mines, which exploded either too soon or uselessly. The fire of his field guns made little impression, and every attempt to carry the main work by escalade failed.[65]

Gleig was writing long after the events and his biography was designed to present Wellington as a hero. Consequently, he did not address the one issue which reaches beyond the how and why of the actual siege. With such inadequate means at his disposal, Wellington's decision to try to take Burgos, and his persistence (some would say obstinacy) when success became increasingly unlikely, remains a problem that cannot be easily resolved.

Gomm certainly considered Wellington's actions as open to criticism:

from the moment the siege of Burgos Castle was seriously undertaken it has always appeared to me that there was more of fondness than firmness, or even obstinacy, in the conduct of an enterprise which all the world saw (and it is absurd to suppose that he himself did not see it) was entered upon with means inadequate, and carried on, certainly, many days after the success of it was more than doubtful.

Yet Gomm had an explanation for Wellington's misjudgement and stubborn persistence.

> Yet he who comments upon these proceedings will do well, in my mind, should he censure, as Lord Chesterfield does, after drawing a picture of Lord Bolingbroke: 'When we contemplate this subject, what is it that we can say but, alas, poor human nature!'[66]

Gomm was writing only a month after the siege was raised.

Nevertheless, it is important to acknowledge Dubreton in an assessment of the allied failure at Burgos. A lesser man might have been tempted to surrender as both supplies and manpower diminished, but Dubreton maintained an active defence from first to last, not only resisting every allied manoeuvre, but also taking the fight to the besiegers to frustrate their plans. His resolve allowed time for the Army of Portugal to recover, gain reinforcements and take the offensive.

Captain Nicolas Marcel of the 69th regiment of the line had no doubt that Dubreton was the true hero of the siege.

> The English army employed all means possible to take Burgos, but General Dubreton and his brave soldiers defended so well that the assaults made by the English were vigorously repulsed: the fusillade was so lively that the palisades six thumbs thick became like broom handles ...[67]

Yet the defenders still held firm.

Finally, there is the criticism, made by many participants, that Wellington weakened the assaults, particularly the early ones, by using detachments rather than whole battalions, as well as Aitchison's claim that numbers were never sufficient to breed confidence. The point is valid, but Aitchison had not been at Badajoz, when whole divisions were sent into the breaches to suffer appalling carnage. He had not witnessed Wellington's reaction to that slaughter, which it is unlikely the commander had forgotten or ever would forget.

Wellington offered Bathurst an explanation for his persistence in a dispatch of 26 October.

> Your Lordship is well aware that I never was very sanguine in my expectation of success in the siege of Burgos, notwithstanding that I considered that success was attainable, even with the means in my power, within a reasonably limited period. If the attack on the first line, made on the 22nd or the 29th, had succeeded, I believe we

should have taken the place, notwithstanding the ability with which the Governor conducted the defence, and the gallantry with which it was executed by the garrison. Our means were very limited; but it appeared to me that if we should succeed, the advantage to the cause would be great, and the final success of the campaign would have been certain.[68]

According to Jones,

A siege is one of the most arduous undertakings on which troops can be employed, – an undertaking in which fatigue, hardships, and personal risk, are the greatest, – one in which the prize can only be gained by complete victory, and where failure is usually attended with severe loss or dire disaster.

Success or failure of a siege frequently decides the fate of a campaign, sometimes of an army ...[69]

For Jones, Burgos was just such a siege.

*Chapter 6*

# Move and Countermove

Events elsewhere in Spain had not only been a factor in Wellington's strategic thinking throughout his expedition against the Army of Portugal, but they were also the reason for the abandonment of the siege of Burgos. The news from Hill had become increasingly worrying and by 22 October the situation was too serious to ignore.

When Wellington left Madrid on 1 September events in Estremadura and Andalusia seemed to be developing to his advantage. On 28 August Hill and his 2nd division were in and around Bienvenida and Usagre. Hill was still engaged in manoeuvring against d'Erlon, but matters were about to take a different turn. Soult was preparing to leave Andalusia. His army, reunited with d'Erlon's forces, which had been engaged with Hill in Estremadura, and joined with the Army of the Centre, would be strong enough to eject the allies from Madrid and force Wellington and Hill's combined forces back to Portugal.

As a result of Soult's decision to join Joseph, his brother, General Pierre Soult's light cavalry left their quarters to follow the march of the infantry. On 28 August they were at Monterubia. From here Captain Hippolyte d'Espinchal of the 2nd hussars took a squadron to Belalcazar to evacuate the two regiments posted there, the 100th of the line and the 21st light.

> The route which we followed to reach the town of Hinojosa was all the more fatiguing because it traversed mountains which were almost inaccessible, forced us to follow the slow march of the infantry and occupied us in making the slowcoaches keep up; otherwise they were infallibly massacred by the brigands who closely followed us.
>
> The day which followed that to Hinojosa was certainly one of the most perilous of my life and death presented itself in various forms, each less reassuring than the others.[1]

The moment of greatest danger was when the cavalry, who were marching as a rear guard to the infantry, found themselves cut off by an avalanche of rocks on a tortuously twisting path while possibly being followed by guerrillas, which was a very uncomfortable situation for any French soldier to find himself in.

From Belalcazar d'Espinchal and the evacuated soldiers made their way to Cordova, where they discovered the town full of troops. The evacuation began during the day and continued during the following days under the protection of General Soult's cavalry.

As Marshal Soult later wrote in his memoirs,

> I had to withdraw a vast network from every part of a huge territory and reassemble it in one place without losing any of its parts, and I had to co-ordinate all the troops marching from opposite directions, sometimes by divisions, sometimes by mere detachments ...[2]

*   *   *

On the 29th the 2nd division under Hill marched for Llerena, where news arrived that the French were on their way to Cordova. The immediate result was a change of direction to the north-west in response to further information that d'Erlon's corps was to serve as Soult's rear guard during a withdrawal to either Murcia or Valencia. There was also confirmation that the siege of Cadiz had been raised, and it was reported that Colonel Skerrett had taken Seville. Although this was not quite the case, Soult having chosen to abandon Seville with all but a small detachment to hold the town, which an Anglo-Spanish force had indeed driven out, the three pieces of news convinced the allies that the French were on the run.

Hill certainly felt confident enough to write to his family on the last day of the month that d'Erlon had left Estremadura. Two days earlier he had sent a dispatch to Wellington with the same information, but Wellington's departure from Madrid meant that he did not receive the news until 8 September.

The new direction of their march now took the 2nd division to Manguilla, Campilla de Llerena, Zalamea de la Serena and Quintana, which was reached on 3 and 4 September. These were particularly difficult roads for artillery. On 4 September Captain William Webber RA recorded in his journal,

> At 4 we marched for Campilla de Llerena, 4 leagues distant, by a very bad road, in some parts almost impassable. The infantry went another way, a league shorter but only passable for them. The country more hilly and enclosed and several mountains were seen at a distance in this day's march ... Water very scarce, muddy and bad.[3]

Nor were conditions any better for the infantry.

> Before daylight, on the 1st September, we directed our steps towards Zalamea, which, after a very fatiguing march of fourteen hours, under a scorching sun, and over a parched desert, we entered and

took possession of considerable stores of grain left behind by the enemy.'[4]

While the allies were at Quintana a Spanish sergeant who had deserted from the French joined them, claiming that Soult was now retiring in haste to Valencia, having abandoned his sick and destroyed his gun carriages. It was even suggested that Maitland had defeated Suchet, while an English force was said to be at Cordova. Webber thought this last must be Skerrett's, up from Seville. 'Supposing all this is true, the general opinion in this place is that Soult will be so completely trapped that he must surrender at discretion in a short time.' A few days later, however, the story had changed. Now Soult was at Cordova, reinforced by Suchet, who had been obliged to evacuate Valencia after his defeat by Maitland. At the same time Ballesteros was rumoured to have taken the greater part of the French force which had been besieging Cadiz, or at least cut off its retreat. Webber judiciously commented, 'I fear good news is magnified as usual and that it now comes too quick to be true, though it is well known everything is going on more successfully than the most sanguine could have expected.'[5]

With such momentous changes to French fortunes in Andalusia, it was no surprise that the rumours grew wilder by the day. As for the true situation in Cordova, where the evacuation had been going on, at 4.00pm on 4 September the French finally

abandoned this beautiful city, object of our regrets, taking away from the inhabitants who had become accustomed to their presence, head-quarters, administration, several manufactures and factories, which had enriched the town while it had never ceased to be under the constant care of its governors.[6]

It was not a totally peaceful departure. Two squadrons of allied cavalry were in close attendance and the French cavalry left under carbine fire for the next stage of the withdrawal.

Meanwhile, Hill's troops remained in and around Quintana for a day before departing for Don Benito. Again there were problems for the artillery.

About half past one, according to orders, we marched. The first part of the road good, but about half way it was so bad and rocky that being dark it was impossible to choose the best part of it, and one of the ammunition wagons upset. Luckily no damage was done except to the perch which was split near the eye bolt. The country open until within 6 miles of this place when we passed between two hills or mountains, the top of one covered by a cloud. After this a most delightful view presented itself – an extensive plain of marsh, 2 leagues square, bounded on the North by the Guadiana river and the mountains on the other side; in other directions by hills forming a continuous chain.

They arrived in a town *en fête*.

High mass is performing in the church. The houses are to be illuminated and fairs are to be held every day this week. Every Spaniard is dressed in his best and the women seem to vie with each other in adorning themselves.

... this town has by some means escaped the ravages of the enemy and the houses are in good order. Perhaps this leniency may be attributed to the easy consent of the inhabitants to comply with the demands they everywhere impose. The French will do no mischief when this is the case, but how despicable is that man who will quietly submit to pay a sum perhaps as large as the value of his house merely to issue the safety of it, when at the same time he is giving shelter and assistance to the enemies of his country.

I am glad to observe that this has not happened in many towns which I have been in and the French have seldom found anything but the bare walls, unless by their rapid movements they have taken the inhabitants by surprise, or unless by their artful intrigues they have duped them with the idea of being spared from contribution. This has been several times practised with success and perhaps the enemy have been as conciliatory as possible till the eve of the move when they have robbed them of everything and even then taken their apparel from their persons: besides breaking their glasses, crockery and everything that did not escape their notice.[7]

On the 8th Wellington wrote to Hill in response to the dispatch that Hill had written on 29 August from Llerena. Having considered Soult's intentions, specifically whether he would march for Granada or La Mancha, and having made the assumption that Hill had marched as far as Trujillo, or even further, he continued,

Upon receipt of this letter I beg you will cross the Tagus at Almaraz, and canton your troops with their right at Almaraz, and their left at Oropesa. Come forward yourself to Oropesa. Colonel Diggens commands a regiment of Portuguese cavalry at Plasencia, or thereabouts; order him to join you. Establish letter parties from Oropesa through the mountains to Avila and thence to Arevalo, to communicate with the guides of this army which are there.

Establish other letter parties direct from Oropesa to Madrid, to communicate with the Light, 3rd and 4th divisions and General [Victor] Alten's cavalry which are there. General Charles Alten is the senior officer.

There was a final reassurance that Wellington would return to Madrid 'as soon as I hear that the plot thickens to the southward.'[8]

A day later Wellington wrote to his brother in Cadiz with instructions for Ballesteros, whose army

should be reinforced as far as may be possible, and that it should carry on operations at all times between the enemy on the one side, and Cadiz and Seville on the other; taking care not to be committed.

I have ordered General Hill to draw nearer to me, and he will cross the Tagus, and move towards Madrid. I shall thus have the whole of the allied British and Portuguese army collected, and communicating by a short communication.

I shall, I hope, be in communication with the army of Galicia by my left; with the army of Estremadura by my right; and I am already in communication with the troops under General O'Donnell from Madrid.

Thus General Ballesteros will always be on the left flank, or rear of the enemy, while I shall be in their front; supported by the Spanish armies of Galicia, Estremadura and Murcia; and it may be hoped, that, unless some accident happens, [the French] will not be long this side of the Ebro.[9]

Hill soon received information to suggest that Soult was under pressure; Ballesteros had taken 2,000 prisoners and two guns in a partial action against the French marshal. Soult was now in Granada, and Ballesteros was maintaining a position six leagues from him. Wellington received the same news and wrote to Bathurst on the 13th that it was now certain Soult was heading for Granada, although he had not yet received confirmation of his arrival, while d'Erlon was making for Jaen. Ballesteros was in pursuit of Soult with 15,000 men, having been reinforced by Spanish troops under General La Cruz, the commander of the successful Anglo-Spanish expedition to Seville. The importance of Ballesteros to Wellington's overall strategy was becoming increasingly evident.

On the 12th there was an abrupt change in the weather when

for the first time since the 6th April, rain fell accompanied by dreadful thunder and lightning, which made old and young cross themselves, but caused me the greatest demonstration of joy, much to the surprise of some priests who seemed to think Purgatory too good for me.[10]

William Swabey RHA, who wrote this, was firmly anti-Spanish, as his diary constantly demonstrates. Nonetheless, he was justified in rejoicing at the arrival of rain, for lack of water had become an increasingly serious problem. The wet weather continued for several days and Wellington's expectation that the rivers would be filled by the autumn rains, making them more of an obstacle for the retiring Army of the South, seemed about to be realized.

As Wellington had informed Bathurst, d'Erlon's corps, having successfully evacuated Cordova, had marched for Jaen, which became d'Erlon's headquarters. D'Espinchal, who had been covering the march, arrived in Jaen on the 11th. Two days later an order arrived from Soult informing d'Erlon that 'the retrograde movements were very shortly coming to a halt in order to regain the offensive immediately the junction with Marshal Suchet was made. The same order of the day gave information of a re-organisation of the cavalry which gave senior command to General Soult, with four brigades under his orders.'[11] Three days later they were engaged in the evacuation of Jaen by infantry, staff and artillery. The 2nd hussars took their position as the covering force, and on the 17th they were witnesses to the destruction of the citadel, which had cost several million francs to convert to a point of defence.

From Jaen General Soult's cavalry were ordered to make the planned junction with Suchet. Marshal Soult then left Granada on the 15th, which enabled Ballesteros to enter the city two days later.

\*   \*   \*

As the French forces completed their abandonment of the south, Hill's Anglo-Portuguese made their way to Trujillo, where headquarters were established on the 14th. The way was rough and rather hilly but, despite the rain which had been falling, the minor rivers remained dry and it was even possible to ford a major river like the Guadiana. The next day headquarters moved on to Torrecillas de la Tiesa, but most of the division remained in Trujillo for several days, awaiting the pontoon train from Elvas, which would make possible a crossing of the Tagus. The rain continued to pour down.

The pontoon train finally arrived during the evening of the 16th, by which time many of the officers had taken the opportunity to explore Trujillo, the birthplace of Pizarro, conquistador of the Incas, as most of them noted in their journals. They also climbed up to the Moorish castle which crowned the town. Webber, a stern critic of French misbehaviour, was nevertheless pleased to note an occasion when the French officers demonstrated 'the humanity and generosity' which they also displayed on many occasions to officers who became their prisoners. Colonel Squires RE had died of exhaustion at Trujillo the previous May, shortly before the town was evacuated by the allies, and before a tomb could be furnished. According to the Alcalde, the French commander, when apprised of the situation, not only instructed the Alcalde to finish the tomb,

> but rendered him every assistance as to money and otherwise to have it completed immediately, with directions that he should be informed when it was so; which being done, he assembled all the French officers and formed a procession and the road to the grave was lined with his men, after which the stone was placed in the most solemn manner. Such conduct is noble.[12]

Less favourable to the Spanish was the discovery of eight guns, hidden under a pile of green wood. They were brass guns from the castle of Miravete, spiked and abandoned by the French after the affair at Almarez. 'Some of the Spaniards it seems, wishing to procure the protection of the enemy in case they should return to Trujillo, took and concealed them from us (perhaps as traitors they had no other policy and safety) and had removed their guns from the forts and the castle' to a house in the town. Webber was particularly grieved when he realised the Alcalde, the very man who, in his opinion, should have been demonstrating loyalty and concern for the welfare of his country, had proved himself degenerate by being a party to the concealment. Swabey was far more explicit, stating quite simply that he would have liked to have the hanging of the man.

The pontoon train left early on the 17th for Almarez, where it was assumed the bridge master would struggle to lay the pontoons against the strong current of the Tagus, causing more delay. On the 19th the troops moved forward to Jaraceijo, which like so many other places had been totally destroyed and could offer no forage, or anything else to the troops while they waited for the bridge to be positioned. Once the pontoons had been successfully put into place, which the bridge master against expectation achieved with little difficulty, the crossing of the Tagus could begin. Several men noted that they were crossing a bridge virtually identical to the one they had themselves destroyed in May, an irony which was not lost on them. The actual crossing was a memorable experience.

> The magnificent scenery for the last two leagues of the road to Almarez, quite overpowers the mind. You move along a high ridge, and descend gradually from it to the Tagus. On the right, large

broken masses of wild, untrodden mountains, clothed in those tints for which there is no name, and which language would in vain describe, bound your view. Far, very far below you, on either side, lie valleys, here verdant with grass, there yellow with corn, and here again, so deep and narrow, that the sun never lights upon their dark and cheerless glens. We crossed the Tagus by a pontoon bridge. The motion of a bridge of this sort, the first time you ever stand on one, is very unpleasant; you stagger, as at sea, and feel quite giddy. We marched over it in files four deep. It is, to be sure, surprising in a modern world, to see with what facility an army moves.[13]

However rapid the flow of the Tagus may have been, Webber on his march to Almaraz noted that the good stone bridges they crossed spanned dry streams. When they reached the pontoon bridge

to our astonishment we found the Portuguese artillery had not crossed more than one gun and all the other eleven with their ammunition were still on this side. It was 10 o'clock and we had expected they would have been all out of our way by 7 or 8.

In fact, the Portuguese artillery did not cross until midday.

Then the infantry came up and were ordered to precede the Horse Artillery. After that, all the baggage of the division was ordered to cross, so that the Horse Artillery could not get their carriages etc over till 5. Then our brigade continued and that the heaviest and carrying the most ammunition.[14]

Although Swabey, of the horse artillery, had preceded Webber, he was equally displeased and more rancorous than his fellow gunner.

General Howard, much to his disgrace, ordered us to halt and put the infantry over notwithstanding the representation of Colonel Tulloch, who had orders to press one of his brigades of Portuguese artillery on to Talavera. General Howard was not satisfied with this arbitrary unmilitary proceeding, but even ordered the baggage (which took two hours to pass the bridge) over before us ... General Howard will be surprised to find his conduct reported to General Hill.[15]

The journals of Webber and Swabey strongly suggest that the artillery harboured an aggrieved sense of being last in the queue, not just when it came to crossing bridges, but in every other respect, particularly the allocation of quarters.

By the evening of the 20th, the whole of the 2nd division was across the Tagus and Wellington's strategy for dealing with Soult could now be executed. Not only was Hill on the road to Toledo and Madrid, but

General Elio had also been instructed to move towards Madrid with the army of Murcia, while Ballesteros was to advance on Alacaraz and protect the fortress of Chinchilla, which dominated the surrounding plain on the borders of La Mancha and Murcia. While it remained in Spanish hands it was an obstacle to Soult's movements. The partisan forces of Bassecourt, Villa Campa and the Empecinado had also been instructed to move towards Madrid.

Wellington wrote to Hill the same day, presuming him to be at Oropesa. On receipt of the letter he was to move all the troops under his command to Toledo, and then send the cavalry forward to La Mancha. The infantry were to be cantoned in Toledo, and also in Aranjuez, where Hill was to make sure men and officers alike respected the king's palaces and gardens.

On the 21st, by which time Wellington was fully engaged in the siege of Burgos, he informed Bathurst that he had received accounts from Hill of the 14th. He was then at Trujillo

and had received my orders, and was to be at Oropesa on the 18th. I have ordered him to march to Toledo, and to defend the Tagus; taking under his command the three divisions of this army, and Lieut. General Alten's and General D'Urban's cavalry, and Don Carlos de España's division of infantry, which are at and near Madrid.

I have not heard that Marshal Soult has yet left Granada. He was still there on the 8th. General Ballesteros had followed the enemy's movements from the Guadalete, and had been very successful. He was at Loja on the 6th.

The enemy had abandoned Andujar and Jaen; and the line of their retreat was certainly through Valencia; but it is not impossible that, when they shall have heard that I have moved to the North, they will endeavor [sic] to pass through La Mancha, which General Hill's position will prevent.'[16]

D'Erlon's corps was still making its way from Jaen to unite with the rest of the Army of the South, and still fighting a dirty war which had characterized the conflict in the Peninsula since its outbreak. On the 18th the corps had reached Casoria

where a terrible act of vengeance was visited on the inhabitants who, two days before, had massacred an entire company of infantry. Nothing was more horrible than the spectacle which met our eyes when we reached this dreadful scene of disaster. At each step the mutilated corpses of the murdered French, the blood-stained rags of their uniforms scattered here and there, the recent marks left in the dust indicated the struggle which each of these unfortunates had put up and the long torment they had suffered before they died. Only their brass shako plates made it possible to identify that they were French soldiers and to which regiment they belonged.

When the inhabitants saw the arrival of a French column, knowing the fate that awaited them, they hastened to flee into the mountains, abandoning their houses, and their furniture which they did not have time to carry away; in a few moments flames destroyed everything from top to bottom and we found nothing in that place of desolation except rubble and ashes to cover the victims of such barbarity.[17]

*   *   *

The 2nd division's march to Toledo was conducted in a fairly leisurely manner. For example, Webber reported covering two and a half leagues with Howard's brigade on the 21st, to Novalmoral de la Mata, and four leagues the following day to La Calzada de Oropesa, where the brigade rested for the day. On the 24th they marched another two and a half leagues to Torralba de Oropesa, and on the 21st six leagues to Talavera, where the division drew together. But there was no need to hurry when Soult's whereabouts were uncertain and French intentions could only be surmised.

One aspect of the advance which impressed itself upon those who experienced it was the attitude of the Spanish. Lieutenant James Hope of the 92nd noted how in Talavera they received

the noisy acclamations of almost the whole population ... The inhabitants talked incessantly of the battle of Talavera, and were perfectly deafening in their praises of Lord Wellington and Sir Rowland Hill. In fact, they never pronounced the name of the latter, but in terms of glowing admiration. His desperate defence of the eminence on the left of the British position, which secured the victory, has gained him an imperishable name in Spain.[18]

Webber also recorded that Hill was being accorded a hero's welcome at every town he passed through, while even Swabey wrote:

What shall I, the enemy of Spanish sentiment, and, though not a hopeless actor in the war for Spanish Independence, yet totally without trust in Spanish patriotism, say, when I found in passing through a village in a populous and highly cultivated country, where we halted for the sake of water, the people coming out *en masse* to greet us not only with *vivas*, but with pitchers of wine and baskets of grapes, the old in tears and the young mad with exultation.

From this village I was sent dreading the conflict I was to undergo from similar civilities, to mark the cantonments at our destination, Domingo Perez, but I had not expected to be stifled by the embraces of old, young, fair, ugly, man, woman, and child, and to be nearly torn in pieces by every pair of respectable people who were ready to fight for the honour of having me in their houses. The bells rang, the authorities went out to meet the troop, and gratitude, a word I have never yet heard sally from the nasty, proud habitation of a Spanish mouth was, they said, the universal debt they were come to pay. The Alcalde, never before accustomed to English soldiers, immediately asked when I would have the meat killed and the rations prepared; a fair indication of what might be done in districts never oppressed by troops moving without a commissariat.[19]

About this time an offer made to Wellington by the Cortes in Cadiz, that he should become commander-in-chief of the Spanish armies, became generally known. It was to provoke a fit of that Spanish pride which Swabey found so uncompromising; and this time Spanish pride would seriously disrupt allied plans and Wellington's strategy.

By the end of September the 2nd division was at Toledo, where Hill received yet another hero's welcome. This welcome extended to his troops, which certainly impressed Hope. He described how the scarlet-clad magistrates, the renowned guerrilla leader El Medico, the governor and all the principal citizens of Toledo came a mile beyond the city gates to welcome Hill and congratulate him on the favourable state of affairs.

As we proceeded from the gates to the grand square, the cheers of welcome which assailed us from every door, every window, and every balcony, were truly electrifying. Joy beamed in every countenance; and amongst numerous loyal ejaculations, 'Long live King George III!' 'Long live Wellington!' 'Long live Hill!' and 'Long live Ferdinand VII!' fell from the lips of delighted thousands. In the principal square, the front of every house was literally covered with the symbols of joy used in Spain on similar occasions, *viz*, quilts of every description, sheets, silk flags, and handkerchiefs, and as we were the first British troops that had ever been in Toledo, the city was most brilliantly illuminated in the evening.[20]

Webber somewhat cynically commented,

the cheering sun appeared just as we began the ascent from the valley (through which the river runs) to the gate, and enabled all the people to meet us there; not that they left their houses to see us, but General Hill had arrived but half an hour earlier and everyone had been anxious to welcome him. Therefore, while outside they thought it better to look at us too.[21]

Whatever the true feelings of the citizens of Toledo, the Anglo-Portuguese troops could certainly be forgiven for thinking they were on a triumphant progress rather than manoeuvring to protect New Castile from the French.

From Toledo the 2nd division advanced to Aranjuez, where there was still no news of either the King or Soult, beyond a general assumption that the French would organize their operations in response to Wellington's at Burgos. But, with no news arriving of the fall of Burgos, anxiety replaced the rather relaxed atmosphere of the advance from Estremadura. Even sightseeing in Aranjuez and excursions to Madrid could not distract from the uneasiness of Hill's troops, including those in and around the capital, as they contemplated their situation.

The extent of the uncertainty was made clear in a dispatch Wellington sent to Hill on 2 October.

> the movements and intentions of Soult and the King do not yet appear to me to be quite clear. They have to guard against the allied force collected at Alicante on the one hand, and against Ballesteros, who I learn is to be about Alcaraz, on the other; and one can hardly believe that they will venture to move towards the Tagus in force by the road of Albacete. If they do not move in force they can effect nothing. If they do, they will expose their interests in Valencia, which is an important resource to them too great to risk. Yet if they do not purpose to move to the Tagus, one cannot understand why the King should have gone to Almanza.
>
> Supposing the march of both to be towards Cuenca, and then towards Soria, in order to communicate with the troops on the Ebro, the object might have been accomplished with equal, if not greater ease, by his movement from Valencia by the route of Utiel and Requena. On the other hand, if the object had been to move to the Tagus, much time has been lost by the route taken by Soult, and a vast distance gone by bad roads; and a junction might have been formed with equal, if not greater ease, by the march of Soult direct from La Carolina or Consuegra; and the march of the King by Albacete into La Mancha. However, the next movement will show what is intended.

As these uncertainties reveal, the initiative was now definitely with the French, after nine months when Wellington had been driving affairs in Spain.

*   *   *

On 25 September d'Erlon's corps, coming up from Jaen, reached Huescar, where they learnt that Soult had abandoned Granada to Ballesteros ten days before. Although this was bitterly regretted, the marshal's arrival

> produced a spontaneous effect; the energy and insouciance so natural to French troops returned with this trust.
>
> We saw nothing more on the retreat that we had just made than those things which were to be expected in war, but which were soon amended by a commander as wise as he was intelligent.
>
> Marshal Soult, like all men of merit and talent, had his detractors, the envious and the jealous who would never have been able to reach the heights of his boots, but it was impossible to deny his having been one of the most remarkable men of the empire, as a soldier and an administrator ...
>
> The Duke of Dalmatia, although he was severe, brusque and only sometimes a little pleasant, had the essential qualities which deserved the esteem, the trust and the devotion of the troops placed under his command.[23]

D'Erlon's infantry had been blockading the fortress of Caravaca, but the blockade was lifted on the 26th because, according to d'Espinchal, the place was judged of little significance. It was true enough that now he had reluctantly abandoned Andalusia, Soult's focus had to be transferred to dealing with Wellington and Hill, not wasting time and effort on minor fortresses. Nevertheless, the French withdrawal towards Valencia allowed the Spanish to move into the territory the enemy had evacuated. On the 22nd General Elio took French-held Consuegra by capitulation.

D'Espinchal's cavalry was at the head of Soult's forces as they marched along the royal road to Valencia. Soult had detached two hundred cavalry to communicate with Suchet's forces, while the Army of the South marched to Albacete to join up with Joseph. D'Espinchal had spent fifteen hours in the saddle when he arrived at Hellin, where he expected to be able to rest. Instead, he discovered that yellow fever was raging in the town, as in much of Murcia. D'Espinchal kept his distance and rode on to Tobara, but some hussars and chasseurs went into Hellin to pillage, with fatal results. In Tobara d'Espinchal met a squadron of dragoons, his first contact with the Army of the Centre. Soult arrived on the 28th and established communication with the outposts of Joseph's army. Five days later, he and Joseph were together at Fuente de Higuera.

The king planned to unite his and Soult's armies, as well as most of Suchet's forces; reluctantly he gave overall command to Soult, mainly because both Jourdan and Suchet refused the position. Soult did agree in general terms, however, with the king's idea that the armies should act together. He believed Ballesteros to be in La Mancha, which was a complication when dealing with the Anglo-Portuguese, either on the Tagus or south of the Ebro. Uniting the Armies of the South and Centre, even without support from Suchet (who claimed the threat from the allied troops in Alicante prevented him from surrendering any of his troops), should force Wellington south to Madrid, whereupon the Army of Portugal would be able to join the other two French armies. Such a force was capable of overwhelming any allied resistance, and Ballesteros would be reduced to a temporary irritant.

Soult's own thinking envisaged that once Wellington had been forced to abandon Burgos, the Army of Portugal would pursue him while the two other French columns advanced to threaten the allied position in central Spain. The stronger of the two, the Army of the South, would follow the line of the Tagus, while the weaker, the Army of the Centre, would march directly on Madrid. In other words, Soult was adopting a Napoleonic strategy with a mass manoeuvre on the Tagus. During his discussions with Joseph he was also unable to resist the chance to point out that time had been wasted bringing him to Valencia when Wellington could have been threatened equally effectively from Andalusia.

For Joseph, however, the priority was to drive the allies out of his capital; all other considerations were secondary to regaining Madrid. He was also still nursing a strong sense of grievance, no less bitter than Soult's resentment that he had been forced to abandon what had become, in effect, his vice-royalty of Andalusia. Joseph's grievances were two-fold: Soult had given no support after the disaster of Salamanca; and the marshal had written to Napoleon in an attempt to convince the Emperor that his own brother was in league with the Cortes at Cadiz against French interests in Spain. Having been advised by Jourdan that the Army of the Centre, acting alone, would not be strong enough to take Madrid from the allies, and also possibly motivated by a need to enforce his position as commander-in-chief of all the French armies, Joseph insisted that Barrois's division and a brigade of light cavalry should be detached from d'Erlon's corps and added to the strength of the Army of the Centre, thus bringing a further 4,000 men to his force of 15,000 troops under arms. Soult protested. Joseph insisted, finally resolving the impasse by giving Barrois's troops a route for a specified date. It was a battle of wills, but even Soult could not disobey a direct order and still keep his command. He satisfied himself with the rather petty rejoinder that the troops were still properly part of the Army of the South, so he would require their commander to report to him as well as to the king.

Joseph's, or rather Jourdan's, plan was that while Soult advanced into La Mancha the strengthened Army of the Centre should march to Cuenca, from where communication would be established with the Army of Portugal via the Samosierra Pass in the Guadarrama mountains and Aranda de Duero. Souham, however, seems to have learnt of this intention too late for it to be put into effect. Nevertheless, the advance on Cuenca was to prove a crucially important movement.

Joseph set 9 October as the date for the advance of the two French columns. Soult objected, claiming that his army was not yet sufficiently collected for an advance, particularly as Conroux's division was still in quarantine after some cases of yellow fever had broken out among the troops who had strayed from the line of march and pillaged while passing through Murcia (like d'Espinchal's cavalry). Also, he needed food and ammunition, and Suchet needed time to supply these vital commodities. To Joseph, this looked like deliberate procrastination on the marshal's part, while to Soult the appointment of d'Erlon to command the Cuenca column seemed a deliberate provocation. In such acrimonious disharmony the French began their manoeuvres to drive Wellington out of Spain.

\* \* \*

For Hill, waiting for the French to make a move, and Wellington, trying to keep an eye on events in Madrid and the Tagus valley, a new problem was emerging. By now, in obedience to the orders he had received, Ballesteros should have been in La Mancha; but there was no news to suggest that he had even left Granada. As Wellington informed Hill on 5 October

> I do not write to General Ballesteros, because I do not know exactly where he is; but I believe that he is at Alcaraz. At least I understand he was ordered there.
>
> Tell him that the best thing I think he can do under existing circumstances, is to hang upon the left flank and rear of the enemy, if they should move by the débouché of Albacete towards the Tagus [Soult's intended route]. If they should move to Cuenca, and the northward, he should come into La Mancha, still holding the same situation relatively with the enemy, and communicating by his own left with your right.[24]

This demonstrates the extent to which Ballesteros was a significant participant in the struggle, but as late as 14 October his whereabouts were still unknown, and Hill was instructed to send him a copy of the Spanish Minister of War's letter which had instructed him to march on Alcaraz. In fact, this would have been a waste of effort, because Ballesteros had opted out of the game as soon as he learnt that Wellington had been offered the position of commander-in-chief of the Spanish armies. Although the Cortes had decided not to publicize the offer until Wellington formally accepted, and Wellington would not accept until he received permission from the British government, such a momentous decision in Spanish terms inevitably leaked out. Ballesteros had been lingering in Granada against Wellington's wishes and the orders of the Cortes. When he heard the news of the offer, a mixture of pique and frustrated ambition provoked him into open rebellion. Depending upon centuries of Anglophobe feeling, he was confident the Spanish would refuse to become servants of the English, as the Portuguese were in his opinion. Unfortunately for him, Salamanca and Madrid had changed people's opinion of Wellington and his Anglo-Portuguese army. Even Ballesteros's own troops did not support him when General Virues, his second-in-command, placed him under arrest on the orders of the Cortes. As a result, he spent the rest of the war in detention.

All this still lay ahead when Wellington was worrying about the whereabouts of Ballesteros and his 4th Army, but Ballesteros had already become inactive before he broke into open rebellion. Consequently, a vital piece in Wellington's strategy was now missing, a dereliction of duty to his country which led Moyle Sherer of the 34th to comment:

> Ballesteros, who might have rendered the most important service by harassing Soult on his route, and uniting his people to ours on the Tagus, obstinately halted in Granada. Ballesteros was a man who wanted neither courage nor ability; but his silly pride would not allow him to receive the orders of Wellington; and, by his ridiculous vanity, the cause was very much injured at a most crucial moment, and it became impossible for us to maintain ourselves in the heart of Spain, or to defend Madrid.[25]

This judgement enjoys the wisdom of hindsight, but there can be little doubt that Ballesteros's contumely made life easier for Soult, both before his arrival in Valencia, and after his departure. On the other hand, Wellington himself might be charged with overconfidence. He does not seem to have anticipated the French strategy of dividing their forces for what became a pincer movement against Hill. Nor did he allow for the inconvenient fact that although the autumn rains might be falling heavily on Burgos, other parts of Spain, most significantly the Tagus valley, could remain relatively dry. What had seemed like the beginning of the autumn wet season in the south had promised more than it delivered.

\*   \*   \*

One reason for bringing Ballesteros up to La Mancha had been to support and protect the vital fortress of Chinchilla, which lay just south-east of Albacete and commanded roads to Valencia and the Tagus. As long as the Spanish continued to hold this fortress, they would seriously impede a French advance north or west. As early as the beginning of October d'Erlon's corps was blockading Chinchilla; but although his artillery maintained a fierce bombardment little was achieved. The position of the fortress was strong, on a dominant height and protected by deep ditches, making defence relatively easy and attack difficult. D'Espinchal recognized Colonel Cearra, in command of the fortress, as a brave and energetic man who was very unlikely to surrender. He was also maintaining fierce artillery fire on the French infantry in the town below.

It is impossible to know how long Chinchilla might have held out; whether the proximity of Ballesteros and his army would have made a difference to the course of events; or whether d'Espinchal's claim that Soult's intended assault would have been successful was justified. It was a natural disaster that determined its fate. On 9 October, during a violent thunderstorm, the keep was struck by lightning, killing or wounding many of the defenders. Crucially, the governor was left seriously concussed, while his sword and its sheath had melted into a single rod. Surrender, probably provoked more by shock than a rational assessment of the situation, was the garrison's immediate response. But the loss of Chinchilla not only opened the road to Almanza for the French; it also forced Bassecourt and Villa Campa to retreat from their forward positions where they had operated successfully as Hill's eyes and ears.

\* \* \*

The allied position now extended along the Tagus valley from Toledo on the right to beyond Aranjuez on the left, with cavalry outposts as far forward as Belmonte to watch the Albacete road. On the day after the fall of Chinchilla Hill received instructions from Wellington, written on the 10th, on how he should conduct a withdrawal from these forward positions if it proved necessary. This was recognition that an attack by the combined forces of Joseph and Soult would overwhelm Hill. But Wellington could not believe 'that Soult and the King can venture to move forward to attack you in the position on the Tagus, without having possession of Murcia and Alicante; unless indeed they propose to give up Valencia entirely.'[26]

A dispatch from Hill to Wellington, also written on the 10th, indicated that there had been no sign of movement by either Joseph or Soult. However, when Sydenham wrote to Henry Wellesley on the same day he reported Hill as believing that the French intended to advance on the Tagus in order to regain Madrid.

> But Lord W. does not appear to think that the movements of the enemy are sufficiently clear and decided to warrant that conclusion, and therefore he will wait for further information before he deter-mines upon what he is to do. The possession of the castle of Burgos is an object of so much importance, that he will not abandon the siege until it is absolutely necessary. If it turns out that the French are moving in force upon the Tagus, he will lose no time in returning to New Castile for the purpose of directing the operations in that quarter in person; and he will leave Sir E. Paget in command of the troops here.

Sydenham also outlined the French options which were being assumed by Wellington. It was known that Soult's troops had been at Albacete for a week, but it was unclear whether this indicated an advance on the Tagus, a search for subsistence, or a move to keep a watch on Ballesteros (who should have been at Alcaraz). If the first, it was strange that there had been no corresponding movement by Suchet and Joseph towards Cuenca.

> This would decide the point; but until we hear of some such move-ment, it is impossible to ascertain Soult's intentions.
>    If the enemy intend to move upon Madrid, they must come in great force, as we shall have 47,000 men on the Tagus, and Ballesteros hanging on their left flank and rear. If they abandon Valencia, or leave an insufficient force for the defence of the city and province, the corps at Alicante will be set free, and can occupy Valencia and follow the rear of the French.[22]

Sydenham's premises turned out to be mistaken in all respects. Assuming that he was accurately reporting Wellington's thinking, it may be surmised that Wellington himself had failed to grasp the purpose of Soult's manoeuvring.

During the following days various stories concerning French move-ments reached Hill's army. On the 11th Webber, at Aranjuez, heard that Soult was advancing, and Hill was concentrating his forces in response. The following day Colonel Tulloh was instructed to take his brigade of artillery across the Tagus to a village on the Madrid road. Swabey, though, had been informed by some Spaniards that, far from advancing on the Tagus, the French were planning to pass the Ebro, much further north.

Hill received another set of instructions from Wellington, including a requirement to mine the bridge at Sacedon, particularly if the rains made the Tagus impassable. He was to feel at liberty to destroy any bridges as

might prove necessary, Toledo and Aranjuez being mentioned specifi-
cally. Two days later, on the 14th, Wellington informed Hill that he
intended to continue operations at Burgos since nothing seemed to be
happening in the south. Joseph, however, began his advance towards
Madrid on the 17th and was at Requeño two days later, while Soult left
Albacete on the 15th. Even before this, however, and before the fall of
Chinchilla, Swabey recorded reports that Soult's advance guard was at
Minaya, twenty-seven leagues from Madrid.

D'Espinchal was confident that with Chinchilla and nearby Peña-Perros
both taken by capitulation the time was ready to force the 'English' from
Madrid. On the 15th d'Erlon's corps was on the road to the capital, where
the enemy was assumed to be preparing for a battle.

Hill had protected his position with a screen of Spanish troops:
Bassecourt at Cuenca; Elio with Frere's horse and a weak infantry division
watching the line that ran from Albacete to Requeña and Tarancón; Penne
Villemur's cavalry and Morillo's infantry at Herencia and Madridejos.
Long's British and Campbell's Portuguese cavalry were at Torbosa,
Villacanes and other places in the vicinity of San Juan de la Zarza, while
d'Urban's cavalry, Carlos de España's Spanish infantry and the troops
of the 2nd division were within a triangle of Madrid, Toledo and
Fuentidueñas. As the French advanced, Hill pulled all except Bassecourt
back behind the Tagus. Bassecourt, in his more exposed position, was
driven out of Cuenca by d'Erlon and made his escape to Alicante.

Yet, as Hill's situation was becoming increasingly untenable, Sydenham
optimistically wrote to Henry Wellesley on the 18th that

> the probability of the French moving in force upon Madrid appears to
> diminish every day; and it would now appear that they intend to
> abandon Valencia, and to move towards Arragon [sic], part along
> the sea coast, and part by the route of Cuenca. The heavy rain, which
> has incommoded us so much here, will probably have filled the
> Tagus ...[23]

The previous day d'Espinchal, with Soult's advance guard, caught up
with the rear guard of a Spanish corps withdrawing to Madrid.
D'Espinchal suffered the loss of three hussars and two chasseurs who
advanced too far and were, in his words, ruthlessly massacred. That
evening, though, the advance guard was at Minaya, where reports were
received that the allies were retreating on Madrid. On the 18th Joseph
joined d'Erlon at Cuenca before moving on to Tarancón, while the head of
Soult's column reached Ocaña by way of San Clemente.

On the 19th Hill informed Wellington that the French forces were
drawing together and that he intended to defend the line of the Tagus

unless the enemy proved too strong. At this point he had no certain knowledge of the strength of Joseph's column, but he appreciated the danger it posed to his position. For this reason, he adjusted the disposition of his own forces. The Tagus was fordable upstream from the confluence with the Jarama, which was a difficult point to defend. This meant that the troops between the Jarama and Fuentidueña, the left of the allied position, were in danger of being cut off. Hill now withdrew behind the Tajuna, a tributary of the Jarama which flowed parallel with the Tagus. In this new position his right held a strong line between Toledo and Añover. Having destroyed the bridges at Aranjuez, Hill now secured the Puente Larga at the confluence of the Jarama and the Henares, and put a bridge of boats upstream from Bayona, on the Jarama. He also brought forward the three divisions from Madrid. The light division, with Elio's troops, were placed on the extreme left at Arganda. At this point, Skerret's force from Cadiz joined Hill, taking up a position at Toledo, on the extreme right.

\* \* \*

On the same day that Hill completed his dispositions, Soult sent d'Espinchal forward to Belmonte to reconnoitre the enemy's movements. Here he encountered several allied vedettes and spent part of the day skirmishing with them. Nor was he able to enter the town until seven in the evening, three hours after it was evacuated by an allied infantry corps which d'Espinchal believed to be 18,000 strong and whose departure the allied cavalry had been covering. The next day he was able to report that 6,000 'English' were in position five leagues from Belmonte while other allied troops were marching on Aranjuez.

Webber, who returned to Aranjuez from Madrid during the evening of the 20th, heard that a piquet of the 13th dragoons had surprised a French piquet near Ocaña. It was obvious that both sides were probing their opponent's positions. In the encounter, Webber reported, an officer and forty-eight men were taken prisoner by the allied cavalry, while the following day

> An officer of the 13th Dragoons came in and brought intelligence of that Regiment having taken 70 men and 2 officers in an affair with some squadrons of cavalry in the morning. The Spaniards were advancing in greater force but were repulsed and driven back to form in the rear of the 13th. This regiment immediately charged and succeeded in the manner mentioned with scarcely any loss.[24]

Despite this small success for the allied cause, however, there could be little doubt that Hill's 31,000 men would have to abandon New Castile when faced with the 60,000 the French were bringing against them.

# PART III

# Retreat

## Chapter 7

# Tactical Withdrawal

It was not until the morning of the 22nd that Souham realised Burgos had been abandoned, by which time the allies had gained a march on him. His first response was to send Maucune with the advance guard into Burgos to congratulate Dubreton on his spirited and ultimately successful defence. The light cavalry were then dispatched to search the roads north and south of the Arlanzon for signs of the retreating allies. They found the abandoned battering train and then, advancing on Urbel, they came into contact with the vedettes of Anson's brigade, whom they successfully drove from San Mamés to the bridge at Buniel.

Wellington, however, could congratulate himself on extricating his army from a difficult situation. As he reported to Bathurst on the 26th, it was not until late on the 22nd that the French began their pursuit, when 10,000 men camped on the southern side of Burgos. By evening the allied troops were at Celada del Camino and Hornillos, while the light cavalry in the rear had reached Estépar and Buniel, having marched since 4.00am along bad roads.

Burroughs described how on the 22nd he rose at daybreak to find the 5th division and the Galicians, the northern column, already on the move.

A party of German Hussars marching by, informed me that the whole of the infantry had passed the skirts of the village, and that the cavalry would arrive presently. Having remounted, and marched about three miles, I overtook the 6th division, and proceeded with it to Celada del Camino, where ... at some little distance, the column was encamped. These troops had arrived here about two hours before, and were cooking their dinners. I had but just come up to my regiment, when the route was announced. The column was soon under arms, and proceeded to Vallefena, which after several halts we did not reach until dark ... There is much inconvenience suffered in coming to a *bivouac* at night, particularly in the present instance, as it was upon vineyard grounds, so that at every step we sank into the soft mound surrounding the trunks of the vines, or else were thrown down by the long branches curling round our limbs.[1]

For Anson's brigade, bringing up the rear of the southern column, the first day of the retreat was a more harassing experience. There was some sharp skirmishing with the French cavalry, acting as an advance guard. Then, when they reached Pampliega in the evening, the peasants informed them that the French were making an advance to the right, which would bring them round the hills close to the village. As a result they had to continue their march to another small village, two miles to the rear.

The following day Souham and Caffarelli brought up all their cavalry, nearly 6,000 men of Curto's light horse, Boyet's dragoons and a brigade under Colonel Merlin from the Army of Portugal, and Lafarrière's brigade from the Army of the North. Their task was to harry the allied rear guard, Anson's and Bock's brigades, together numbering 1,300 men, and 1,000 lancers of Julian Sanchez's irregular cavalry. In front of them were the rear units of the allied infantry, the two light battalions of the King's German Legion which comprised Halkett's brigade of the 7th division. They had Bull's battery with them, under the command of Major Dowman and Captain Ramsey.

The French cavalry caught up with the allied cavalry at Celada del Camino where Anson's brigade was posted at the Hormanza stream, on the edge of the village and in front of a ravine. Halkett's two battalions were in the bushes above the water. Sanchez's lancers were beyond the Arlanzon, while the late partisan leader Martinez's guerrillas, under the command of Matiez, were further to the left on higher ground. When the French drove in the allied piquets the 11th light dragoons under Major Money counter-charged, with Bull's guns in support. A running fight now developed as the two sides skirmished for three hours.

Anson was able to withdraw his troops under cover of the 16th light dragoons, but even as he was retiring Martinez's guerrillas, who had been dislodged from their position by Curto's hussars, were driven into the left flank of Anson's brigade. The result was a chaotic mêlée of British, Spanish and French cavalry, which resulted in the French taking thirty prisoners, including Colonel Pelly and seven men of the 16th. Matters might have been worse had the French not been as disorganized as the allies, so that they needed time to re-form before they could continue the combat.

Anson was able to bring his force back to Villaldemiro, covered by the two German light battalions, while the guns went to Venta de Pozo. By the time the French were sufficiently organized to renew the attack, all the allied forces, including Bock's heavy German cavalry, were behind the stream at Venta de Pozo and the two light battalions were retiring on Villodrigo.

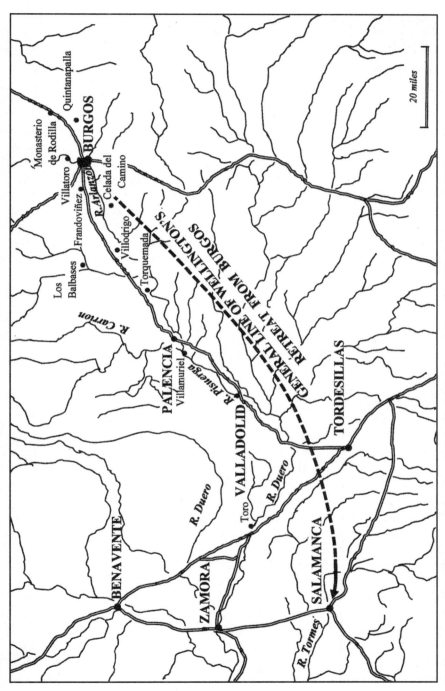

*Wellington's retreat from Burgos to Salamanca via Palencia, 22 October to 9 November 1812 (from a map of 1796).*

At this point Lafarrière's brigade, comprising the Berg lancers, 15th chasseurs and a legion of gendarmes under Faverot, came into the fight. The allies were now under the command of Sir Stapleton Cotton, who had very recently joined from sick leave. Cotton seems to have decided that it would be most effective to allow some of the French to cross the bridge at Venta de Pozo, then deal with them before they were too strong and before other French cavalry could come up in support. The German heavy cavalry was already to the left of the guns and Cotton decided to move the light cavalry to the right. Unfortunately, this man-oeuvre masked the guns just as the French were crossing the bridge. To add to the gunners' problems, even when they had a clear line of fire they could not achieve the required elevation. By the time this became apparent eight French squadrons were lining the river bank on the allied side.

Cotton now ordered Bock's brigade to charge the gendarmes and the left of the chasseurs, while Anson's brigade advanced more slowly on the right towards the chasseurs and the lancers. The Germans were not initially seriously outnumbered, but the arrival of two further squadrons of gendarmes tipped the balance. Also Boyer had found a further crossing point at Los Balbases and now charged from the left. In the confusion, no one could be sure exactly what had happened. The German charge failed, though, and it was only the speed of the heavy cavalry horses that saved their riders from destruction.

Anson and Bock now fell back on Villodrigo, where the two light battalions were in position and formed square when attacked by Boyer. They fired on the advancing cavalry and inflicted heavy casualties. The infantry then retired, keeping the French at bay and enabling the allied cavalry to re-form. The French followed slowly and cautiously; nor did they renew the attack. As darkness fell, they bivouacked at Villodrigo while the allies halted for two hours at Quintana del Puente before marching on to Torquemada, which they reached at 2.00am.

The allies had suffered 230 casualties, of which seventy were prisoners, while the French had lost over 300 men, many to the fire of the King's German Legion battalions.

Burroughs, in his account, explained the cause of the initial confusion, although he thought it was the cavalry 'of that meritorious officer, Don Julian de la Sanchez' who were driven in by the French, whereupon 'they came flying upon the British cavalry, mixed with the enemy, in pursuit. Here the differences of language, with the similarity of the Spanish to the French uniforms, created much confusion and our light dragoons, under Sir Stapleton Cotton, (now Lord Combermere) having done everything bravery could effect, were overpowered by numbers and obliged to retire.'[2] He also noted that Wellington and his staff were forced to take cover in one of the infantry squares.

Browne was full of praise for the light infantry, who

> threw themselves into squares, & in the most gallant and determined manner resisted & repelled every attempt of this formidable body of cavalry to break them. The French experienced considerable loss, and our rear guard got clear off. This was one of several occasions on which I had an opportunity of observing the inefficiency of cavalry attacks on squares of infantry.[3]

Dansey, who was present at the action as aide-de-camp to Major Dowman, was similarly complimentary to the Germans who

> behaved very well this day being placed in ambush behind the banks of a stream which crossed the road, our cavalry retreated quickly over the bridge, when the enemy's rapidly advancing were received with a heavy and destructive fire from the Germans, which considerably checked them, and the Germans retired without loss in a compact and invulnerable column.[4]

It was obviously a disturbing experience for a civilian to find himself in the middle of this fracas, as Sydenham reported to Henry Wellesley.

> In consequence of the great superiority of the enemy in cavalry, we were a good deal pressed in our march from Celada del Camino to Quintana Puente. I twice thought that Anson's brigade (which is weak in numbers and much exhausted by constant service) would have been annihilated, and I believe we owed the preservation of that and of the German heavy brigade to the admirable steadiness of Halkett's two light German battalions ... We had literally to fight our way for four miles; retiring, halting, charging, and again retiring. I may be permitted to say *we*, for I was in the thick of it, and never witnessed such a scene of anxiety, uproar, and confusion. Notwithstanding all our difficulties we made some prisoners, and destroyed at least three times as many as we lost. Throughout the whole of this trying occasion Cotton behaved with great coolness, judgement, and gallantry. I was close to him the whole time, and did not observe him for an instant disturbed or confused.[5]

Wellington came to the same conclusion as Burroughs about the confusion of uniforms, ('five squadrons on the enemy ... were mistaken for Spaniards, and they fell upon the flank and rear of our troops') and as Sydenham about Cotton, informing Bathurst that, 'The exertions and conduct of Lieut. General Sir Stapleton Cotton, and of the officers and staff attached to him, throughout this day were highly meritorious ...' There was also praise for the 'great steadiness' of the cavalry and the light infantry brigades and the horse artillery, who 'distinguished themselves.'[6]

Not surprisingly, a French view praised the French cavalry. Marcel was under the impression that the enemy believed the

> twelve squadrons of French gendarmerie were composed of young men, newly recruited, who would not be able to resist them. They waited for them on firm ground but they did not take long to recognize that the sabre cuts that were administered were not delivered by conscripts; ... The English lost 1,800 prisoners and a good number of horses because more than 800 of theirs were sabred ...[7]

Marcel, however, made only a vague reference to French losses, although he was obviously impressed by Colonel Thévenet of the Gendarmes who received fourteen sabre cuts, and made no reference to the German light battalions that effectively brought the French advance to a halt.

\*   \*   \*

While the rear guard was engaged in this long-running fight, the rest of the allied army marched to Cordovilla and Torquemada. It was a frustrating experience for the northern column, heading for Cordovilla.

> On the 23rd we marched again about 5 leagues and halted, as we supposed, for the day. But scarcely had we commenced to cook when we embarked on a second route, which extended for 3 leagues more, this being accomplished some time in the night. As the days began to shorten during this latter end of October, we of course expected to have a good nap after this march; but when about to lie down, a 3rd route awaited us for 2 leagues more. There was no use in grumbling and to the road we went, hungry, wet, and weary ... We lost a number of men this night, worn down with hunger and fatigue.[8]

However exhausting the fifty miles Douglas claimed to have marched, this route kept the 5th division and the Galicians away from the temptations the southern column discovered at Torquemada. Green, who was with the southern column, also reported a long march, nearly thirty miles, which took a heavy toll. Already men were falling from the ranks, totally exhausted. According to Green some simply expired on the spot. The pace of the retreat was also taking its toll on the horses, even the best of them collapsing under the strain of the march. It is no wonder, therefore, that when the exhausted troops discovered the wine vats of Torquemada, they could not resist the chance to reward themselves for their efforts. Wheeler believed there was

> some excuse, from Burgos to Salamanca is chiefly a wine country, and as there has been a good harvest, and the new wine was in tanks particularly about Valladolid the soldiers ran mad. I remember seeing a soldier fully accoutred with his knapsack on in a large tank, he had either fell [sic] in or had been pushed in by his comrades, there he lay dead. I saw a Dragoon fire his pistol into a large vat containing several thousands of gallons, in a few minutes we were up to our knees in wine fighting like tigers for it.[9]

The following morning many in the army were drunk. According to Ensign Mainwaring of the 51st:

> Some of them were found dead, literally drowned in wine, it having overflowed in the cellar and suffocated the poor wretches who were too drunk to escape. Next morning, at daybreak, when we stood to our arms to recommence the march, the scene was one, perhaps, without parallel in the annals of military history; for I scarcely exaggerate when I say that, with the exception of the officers, the whole army was drunk.[10]

Mills similarly maintained that there was scarcely a man sober in the morning, and it was a wonder that most of them had been able to march. It had been necessary for officers from every regiment, as well as a strong rear guard, to be left behind in order to keep the men going, while about 500 stragglers were lost to the enemy.

Alexander Dickson of the Portuguese infantry had one such man. His guns were attached to the 5th division for most of the retreat from Burgos but he had temporarily left this division at Tardajos as they marched to the right. Consequently, he moved with his guns to

> Torquemada where such a scene of drunkenness occurred as would have disgraced even a Billingsgate rabble. The wine vaults were broken open by the troops & hardly 500 men in all the troops in my brigade, the 1st & 6th divisions, were effective.

Subsequently,

> The [5th] division arrives at Torquemada & I join it & we march for Villamuriel. Previous to moving from Torquemada I ducked Drivers Henderson, Mitchell, Ash, Farmer, O'Neal for being drunk, and Driver Doran was so completely inebriated that he was obliged to be left behind[11]

It is worth noting that the artillery drivers had a very bad reputation for indiscipline, although few soldiers could resist wine, and with wine came the breakdown of order so that the army quickly became a rabble.

Bingham's brigade in the 6th division probably regarded themselves as hard done by, but Bingham congratulated himself that

> The brigade I commanded was fortunately farthest from the scene of disorder, and it was not till towards morning that our people made the discovery. I heard a noise, and got up and found some men of the 61st, drinking wine out of a camp kettle, which I immediately overset. I immediately awakened all the officers, and as we had the officers of three Regiments, to somewhat about 1,000 men, we contrived to keep the people sober; and so we were able to undertake the post of rear guard . . .[12]

Despite the state of the men, many of whom were still wine-sick and befuddled, the allies were able to cross the Carrion at Palencia, Villa-muriel and Dueñas unmolested by the French. Wellington now took up a position on the Carrion, placing the 5th division and the Galicians, who had found no wine at Cordovilla, on the left, closest to Palencia, and extending downstream to Villamuriel. Cabrero's Galician division was given the task of destroying the bridge in Palencia, supported by the 3rd Royals, while Losada's division joined the 5th division in Villamuriel, the site of the next bridge downstream from Palencia. The 1st, 6th and 7th divisions extended the allied line to the Pisuerga, and set about destroy-ing all the bridges from Villamuriel to the confluence of the Carrion and the Pisuerga.

Souham had followed the allies to Torquemada, where he made a demonstration of his presence by cannonading the allied rear guard. He was then forced to halt at Magaz. His troops had found yet more wine at Torquemada and were soon in a worse state than the departing Anglo-Portuguese. Souham was able to send Foy with two divisions to Palencia, however, while Maucune, also with two divisions, was ordered to attack the bridges at Villamuriel and San Isidro. Both French generals had a cavalry division in support.

Douglas reached Palencia with his battalion after dark. They found the bridge over the Carrion

> nearly blocked with men, baggage, guns and every species of trumpery attendant on an army. We made our way with no small difficulty, and encamped for the night on the heights facing the bridge, with Placencia [sic] on the left. This is a beautiful town

situated at the foot of a mountain. A dry canal ran nearly parallel with the river, to near the town. A dilapidated bridge over the canal led to a beautiful green, ere you reached the town, where a noble bridge crossed the river leading into it.

This was the bridge which Wellington had ordered to be blown up.

unfortunately the dragoon who carried the order lost his way in the dark and did not reach the Division until 8 o'clock in the morning, by which time the bridge ought to have been destroyed. The accident was the sole cause of the disasters of the day.[13]

Although Douglas offers one explanation for what he termed the sub-sequent 'disasters' of the 25th (others in the 5th division would have disagreed with this judgement), the determination of Cabrero to hold Palencia, even though it was on the wrong side of the river for the allies now the Carrion had been crossed, was another contributory factor in the events that followed.

On the right of Wellington's position was the 1st division, which was strengthened on the 24th by the arrival of a brigade of guards (1st foot guards) from Corunna. The 1st division, like the other divisions of the southern column, had not marched well during the day,

for it was with great difficulty the men who had indulged themselves could keep up with their regiments. This circumstance did not pass unobserved by General Paget, who, when the columns halted for the evening, formed it into brigades, and addressed it. He began by expressing his regret, at the scene he had witnessed that day; which cast a severe reflection on our character as soldiers, whose particular province is to observe discipline. He professed himself anxious to further the comforts of the private, as of the officer, but it was more especially incumbent on the officer to look after his men; and Sir Edward concluded, by avowing his determination to inflict exem-plary punishment, should a similar outrage occur. As he spoke, the evening breeze blew aside his cloak, and exposed the arm which had suffered amputation in the passage of the Douro, at Oporto, in 1809; and this, with the peculiar expression of his countenance, rendered the address doubly impressive.[14]

As the day wore on working parties from all the divisions were employed in mining the bridges across the Carrion and making the necessary preparations to destroy them. Only at Palencia was nothing happening; and Palencia was the site of the most crucial bridge.

Elsewhere the commissariat, with the sick, wounded and baggage, was on the way to Valladolid, where Daniell, who arrived in the city at 11.00pm, encountered a chaotic scene.

> The civil authorities of the town were at their posts answering the numerous requisitions making upon them for billets, means of transport, guides, etc. Our retreat had been so sudden and rapid that it was not without the greatest difficulty that we were able to bring off our numerous sick and wounded men: and the magistrates of Valladolid naturally giving the preference of the demands made upon them by the commissaries of the Spanish army, a great portion of them had not yet been able to cross the Douro.[15]

According to Daniell, this was the reason Wellington chose to make a stand on the Carrion.

*    *    *

Foy, as enterprising as ever, was not deterred when he reached Palencia and found the gates

> closed and barricaded, a regiment of Spanish cavalry around the ramparts, a part of the English 5th division and some troops of the army of Galicia in the town. After having put the cavalry to flight, the tirailleurs approached the gate; the Spanish who were behind it said they would open it if the general approached. I sent an aide de camp and a trumpeter; they were allowed to approach and were fired upon from the ramparts, which killed a horse. I advanced the artillery; the gate was stove in by cannon shot. Brigadier Chemineau, at the head of the 2nd battalion of the 69th, entered the town with the bayonet and knocked over the English in the streets and, despite a lively fusillade, took the bridge over the Carrion which the enemy tried to blow up; the powder for the explosion was in place. The artillery and the rest of the division debouched on the right bank of the river. We pursued the enemy; they had cannon; ours did them a lot of harm; a single shot killed three scarlet dragoons. The infantry pursued the enemy to kill them, right up to the entry to Paramo.[16]

Douglas told a rather different story. Once the artificers and miners of the 5th division arrived to mine the bridge,

> We were formed on a delightful green close to the river which separated us from the town, in open column of companies, not expecting the enemy to be so convenient; and as proof of our ignorance of the enemy being in the vicinity, the shoemakers of the different

companies marched into the town to procure leather for the repair of the men's shoes, and everything went on as if in the most secure camp. By this time the enemy were moving down the hills which overlooked the town, keeping up a desultory fire, which was taken for the stragglers shooting pigs; when all of a hurry our leather merchants came running down the lanes and spread the alarm of the enemy being in the town. Scarcely had they reached the column when some close firing took place on the bridge, and the enemy got possession of it. The Engineer Officer comes running to Col Campbell and says, 'Col Campbell, the bridge is taken. You are at liberty to act as you please with your Battalion.' There were a handful of men widely separated from any support, with Foy's division both in front and flank, which rendered our only safety in an instant retreat. But before the battalion went to the rightabout a round shot from the opposite side of the river took down 10 men of the Battalion, 1 dragoon and 2 horses.

There was another bridge to cross, the dilapidated bridge across the dry canal, but this position was vulnerable to the guns that Foy had brought up, and to cavalry fording the river.

The Battalion got more closely locked up than in the open space, which the enemy seemed to be aware of, as they ceased the fire, which I imagined was for the purpose of elevating the guns for the bridge, so that I let the main body pass before I crossed it. I was not wrong in my conjecture, for as the Battalion was crossing, the guns opened up in great style, but almost every shot flew over the column.

Foy claimed to have taken a hundred prisoners, with sixty men killed. He also referred to a great deal of baggage and 100,000 rations of biscuit that came into his possession. Douglas, however, explained that

As to our baggage, it was left with the Division, while we made the excursion. Consequently, it was not within their grasp, and even had they got every ounce that belonged to the Battalion, it would have fallen far short of abundance. As to prisoners, I was nearly the last man over the bridge, and I am quite confident we did not lose a single man as prisoner with the exception of those who fell badly wounded, and whom it was impossible to get away.[17]

The Royals made their escape when two light Spanish guns came up and held off the pursuing cavalry. They then ascended the steep hill that rises from the Carrion, where they re-formed before marching for Villa-muriel to join the rest of the division. They marched into a crisis, because the French were now in possession of the dry canal behind the village, a state of affairs which, according to Douglas, General Oswald, in command of the division, should have been prevented – although, not having been present at the beginning of the fight, he was repeating a judgement that Napier had made in his account of the action at Villamuriel.

Oswald had only recently arrived to command the division during the extended absence of the popular General James Leith, who was still recovering from the wound he had received at Salamanca. Inevitably, because he was not known to the men, he was the butt of criticism. Douglas, however, when he arrived in the middle of a fierce action, misread the situation.

The morning of the 25th was foggy, but by 8.00am the worst of the fog had dispersed. An hour later the 5th division became aware of Maucune's advance, but they were already in position to receive the enemy. Some of the troops were in the village, on the west bank of the Carrion; others were in the dry canal. James Hale of the1/9th makes clear in his account that his battalion were near the bridge, 200 men close to the bridge itself and the rest of the battalion extended along the river. This suggests that Barnes's brigade formed the front line, with Pringle's and Spry's (Portuguese) brigades further back. But since Barnes's brigade was missing the Royals, it is possible that men from the other two brigades were in close support. The 8th caçadores were definitely along the river bank, guarding a ford. Lawson's battery and Dickson's guns were behind the division, on the rising ground. Losada's Galician division was also on the high ground, acting as a reserve.

The guns were the first casualties. Two pieces were quickly disabled when the French artillery opened up, and the gunners had to draw back, higher up the hill. There were also some casualties among the troops in the dry canal, including a British major in the Portuguese service who was decapitated while reading a newspaper.

The French objective was the bridge. Having softened up the enemy with cannon fire and

> seeing so small a party to defend the bridge, they made a grand push for that place, but fortunately, before they could make their object, the bridge blew up, which put a stop to their pursuit: so then they extended themselves along the river, in about the same direction that we were, by which a sharp skirmishing immediately took place, and continued about four hours.[18]

It was during this extended skirmish that Wellington learnt of Foy's success in Palencia. 'This rendered it necessary to change our front, and I directed Major General Oswald to throw back our left, and the Spanish troops on the heights and to maintain the Carrion with the right of the 5th division.' As intended, this move successfully halted a French advance from Palencia and allowed Cabrera's Galicians, who like the Royals had made their escape over the high ground, to re-form on Losada's division.

Maucune had sent General Gaulthier to find another crossing point. Gaulthier was frustrated at San Isidro, where the bridge had been successfully blown up. At Baños the bridge had survived the attempt to destroy it, only the parapets collapsing when the mine was fired, and Gaulthier had the satisfaction of taking the working party prisoner. Nevertheless, Gaulthier advanced no further, nor did possession of Baños allow Maucune to cross the Carrion, for which he now needed to locate a ford. The 8th caçadores came under heavy fire from the French voltigeurs on the opposite bank of the river and this strong resistance offered by the Portuguese may well have led the French to realize that they were guarding a ford. Napier, however, gives a more colourful version of how a ford was finally located:

> suddenly a horseman darting out at full speed from the column, rode down under a flight of bullets, to the bridge, calling out that he was a deserter; he reached the edge of the chasm made by the explosion, and then violently checking his foaming horse, held up his hands, exclaiming that he was a lost man, and with hurried accents asked if there was no ford near. The good-natured soldiers pointed to one a little way off and the gallant fellow having looked earnestly for a few moments as if to fix the exact point, wheeled his horse round, kissed his hand in derision, and bending over his saddle-bow dashed back to his own comrades, amidst showers of shot, and shouts of laughter from both sides. The next moment Maucune's column covered by a concentrated fire of guns passed the river at the ford thus discovered, made some prisoners in the village, and lined the dry bank of the canal.[19]

Napier did not acknowledge the source of this story and there is no corroborating evidence. Hale's silence is particularly surprising since he was in an ideal position to witness the incident. By whatever means, though, the French found a crossing point for cavalry. One company of the 9th was positioned in a grist mill, which was particularly convenient for firing across the river. They were so busy skirmishing with the French tirailleurs across the water that they were taken totally by surprise when a troop of French cavalry suddenly rushed the mill. As a result the whole party were taken prisoner before the rest of the battalion could do anything to help them.

Douglas placed the ford to the left of the town (from the allied perspective). As it was only fordable by cavalry, he described how each rider took up an infantryman behind and carried him somewhat precariously to the other side. The infantrymen then scrambled down to terra firma. However the crossing was achieved, once the French were able to get their troops on the allied side of the river they could drive the Anglo-Portuguese back behind the dry canal and also effect a temporary repair of the bridge, using ladders. When a second ford was located, Maucune's forces quickly took possession of the village and the canal.

With the French at Palencia and now on the right bank of the Carrion at Villamuriel it was obvious to Wellington that his only option was an allied retreat from his current position. First, though, the French needed to be driven from their newly-gained position, even though Maucune (like Foy in Palencia) seemed disinclined to advance his troops any further, possibly on Souham's orders. Wellington now 'made Major General Pringle and Brig, General Barnes attack these troops, under the orders of Major General Oswald; in which attack the Spanish troops co-operated, and they were driven across the river with considerable loss.'[20]

Napier elaborated on this terse account. In his version Wellington overruled Oswald's doubts, giving orders for Barnes's brigade to attack the main body of the French, while Pringle's brigade cleared the canal. Further left, the Galicians and a company of Brunswick Oels riflemen attached to the 5th division were used to provide strong support. Barnes's brigade immediately launched their attack.

> The Royals and the 38th went, which was none of the easiest jobs as it was very steep and broken. The fire of the enemy slackened on seeing us move down until we came on a level with their guns, and then the play began. Our first fire and advancing with the bayonet cleared the canal and here, if Wellington's orders had been obeyed, our loss would have been trifling as we were to halt and keep possession of it … But, instead of occupying this post, we were ordered to follow the fugitives to the river's brink, exposed to a front and flanking fire of round and grape shot with occasional shells.[21]

Douglas, of course, was not privy to Wellington's orders, and also seems to have misremembered which brigade was given which task.

Hale, also in Barnes's brigade, reported how the brigade was ordered to stand to their arms and then charge the French. They enthusiastically obeyed the order, quickly capturing about 400 prisoners, while a great number were killed or wounded as they made a desperate effort to escape across the river.

Pringle's brigade, meanwhile, had marched in close support, finishing the work of clearing the canal, then extending to the left to assist the Galicians, who were under frontal attack and in a state of disarray. The Spanish were rallied by Wellington's liaison officer, Miguel Alava, who, according to Sydenham,

> behaved with great spirit and resolution at Dueñas [Villamuriel], in rallying his countrymen and leading them against the French. The moment he saw the Spaniards give way, he drew his sword and put himself at the head of them, abusing and licking them till he got them to turn and re-attack the French.[24]

The steadiness of Pringle's brigade, combined with Alava's efforts, during which he was wounded, enabled the Galicians, who had been under heavy French artillery fire, to re-form and return to the attack. They followed the French into the river and inflicted heavy casualties. As for Pringle's brigade, the 2/30th and 2/44th particularly distinguished themselves when they gallantly advanced in line and, against seventeen pieces of cannon, cleared the village, which had been in French hands, and took more prisoners than their own total numbers. At the same time the third battalion in the brigade, the 1/4th, supported Barnes's brigade.

Although infantry and artillery continued to fire into the night, the French had effectively been pushed back to where they started. The fighting had been fierce; the allied troops used more than their allotted sixty rounds of ammunition during a struggle which lasted all day. The position had been held, however, and the rest of the allied army was able to retire during the night, crossing the Pisuerga at Cabezon, while the 5th division covered them at Villamuriel. In the early hours of the 26th, the 5th division followed them, unmolested.

Not surprisingly, Gomm was soon writing to his sister:

> The Gazette will make you acquainted with the particulars of a heavy day the 5th division passed at the Bridge of Villa Muriel [sic] on the 25th. We lost nearly 600 men, but did, I believe, all that was expected of us.[24]

As for Dickson, he recorded that they remained

> in position at Villamuriel and were attacked by the enemy, the 5th division only having care of that post. My brigade losses, 3 killed, 6 wounded. One officer wounded and a gun carriage disabled with one horse & one mule wounded. Most of the men again drunk & in the morning of the 26th Gunner Reed so mutinous that I was obliged to send him away to the provost guard. Gunner Jones deserts.[35]

It seems that even when the French were on their tail, some men remained out of control, a point which Wellington would later make much of, although Dickson does not explain where his men had found more wine, unless they had brought it with them from Torquemada. It is unlikely, however, that this indiscipline was widespread in the 5th division, bearing in mind the strong and successful resistance they had just offered to the French.

*   *   *

A further French attack had seemed inevitable, but by nightfall on the 26th the allied army was lining the left bank of the Pisuerga from Cubillas de Santa Marta to Valladolid unchallenged.

> As the country was advantageous for the employment of cavalry, and the enemy greatly outnumbering us in this species of force, we expected this day they would harass us much. Accordingly, before we marched, the men practised a little drill in forming squares with celerity, to repel the charge; but the enemy contented himself with narrowly observing and following our course.[26]

If Wellington was popularly regarded as a cautious commander, Souham seemed intent on giving him a lesson in caution.

The allies were now in a strong position. Two bridges across the Duero, at Tudela and Ponte Duero, were within easy reach and there were good roads south and west to Medina del Campo, Arevalo and Olmedo. To make the position even stronger, the 1st division was sent to secure the bridge at Cabezon, over the Carrion. This position was held so that the sick and the stores could be taken across the Duero. It also allowed time for Commissary General Kennedy, who had joined the army from sick leave a week before, to put right some serious mismanagement which had occurred during his absence. This principally involved making arrangements for the magazines in Estremadura to be removed, and stores to be brought up along the lines of the present retreat. He did his best but the

> operation in some measure failed, the greatest distress was incurred, and the commissariat lost nearly the whole of the animals and carriages employed; the villages were abandoned, and the under-commissaries were bewildered, or paralyzed, by the terrible disorder thus spread along the lines of communication.[27]

Another foggy morning on the 27th cleared at midday to reveal a scene similar to Villamuriel two days before. This time the French were encamped three miles away.

rd Wellington, from an 1810 portrait after
pner. (*Author's collection*)

2. Marshal Nicolas-Jean-de-Dieu Soult, Duke of
Dalmatia. (*Author's collection*)

4. Field Marshal Sir William Maynard Gomm.
(*Author's collection*)

seph Bonaparte. (*Author's collection*)

5. General Francisco Ballesteros. (*Private collection*)

6. General Jean Baptiste Drouet, Count d'Er[
(*Private collection*)

7. General Sir Stapleton Cotton. (*Private collection*)

8. Marshal Jean Baptiste Jourdan. (*Private colle[

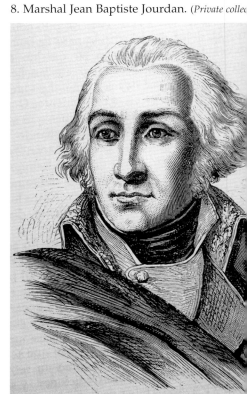

9. General Maximilien-Sébastien Foy.
(*Author's collection*)

10. Lt. Col. William Tomkinson. (*Author's collection*)

11. Major the Hon. Edward Charles Cocks.
(*Courtesy of the Council of the National Army Museum, London*)

12. Wellington's arrival in Madrid.
(*Courtesy of the Council of the
National Army Museum, London*)

13. Bronze medallion commemorating
Wellington's arrival in Madrid.
(*Courtesy of the Council of the National Army Museum, London*)

Wellington receives the keys to Madrid. (*Courtesy of the Council of the National Army Museum, London*)

Site of escalade at Burgos, 23 September 1812. (*Author's collection*)

16. Roman bridge at Palencia. (*Author's collection*)

17. Bridge at Villamuriel. (*Author's collection*)

ridge at Puente Larga. (*Author's collection*)

ridge at Tordecillas. (*Author's collection*)

20. Bridge at Alba de Tormes. (*Author's collection*)

21. Ford near San Muñoz. (*Author's collection*)

With a party of cavalry masking some light artillery, they approached the bridge [at Cabezon], and several shots were exchanged on both sides; one of which severely wounded Colonel Robe, of the artillery. They were suffered to post their videttes [sic] on the opposite side of the river, and their sentries near them. Their officers were plainly seen walking to and fro upon the road, with segars in their mouths, talking to one another with all possible *nonchalance*, although within range of our cannon.[28]

Souham left a division at Cabezon and extended his right to Cigales, Simancas and Valladolid. Now that Wellington could see the full strength of Souham's forces, he wrote to Hill:

the enemy are infinitely superior to us in cavalry, and from what I saw today, very superior in infantry. We must retire, therefore, and the Duero is no barrier for us. If we go, and we cannot hold our ground beyond the Duero, your situation will become delicate. We certainly cannot stand against the numbers at present opposed to us in any situation, and it appears to me, therefore, to be necessary that you, as well as we, should retire. The only doubt which I entertain is respecting the road which you should take, and that doubt originates in the insufficiency of this army to stop the army opposed to it a sufficient length of time to enable you to reach the Adaja.

Wellington intended to remain the next day on the Pisuerga, and then on the Duero for as long as possible, before withdrawing to Arevalo, which he proposed to reach on 3 November.

If I should not be able to hold my ground as long as I expect, either on the Pisuerga or the Duero, I shall apprize you of it at the first moment, and shall suggest your line of retreat ...[29]

When Wellington realized that Souham had detached his right to take possession of Valladolid, he sent the 7th division, under the newly arrived Lord Dalhousie, to defend the town. The French had already positioned a battery which caused problems for Daniell, who was engaged in getting the last of the sick and wounded across the Duero:

they were actually at this moment cannonading the suburbs of the town, and the hospital waggons which were running down the road with the sick were exposed to their fire: this, with the noise of the artillery and cavalry galloping through the streets, and the trumpets sounding the retreat, produced a scene of bustle and alarm not easily described ... The rain fell in torrents, and some of the poor wounded, from their infirm state and want of conveyance, fell by the roadside. Every one seemed to act upon the principal of self-preservation.[30]

On the 28th the French drove the caçadores of the 7th division from the suburbs of Valladolid, but Souham then decided the bridge across the Pisuerga was too strong to attack. Notwithstanding this caution, the French still took the opportunity to fire into the camp of the 51st, killing a sergeant's wife who was preparing her husband's breakfast. The disturbance also left Wheeler in what he realised was a singularly ridiculous position:

> Mounted on a refractory mule, a red worsted night cap hanging half way down my back containing several little articles, viz. chocolate, tobacco etc. half a dozen canteens full of wine, some upside down and the stoppers coming out, two haversacks full of bread, slung across my shoulders, and a monstrous large loaf under my arm, the mule in a gallop, the tail of my watch coat waving in the wind, and your humble servant a shocking bad rider, how I kept my seat I am puzzled to tell, but keep it I did.[31]

Wheeler had taken charge of one of the battalion mules with extreme reluctance; the effect of cannon fire on 'Betsy' seemed to justify this.

Green, however, thought there was a definite insouciance about the allied soldiers as they found themselves in this uncomfortable situation. Despite the guns which played on the bridge, the men believed themselves well protected by some strong buildings and some defensive breastworks. Even when they wandered into nearby gardens to gather potatoes and came under French musketry fire they were not intimidated and continued to collect the potatoes.

Burroughs was of the opinion that the French actually attacked the bridge with the intention of taking it, which suggests the determined nature of their fire.

> On the 28th October, about seven o'clock in the morning, a very heavy cannonade was heard in the direction of Valladolid. The spires of whose churches were rising to our view. The enemy, as was expected, had assaulted the bridge, and, at different times, but were constantly repulsed by a part of the 7th division, and in these attacks, the houses of the neighbourhood, suffered considerable injury.[32]

In fact, it would seem that Souham's chosen tactic was to make the area around the bridge too uncomfortable for the 7th division to remain in position. He was also searching for an easier crossing point; the nearest bridge was at Simancas on the Duero, but this had been secured by Halkett's German light battalions. They offered an obstinate defence long enough for the bridge to be blown up. Halkett then sent his Brunswick battalion to Tordesillas to secure the bridge over the Duero.

At this point, many officers could see no good outcome for the campaign. Mills wrote to his brother on the 28th,

> What is to become of our affairs here? Our army consists of 14,000 British and Portuguese and as many Spaniards. The French have 35,000. The Marquis has ruined his character, has lost 2,000 men in the siege, wasted two months of the most precious time and brought a most formidable army upon him. He has exposed his troops to five weeks of constant rain and brought on a great deal of sickness. Soult threatens Madrid with an immense army; Hill has an inferior and motley crew. In short, I think it all stands on the hazard of a die.[33]

It might be argued that Wellington was not a weather god, and wherever he had campaigned the excessive rain would have been a problem, while Hill's 'motley crew' included the 3rd and light divisions, two of the best fighting divisions in the army. Furthermore, once Soult was forced by Joseph to leave Andalusia, he was always going to threaten the allies with 'an immense army'. The significance of Mills's comments, though, lies in the state of mind that produced them, rather than the content of the actual comments.

On 30 October Foy sent a dispatch to Souham describing events which had occurred late in the afternoon of the previous day. He had reached Tordesillas to find that the main arch of the bridge had been destroyed as Halkett had ordered. On the far side of the river was an outlying piquet of Halkett's Brunswickers, who had taken up a position in a medieval watch tower. The rest of the battalion was camped in pine woods some distance to the rear. All the boats had been destroyed. Indeed, all necessary precautions had been taken except the most important, the need to keep a careful watch, but the Germans were obviously enjoying a false sense of security.

Foy's problem was simple enough. How to get troops across the Duero, which is wide at Tordesillas and was flowing strongly after the torrential rains of the past few weeks?

> I asked among the 1st division and the engineer sappers for volunteer swimmers; immediately 11 officers and 44 NCOs and soldiers presented themselves; they jumped into the water under a hail of bullets, the officers holding their swords in their mouths, the soldiers carrying their muskets and cartridges on two planks hastily assembled to form a raft. They reached the left bank, despite the enemy's very

lively fire, and although the muskets were wet, officers and soldiers ran totally naked to the tower, took it with sword and bayonet, overwhelmed 9 men who surrendered at the debouche of the bridge, and took two other prisoners on the platform of the tower. The Brunswick battalion took up their weapons; struck with terror at the sight of such a bold stroke, they fled and retired to the lane of San Martin del Monte.[34]

As Foy claimed, this was certainly a bold stroke, which was actually proposed and then directed by Captain Guingret of the 6th voltigeurs, aided by Lieutenant Rose of the 69th of the line. Foy's account, however, is a little disingenuous in its reference to 'a hail of bullets' and 'very lively fire'. Even allowing for the inaccuracy of musket fire it seems unlikely that the Brunswickers could have failed to inflict casualties had they been aware of what was happening, particularly at such close range. (Foy makes no reference to any losses.) In the fading light and secure in their tower, the piquet seems to have been keeping a casual watch at best, and the men were taken by surprise. They did flee, however, while the major in command, instead of organizing the battalion to resist fifty-five naked men, sent for orders from Halkett, who was not in the vicinity. As a result, all the 7th division could do once the debacle became known was to block the roads from the bridgehead; but they could not prevent Foy from repairing the bridge.

With the French now threatening Valladolid, Simancas and Tordesillas, Wellington took the decision to abandon Valladolid and Cabezon and move west. He drew in the 1st, 5th and 6th divisions, who all came under French fire, and the allied forces reached Puente Duero after a three-league march. The narrowness of the bridge across the Duero caused considerable delay as the baggage and the commissariat mules passed over, and even Wellington and his staff were obliged to wait. Burroughs noticed that although Wellington looked well physically it was possible to detect the anxiety he was feeling in his expression. By nightfall the whole army was on the left of the Duero, the 7th division, the last to cross, having destroyed the bridge across the Pisuerga before they left Valladolid.

Wellington now formed a line of battle 1,200 yards from the Duero. This provoked the French, who were engaged in repairing the recently destroyed bridges, to strengthen the bridgehead at Tordesillas in anticipation of an allied attack. Wellington, however, had no offensive intentions, and settled into headquarters first at Boecilla, then at Rueda. On the 30th he reported to Hill:

The enemy are collected at and about Tordesillas, and last night obtained the bridge at that place by the misconduct, I believe, of the

Brunswick corps. The army are formed in front of the enemy, and I hope that the latter cannot pass the Duero till you shall be near me.[35]

Souham was equally inclined to bide his time, spending six days in Valladolid, although he still probed for further crossing points because, until the bridges destroyed by the allies had been repaired, there was no practicable way of challenging Wellington's strong position. He also lost the contingent from the Army of the North when news of disturbances in Bilbao and Pamplona drew Caffarelli back to his area of command.

Wellington himself was in a much more positive frame of mind when he wrote to Beresford, who was in Lisbon, on the 31st.

you will see what a scrape we have been in, and how well we have got out of it. I say we have got out of it, because the enemy show no inclination to force the passage of the Duero. I have the army posted on the heights opposite the bridge of Tordesillas, of which they have possession. The bridge of Toro is destroyed, and I hope that of Zamora; and at all events they cannot cross at either before Hill and I shall join, when they will probably feel no inclination to cross.

To Sir Charles Stuart, also in Lisbon, he was a little less sanguine. Although he claimed to 'have got clear, in a handsome manner, of the worst scrape I ever was in,' he perceived himself as being seriously outnumbered.

Caffarelli's troops are certainly here; and the enemy have at least 40,000 infantry and 5,000 cavalry. I have not 20,000 British and Portuguese. Amongst the British are all the foreign troops in the army; and I have not 1,500 English cavalry; and only 24 pieces of artillery. I was shocked when I saw how the Spaniards fought on the 25th; and when I saw the whole of the enemy's army, it was very clear to me that they ought to eat us up. I detained them two days on the Carrion, three on the Pisuerga, and they do not appear inclined to pass the Duero at all. Hill will be at Arevalo on the 3rd or 4th.[36]

\*   \*   \*

Although Wellington had extricated his army from a perilous situation, the mood of that army remained volatile. Aitchison probably summed up the feelings of many of his fellow officers, and of the men, when he told his father,

Since I wrote to you on the 19th instant most important events to this army and the cause of Spain have taken place, but I am sorry to say that they have not been of that promising nature as those which occurred in the early part of the campaign. We have returned to the Douro where our offensive operations, I fear, may be considered as already terminated for the present year. As it would only add to the melancholy which their non-accomplishment has created, I shall now revert to the brilliant prospects of this army opened by the victory of Salamanca and increased by the surrender of Madrid ...[37]

Unfortunately, in the present circumstances, the successes of the first eight months of 1812 had made the taste of subsequent failure all the sourer. Major Samuel Rice of the 51st was particularly scathing in a letter to his brother.

> our movements have been retrograde – I won't call it in this place *retreating*, because it is possibly only a little run on the part of our Most Noble and Gallant Marquis, whose judgement and military abilities are inferior *nulli* – not even Bony the Great ... The fact of the matter is, we were doing too much for our means, and, *entre nous*, are lucky in getting clear off. Our movements have been rapid, and not a little pressed; dire destruction of bridges &c, in fact all the agreeables attending retrograde movements ...
>
> Our sufferings have not been a little; the weather horribly cold and wet; not once under cover for these last two months. The poor soldiers dreadfully off; but I must not depict all the miseries; the truth must not be told all the times.[38]

Others, however, shared Wellington's more optimistic beliefs. Rous, for instance, told his father that they were now making a good and easy retreat and expected to join Hill in the near future. When this happened they would give the French the same treatment they had handed out at Salamanca, possibly in the same place. Although Gomm might have taken issue with Rous's reference to an easy retreat, since he referred to 'fatiguing marches and bad weather', like Rous he anticipated 'a great battle that will shortly set matters to rights amongst us.'[39] As for Dansey, while he conceded that 'Our operations at Burgos were certainly not of a very brilliant aspect,' he maintained that 'under God and Lord Wellington no one can be desponding, and even in our retreat we anticipate nothing but success.'[40] Sydenham, from his civilian perspective, assured Henry Wellesley that they could remain where they were for as long as they chose. Looking at the wider picture, he believed that only Maucune's division of the Army of Portugal was as far forward as Tordesillas (it was actually Foy's division), and Caffarelli's division of the Army of the North at Toro. As for the rest of Souham's forces, both infantry and cavalry, they appeared to be dispersed in cantonments.

Nevertheless, even the most optimistic would have been forced to concede that the army was in a deplorable condition. Captain William Hay rejoined his regiment, the 12th dragoons, at this stage of the retreat and was shocked by what he discovered.

how mortified I felt to see the sad change worked on them in the few months I had been absent! On reporting myself ... from the 52nd [his previous regiment] to the headquarters of the 12th, I found the men in new uniforms, and the horses and appointments in the best condition. At that time they had but recently arrived from England, and it was a treat to look upon so neat and clean a corps. But what a difference one campaign had made; the men's clothes were actually in rags, some one colour, some another; some in worn-out helmets, some in none; others in forage caps or with handkerchiefs tied round their heads; the horses in a most woeful state, many quite unfit to carry the weight of the rider and his baggage. The edge was indeed off all but the spirit of the dragoons and the blade of his sabre; these continued the same ever, under all privations, willing and ready to work.[41]

On 3 November Wellington informed Hill:

We are all quiet on this side. The enemy have repaired the bridges at Toro and Tordesillas, but have shown no inclination to pass either. It is reported that Caffarelli's two divisions have returned to the north; but of that I have no certainty. If it be so, I conclude that the preparations to cross the river are made to be taken advantage of when the troops of the Armies of the Centre and of the South approach us.

Under these circumstances, you become the guide of our movements, at least for the present. Unless you should be pressed by the enemy, I recommend you to halt a day upon the Adaja at Blasco Sancho or Arevalo, keeping your cavalry well out of the road towards Villa Castin, to give time for stragglers, baggage &c, to come up; and give me timely notice of any movement towards you, or in the valley of the Tagus.

Hill was also required, should he move from the Adaja, to 'take care that all our stores and people (including my hounds at Arevalo) move off.'[42]

By this point Wellington and Hill were in close communication.

At 6 o'clock on the morning of the 5th, Sir Rowland Hill, having received intelligence that the enemy's armies were rapidly advancing on his rear, ordered me to proceed without delay to the headquarters of Lord Wellington at Rueda, and communicate to his Lordship the course of events on the Adaja.

Lieutenant Andrew Leith Hay, aide-de-camp to his uncle, General Leith, had volunteered to serve during Leith's absence in an unattached role. He was an experienced exploring officer and covered the fifty-two miles to Rueda by ten o'clock.

> I found Lord Wellington inhabiting a very indifferent quarter in the village of Rueda, but, notwithstanding the reverse he had sustained, apparently in the same excellent spirits, the same collected, clear, distinct frame of mind, that never varied or forsook him, during the numberless embarrassing events and anxious occasions that naturally occurred to agitate a commander during the long arduous struggle which he conducted with such firmness and judgement.[43]

In his reply to the dispatch Leith Hay carried, Wellington informed Hill that the 5th division and Ponsonby's cavalry had been sent to Aleajos early that morning in response to a French movement in that direction. Wellington himself intended to establish his headquarters at Nava del Rey on the 6th. If Hill now marched for Madrigal or Fuente el Sol they would be tolerably well connected. Hill was also warned in a further dispatch not to let the French advance guard get too close to him.

Although disquieting comments were being written in letters and journals, the writers themselves were in a familiar world and generally understood what was happening, if not why, since Wellington was not inclined to reveal his intentions to his subordinates. It was a different matter for Francis Seymour Larpent, a civilian lawyer sent out to act as judge-advocate general to the armies in Spain. He reached Rueda on 4 November. His account of what then happened conveys the bemusement and increasing frustration of a civilian who now found himself in a military world.

> When here, I had my beasts standing loaded in the streets, before I could get a quarter. The people were civil, but I had to go to the Quarter Master-General, Adjutant-General, to the billet-manager, to the Military Secretary. &c, &c. One said, 'go here,' another said, 'go there,' a third sent a serjeant [sic] to enquire, and then thought no more about it; another I was referred to to turn any one out for me, but I was to find out who was to turn out, and when it came to the point nothing was done.
>
>   At last I got an indifferent quarter vacated by a Commissary, without any stable, only a shed with holes through the floor into the cellar below. My animals therefore stood all night in the entrance of the passage. I then drew for provisions, &c, and at eight o'clock got a piece of warm killed beef fried; of course, it was like Indian rubber.[44]

Nor was Larpent destined to enjoy much leisure. The following day Wellington invited him to dinner, but also sent him fifty cases pending against officers to examine.

On the 6th Wellington pulled back his other divisions in response to a French advance in strength on Toro the previous night. He informed Hill that the following day he would march to Pitiegua in order to cover the Toro to Salamanca road. As a result of the French movement, Hill was advised to 'march at an early hour, and pass Peñaranda, and encamp either at Nava de Sortrobal along that river [Tormes], or at Coca, Tordillos, and Peñarandilla, further in the rear, as you may think proper ...' Of more concern was the position of the French. 'Have you any account of the enemy moving in the valley of the Tagus? or whether the King has stopped at Madrid? or what force has followed you? It appears last night nothing but cavalry.'[45]

Later Wellington reported that the French had not moved beyond Toro, but he still intended to take up a position in front of Salamanca the next day, and advised Hill to march for Alba de Tormes. As soon as he arrived there he was to send the 3rd, 4th and light divisions, de España's troops and Victor Alten's cavalry to join the main army in its Salamanca position, while the 2nd division should stay at Alba with the remaining cavalry.

Souham was also trying to establish communications, in his case with the other French armies. He crossed the repaired bridge at Tordesillas and sent scouts to locate Soult. He was still moving cautiously, though, because he suspected that Wellington's withdrawal from Rueda was a ruse designed to lure him into a trap. The following day, the 7th, he was in close contact with the forces of Soult and the king. The French could now focus on a combined operation to deal with the allied army.

By the 8th Wellington's headquarters were as planned at Pitiegua and his army was in the position it had held in June, at the start of the Salamanca campaign, forming a semi-circle on the left bank of the Tormes from Aldea Lengua to San Christoval. The weather was deteriorating fast and as many troops as could be accommodated were crammed into the small villages in the region. Many were still bivouacking, though, and cases of dysentery and rheumatism were rising. Bingham, thinking of the welfare of his brigade, was pleased when tents were distributed, and regarded himself as particularly fortunate to enjoy the comforts of clean quarters. However, physical conditions were not always the worst of a man's misfortunes, and Bingham continued his letter to his mother:

all these misfortunes, incidental to a campaign, I could bear with patience, but I cannot bear with equanimity, General Clinton, who is one of the greatest fools I ever met with. He expects men are made like the little wooden figures you move and manoeuvre on a table with so much facility. Now he makes no allowance for weather, fatigue, or any other cause. I wish every day I was clear of him and the trade of war, altogether, if carried on by such masters.[46]

Wellington might well have agreed with the tenor of these comments, for Clinton's conduct in August, which had allowed Clausel to advance unchallenged on Valladolid, had been a contributory factor in the decision to leave Madrid, the consequences of which were now evident.

For Wellington, with his army in position and Hill within reach, there were now two options: offer battle or retreat. But he was aware that neither was what his army needed, as he explained to Bathurst.

The two corps of the army, particularly that which has been in the north, are in want of rest. They have been in the field, and almost constantly marching since the month of January last; their clothes and equipments are much worn, and a short period in cantonments would be very useful to them. The cavalry likewise are weak in numbers, and the horses rather low in condition. I should wish therefore to be able to canton the troops for a short time, and I should prefer the cantonments on the Tormes to those further in the rear.[47]

Yet all his options, including what would be best for his army, depended upon the intentions of the French.

## Chapter 8

# Front Line Abandoned

As Wellington began his retreat from Burgos, Hill was establishing his position behind the Tagus. By 25 October the extreme right of his line, at Toledo and Añover, was held by the newly-arrived Colonel Skerrett, with the 4,000 men he had brought up from Cadiz. To the left, the four brigades of the 2nd division held Aranjuez and Colmenar de Oreja. Penne Villemur and Morillo were between Belmonte de Tajo and the Villamanrique fords, while Elio and Freire controlled the area around Fuentidueña and watched the road from Valencia. The 3rd and 4th divisions were close together at Valdemoro and Ciempozuelos, behind Aranjuez, and the light division was at Alcala, five leagues from Madrid. These three divisions were acting as a reserve, along with de España's Spaniards at Campo Real and Hamilton's Portuguese at Chinchon. The advance cavalry was still forward, but withdrawing slowly from Ocaña. These dispositions enabled Hill to concentrate at either Aranjuez or Fuentidueña, the two obvious crossing points of the Tagus. D'Urban wrote approvingly of Hill's disposition: 'there can be no doubt that Sir Rowland's determination is right. Of course he intends to contest the difficult ground between the Tagus and Henares with a strong and clear Advance Guard and fight behind the latter.'[1]

In preparation for a defence of the Tagus Hill's forces were strengthening their positions. This could sometimes prove frustrating. At Aranjuez Captain George Wood of the 82nd was

> sent with a party of men to the river that divided us, to throw up breastworks at the bridge, in order to obstruct the enemy should they attempt to cross; but, after being at work the whole day, I had the mortification of seeing all our labour blown into the air, according to orders received for that purpose, the more effectually to prevent their crossing.[2]

Joseph had arrived at Cuenca on the 23rd and found d'Erlon waiting for him. The next day Webber, who was at Villamaurique, learnt from the Alcalde that the French were only eight miles away at Santa Cruz de la Zarza, on the opposite side of the river. This rumour may have accelerated

Soult's actual progress, but he was definitely at Santa Cruz on the 25th, having met Freire's retiring Murcian horse at Tarancón and Long's 9th and 13th light dragoons and the 2nd hussars of the King's German Legion at Ocaña. According to d'Espinchal, on the 24th, while

> marching at the head of the division, we closely followed the retrograde movement of the English, during which Lieutenant Ducis vigorously charged at the head of the tirailleurs, and took five English hussars prisoner, who told us that the army was concentrating on the Tagus.[3]

Presumably, this was an encounter with Long's cavalry, just outside Ocaña, in which case, if they were hussars rather than dragoons, then they were German, not 'English', but this was a distinction of little significance to the French. The following day d'Espinchal was sent by General Soult to Tarancón. On his way he learnt that the enemy were in front of the village.

> Three Spanish squadrons, making as if to stand, were immediately forced in and chased almost to Velineon, seven men being killed and nineteen made prisoner; the light infantry, who were following our movements at a quick pace contributed not a little to this success. In the evening we established out bivouacs before Santa Cruz.[4]

While d'Espinchal was moving closer to the Army of the Centre and challenging allied cavalry at every opportunity, Webber had moved out to Fuentidueña, where he had joined Howard's brigade and Freire's horse, who had retreated successfully from Tarancón, despite the encounter with the French referred to above, and now watched for the enemy on the right bank of the Tagus. Webber posted two guns on a hill outside the town to protect the Spanish pontoon bridge, but, from the reports received, he fully expected to be driven back. Yet although Soult was at Santa Cruz with 10,000 men, his immediate objectives were unclear to the allies. A report from about this time suggested that his first objective was Aranjuez, then Madrid. D'Urban on the other hand interpreted Soult's manoeuvring as a feint to his left to cover his true movement to the right.

Nevertheless, there could be no doubt that the French were drawing closer.

> At Aranjuez there was unusual bustle; the Enemy in front were making demonstrations of advancing on that Road, & on our part every precaution was making, all the heavy Baggage, Forge & Forage Waggons &c &c were moving to the rear for the purpose of crossing the River, and the several Bridges were mined and ready to be blown

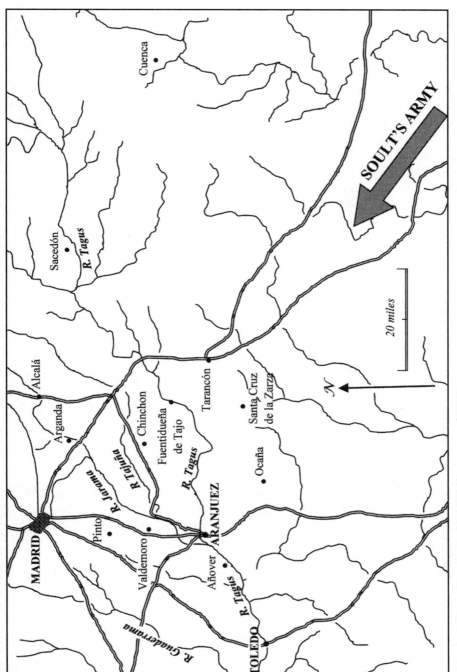

The area to the south and east of Madrid (from a map of 1796).

up. On the following day however it was ascertained they had taken
a direction to their right.[5]

This was a movement which seemed to confirm D'Urban's interpretation
of Soult's intentions.

In fact, these were only minor movements on Soult's part as he waited
for the whole of his army to come up and link with the force at Cuenca.
Then there could be a general advance which would threaten Hill's
position. Soult had already nominated the 28th as the day for the attack on
the allies. Believing that the French were moving to the right, however,
Hill made some further adjustments to his position. The 2nd division
crossed to the right bank of the Tagus and then extended left on the
Jarama, while the light division was brought down from Alcala to
Arganda. This enabled Hill to make a show on two fronts and protect the
roads from the Tagus, the Jarama and the Henares to Madrid.

Howard's brigade in the 2nd division was ordered for Colmenar, to
defend the Tagus between Fuentidueña and Aranjuez. Hope described
how:

> On our arrival we found the Spanish corps of Generals Elio and
> Freyre [sic] in bivouac close to the village. On the 27th, the enemy
> appeared on a height opposite to Duenna, where they pushed for-
> ward a strong reconnoitring party towards the bridge. To prevent
> them finding out the state of the bridge, the 60th Rifle Company lined
> the bank of the Tagus, and kept up a smart fire on their advance
> guard of cavalry, but the shots being rather long, very little execution
> was done. In about an hour they retired altogether out of our view.
>
> The day being unusually fine, some men of the brigade were enjoy-
> ing themselves in the limpid stream, when the enemy descended the
> heights to reconnoitre the bridge. Warned of the rapid approach of
> the enemy, our men quitted the water, and remained on the left bank
> till the enemy was quite close to them. Before leaping into the river
> to return to their own side of it, one of them placed himself in a
> nameless attitude, which roused the ire of the Gallic soldiers to such a
> pitch, that one of them, foaming with rage, galloped forward almost
> to the verge of the river, and deliberately levelled his carbine at the
> unprotected person of the poor fellow who was still in the water. This
> cowardly act called forth such a spontaneous and deafening shout of
> indignation from every mouth in our brigade, that the arm of the
> assassin was paralyzed. The hand which grasped the weapon from
> which the messenger of death was to be sped, dropped as if by magic
> by his side, and then, covered with confusion, and heartily ashamed

of his conduct, he wheeled his horse to the right-about, and rode off at full speed.[6]

As for the light division, they first marched as ordered to Arganda, closer to the rest of the allied line, but the changing situation made this move unnecessary. They then assembled in the dark and marched back to Alcala, which they reached after daylight. After a brief rest, they spent the afternoon marching to Barajas. As Kincaid commented, 'If any one thing is more particularly damned than another it is a march of this kind.'[7]

On the 27th, two days after the departure of the baggage, sick and stores from Aranjuez, and while the light division were making their 'damned' march, the last infantry were evacuated from the town, across Captain Goldfinch RE's bridge. Ensign George Bell had only just joined his regiment, the 34th, in time to cross the Tagus:

> one bridge on fire, the other about to be blown up – a little later and I should have been on the wrong side! The two bridges had not been destroyed more than an hour or so when the French cavalry approached and sent their videttes [sic] down to the river to look after our locality. It might have been very inhospitable, but they received a very ugly discharge of musketry from our riflemen, who lined the banks under cover of the evergreen shrubs and bushes.[8]

This was about 4.00pm, by which time the Puente de la Reyna had been blown up. About five hours later the 2nd division received orders to march for Chinchon, which they reached the following morning. Hill had realised that the Tagus was fordable in too many places and also had a difficult hinterland. He decided instead to defend a line running north to south from Guadalajara to Puente Larga.

On the 28th, after a thirty-minute rest at Chinchon, the 2nd division marched on to Puente Larga, on the Jarama. Reaching the river at 5.00pm they crossed to the right bank and ascended the heights, having covered forty miles in twenty-four hours. One young man who suffered from all this marching was Ensign Bell. Having taken his boots off during one of the halts he then fell asleep. Waking to find himself alone, he tried to get his boots back on, but could only force one foot home. He then proceeded to limp in pursuit of his battalion with the other boot half on and half off. Not surprisingly, he was fairly knocked up when he finally caught up with them.

Captain Goldfinch now set about mining the bridge, which was defended by strong piquets. Skerrett's 1,600 men from Cadiz, who had arrived in Aranjuez from Toledo three days before and left two days later, were in position to defend the bridge. Elsewhere, the 4th division was at

Añover, the 3rd division and Hamilton's Portuguese at Valdemoro and San Martin de la Vega, the light division back at Alcala, where they had been joined by de España and Morillo, and Elio at Guadalajara. The allied cavalry were all forward, holding the Tagus, but with instruction to withdraw to the Tajuña if the French crossed the river and drove them in.

The following day Soult brought an infantry division up to Aranjuez and repaired the bridge so that he could make an advance beyond the Tagus, although he made no further forward movement at this point. However, he met the king at Ocaña so that plans could be confirmed for the general advance against the allies the following day, a day later than Soult had originally intended. D'Erlon crossed the Tagus at Fuentidueña and Villamanrique in preparation for this forward movement. Soult had also heard rumours that Wellington was coming to Madrid, and he urged Joseph to come up to Aranjuez and Puente Larga, so that the French could present a united front. On Jourdan's advice the king agreed.

At this point Hill received the dispatch from Wellington, written two days earlier, which instructed him to retreat in concert with the retreat of the Burgos troops. There were also orders for the disposition of the Spanish troops:

> Let Don Carlos' division, Morillo's and Penne Villemur's, retire with you; desire Generals Elio, Bassecourt, and Villa Campa, to join General Ballesteros by the bridge of Toledo, if you should have left that entire, or by that of Talavera, or that of Arzobispo if you should not; and desire the Empecinado to go to his old ground about Guadalaxara. Tell them all that we shall soon be able to set matters on their legs again, but that it is impossible for the British army to resist the armies of the North; the centre; of Soult; and that of Portugal; and part of that of Suchet; in co-operation at the same moment.[9]

The reference to Ballesteros is particularly significant. Obviously, Wellington had no news of that general's defection, and was still allotting him a role which would keep him as a constant irritant on Soult's flank. In a postscript, Wellington approved Hill's decision to hold the Jarama, although he pointed out that it could be turned on both the right and the left.

In response to this dispatch Hill ordered an immediate retreat. Skerrett remained at Puente Larga to hold the bridge and protect Hill's right wing, which was threatened by Soult. The light division, with de España's and Morillo's Spaniards, marched from Alcala to El Pardo north of Madrid, which they reached at midnight. The 3rd division and Hamilton's Portugese followed a route south of Madrid to Aravaca. The 4th division marched all night from Añover to Valdemoro where, unfortunately, they discovered the wine vats. The result was inevitable – widespread drunkenness. Although the division joined the rest of the right wing at Aravaca the next morning they left behind 300 drunken stragglers for the French to pick up. (D'Espinchal claimed that they took more than 1,200 prisoners.) The commander of the 4th division, General Sir Lowry Cole, who had returned after recovering from the wound he suffered at Salamanca, remained with Skerrett at Puente Larga, having temporarily attached the Cadiz troops as his rear guard. Finally, the 2nd division crossed the Jarama.

> we came on the great road about seven leagues from [Madrid] where a bridge crosses the Guadarama [sic], which the Sappers and Miners were preparing to blow up, and a party of the Guards that had arrived from Cadiz were on duty protecting them while the operations were going on. It was about twelve o'clock at night when we reached the bridge; and when the division was partly over, some one called out that the mine was sprung. As the bridge was very crowded at the time, a scene of indescribable confusion ensued. Some fell back, while others rushed forward; several were pressed over the parapets, and a great many trampled upon and severely bruised. Order was at length restored, and we resumed our march.[10]

They marched to Madrid by way of Valdemoro.

Bell, who claimed never to have lost his appetite, although his feet often failed him, was dismayed to find himself in Madrid without a dollar to buy a loaf of bread or a sausage, both of which he earnestly desired. Nevertheless, he had taken the precaution of putting two pounds of biscuit into his haversack, as subsistence for the next two days. Then the bugles sounded.

> I rolled my blanket, strapped it on my back, and waited for the assembly call, when the 88th Regiment, or Connaught Rangers, passed by as merry as larks, singing and cracking their Irish jokes. They were regular bronze fellows, hard as nails, and as ready for a fight as for a ration of rum. One fellow took a side glance at me and said, not in a very undertone, 'I think that young gentleman would be better at home with his mother!' I was very indignant at this remark and kept it to myself. I knew they were a crack regiment, and esteemed them for their remarkable bravery at all times.[11]

> The next morning [the 30th] we passed close under the walls of the capital, three miles from which, on the road to the Escurial, we encamped. During the march, the rain poured in torrents, nor did it

terminate with our fatiguing march, but continued with unabated violence till sunset. By this time the soldiers were rendered almost unfit for duty, having no tents to shelter them from the storm.[12]

Skerrett, holding the position at Puente Larga with his five battalions and a Portuguese battery in support, shared the discomfort of the weather. The rain and mist also worked to his advantage since it prevented the cavalry Soult sent to assess the strength of the force holding the sixteen-arched bridge from gaining an accurate picture. Nevertheless, Soult sent Raymond's division to dislodge the defenders and there ensued a musketry and artillery struggle which lasted for several hours.

D'Espinchal, who was present, described the course of events when the French realised the 'English' had taken up an entrenched position and could not easily be moved.

The four companies of the 13th light, under my orders, attacked with the greatest resolution a large post placed in the middle of strong barricades, and cleared it; but the enemy, returning strongly and furiously, regained the position, from where he was chased in good style with the support of a battery of six pieces; then the general [Soult] thinking that the English were going to make a retreat, sent his aide-de-camp, Captain Léng, to me with the order to go forward and make a lively charge against the rear guard; but we received at half-range from a masked battery three discharges of ammunition which instantly laid low an officer, seven hussars and nine horses.

At this moment Marshal Soult arrived with twelve guns, which forced the defenders to withdraw; but 'the enemy, with admirable courage, re-formed in column, a short distance in the rear.'[13] D'Espinchal charged again and this time Skerrett's men retreated, a move d'Espinchal ascribed to the large number of allied dead and wounded. Not that the damage was all on one side. When nightfall brought the combat to an end, the French had close on 100 men killed or wounded. Three officers lay dead and two were seriously wounded, requiring instant amputation. Even d'Espinchal had to withdraw from the fight when a hail of bullets shattered his helmet.

In fact, it was Soult who withdrew his artillery and voltigeurs, thus ending the fight and leaving Skerrett in possession of the bridge. He permitted the French to remove their wounded. As for his own losses, these amounted to sixty men killed and wounded. The French were left with little to console them; the night was damp and cold and they had neither food nor forage.

Swabey was a witness to the struggle from

the heights above the Jarama bridge where there had been all day a smart fire, these hills form an excellent position and we thought we were certainly intended to fight. The bridge, guarded by the 57th, but from the nature of the ground commanded by the French artillery, was charged twice by French infantry and three times by cavalry, but they could not make any impression.[14]

This is a rather different interpretation of what happened from d'Espinchal's, even though Swabey seems not to have noticed that Skerrett's force was a detachment of battalions, the 3rd battalion 1st foot guards, the 2/47th, 2/87th, 20th Portuguese and three companies of the 3/95th. A further detail which adds to Skerrett's achievement was the fact that the Portuguese artillery ran out of ammunition before the combat was over and the infantry had to hold the position unsupported against French infantry, cavalry and artillery.

Skerrett, whose stand at Puente Larga had enabled all the other allied units to withdraw unmolested, waited until dark before retiring to El Pardo, on the north side of Madrid. He had bought time for Hill just as the 5th division did for Wellington at Villamuriel. Nevertheless, as in Wellington's army, the mood of the troops was generally dispirited. Webber, for example, wrote in his diary

I never recollected on any occasion ... being more melancholy and depressed than in passing by the Puente de Toledo and giving up Madrid to the plunder and wanton cruelty of the enemy. I would willingly have lost a limb in a battle to have saved it, and I know every man felt the same sentiments.

The unfortunate people were so confident of our protection and means of defence, that they would never listen to the possibility of being once more under the French yoke. Therefore their fall was the greater and their sad reverse of fortune so unexpected and they so unprepared for it that every feeling mind must have participated in their grief and distress.[15]

Others shared Webber's feelings and his hope that the rains would delay Soult long enough for Wellington to join with the Burgos army before the French could cross the Tagus. Some, like Captain Jonathan Leach of the 95th, also recorded a more personal sense of loss.

The moment of our departure had now arrived: the rearguard of cavalry was gradually falling back towards the heights; and, in a dark, gloomy afternoon, on the 31st October, we bade farewell to that city, in which I passed some of the happiest days of my life, and shall ever look back on with mixed sensations of pleasure and regret. The rains of winter had already commenced; the prospect of a long and dreary retreat, of wet camps and bivouacs, and the long train of privations and vicissitudes which winter campaigning more especially brings with it, stared us in the face.[16]

*   *   *

Wellington had previously made some suggestion that Hill would be able to withdraw along the Tagus valley. Once Soult crossed the Tagus at Aranuez and Fuentidueña, where the 2nd division had failed to destroy the bridge of boats, this line of retreat was no longer an option. Instead, Hill accepted that he would have to take his army over the Sierra de Guadarrama.

The allied rear guard finally left Madrid on 31 October, the light division covering the troops that had marched up from Arganda and Aranuez. First, though, the stores at La China, in the Retiro, had to be destroyed, despite the demands of the mob who wanted them handed out. In fact, some food was saved for the poorest citizens. The initial destruction was mismanaged. According to Grattan of the 88th, a storekeeper of the ordnance department was blown to pieces when he ventured into the building after he had lit the match. Swabey recorded that several other men had been killed. The following day he accompanied a King's German Legion artillery officer back to the building to complete the destruction. This German officer observed

a degree of recklessness in the preparations; however, there was no time to lose and I went out to ascertain that there were no persons within reach of danger. Whether by accident, or because my companion was jealous of my presence, I cannot say and never ascertained, but I had hardly got into the open, and by no means indeed out of danger, when up flew the corner of the building into the air and the breach was indeed effectively made. My first act was to rush into the vaults of the building which I did without a light. It seemed in vain to hope that the perpetrator of this rash act, rash if designed, could have escaped, and my only idea was to recover his body, but to my utter terror and dismay I ran against him in the dark vault: a feeling of horror came over me, and my first impression that I had encountered his spirit gave way to greater anxiety as I led this walking cinder to the light. Here, as soon as I could see him, was a spectacle! Every hair on his head was singed, and he was perfectly black and blind, yet though he was scorched by the explosion he was not burnt, and I understood afterwards that in spite of much suffering he recovered. This gallant fellow's idea was that he would rather perish than not succeed in the duty that had been assigned him, and which had not been effectually done in the first instance. I have no doubt that the great strength and weight of the building, together with the immense subterranean vaults which offered insufficient resistance at any one point, rendered the operation less simple and easy than might have appeared to a mere spectator.[17]

The army now moved north towards the mountains. While the 3rd and 4th division marched directly to Guadarrama, the 2nd and light divisions followed the Escurial road, with the cavalry covering the retreat. Soult brought his troops up to Valdemoro where he halted to await the rest of his troops, who were coming up from Ocaña, and the Army of the Centre, which was still on the far side of the Jarama. The rumours about Wellington moving south had persuaded him to move cautiously and at full strength. On 1 November the French cavalry entered Madrid, although most of Soult's force was at Getafé. He also sent scouting parties to locate the allies and ascertain their line of march.

By this time most of the allied army was bivouacking near the Escurial. There was some excitement when two wild boars came galloping through the lines of the light division and caused mayhem. In the confusion a soldier of the 52nd was upended by one of the panicking animals, which then bounded over him. The soldier was lucky to escape unscathed. According to Kincaid, there were also hares in the park.

It is amusing, on a division's first taking up its ground, to see the number of hares that are every instant starting up among the men, and the scrambling and shouting of the soldier for the prize. This day, when the usual shout was given, every man ran, with his cap in his hand, to endeavour to capture poor puss, imagined, but which turned out to be two wild boars, who contrived to make room for themselves so long as long as there was nothing but men's caps to contend with; but they very soon had as many bayonets as bristles in their backs.[18]

Hill's army crossed the Sierra de Guadarrama during the next two days. The ascent was a three-hour zig-zag march, although, according to Sherer, 'The ascent to the top is four miles, but the royal road is so fine, and so admirably laid down, that your cannon meet with no obstacle, which an additional pair of horses, or a drag rope cannot overcome.' Nor was the climb without its compensations:

the southern face of the Guadarrama mountains is bare, brown, and rocky, but the northern side most majestically wild; large projecting masses of rock, dark, and thick plantations of the mountain fir; and steep patches of the liveliest verdure, all boldly blended, are the features of this grand and uncommon scene.[19]

As Swabey crossed the mountains, however, he 'began to realize the miseries of the retreat; animals knocked up, men and women failing, and every kind of woe ...' This observation is significant because it was written in a diary, which indicates that the distress, usually associated with the end of the retreat, was evident from the start. Swabey also witnessed the

> massacre of some unfortunate French prisoners by a Spanish escort, who with the utmost composure shot them like dogs. We were not near enough to arrest their cursed purpose, but when we remonstrated were told that we frequently served them the same, and moreover, they had requested to be shot. Inhuman wretches! They had reduced them to despair by starvation, and thought their deeds justified by the desperate request.

Needless to say, 'this dastardly revenge' only strengthened Swabey's prejudice against the Spanish.[20]

As the allies crossed the mountains and reached Villacastin, the armies of the South and the Centre were finally united. Soult now decided to cross the Sierra de Guadarrama in pursuit, while Joseph entered his capital in triumph, although without the deliriously joyful welcome accorded to Wellington less than three months before. He then garrisoned the Retiro as a sign of his power. Towards evening on the 3rd d'Espinchal, in the advance guard of Soult's forces, came upon two 'English battalions serving as escort to a large column of carriages: this troop put down their arms without firing a shot'. Thus the whole column fell into French hands, although, to d'Espinchal's disgust, there followed some flagrant pillaging by his own troops, who preferred this activity to fighting the enemy. As d'Espinchal watched in horror the bivouac began to resemble a Bedouin camp. His men had found wine and quickly became drunk, which led to brutality against the prisoners who had been taken with the baggage waggons, particularly the women. With his men totally out of control, d'Espinchal set up a false alarm to bring this Saturnalia to an end.

Swabey, who was with this column of vehicles, merely reported that the brigade lost some baggage and that two men were taken prisoner who were employed by the Commissary, a laconic comment on what to him was a minor incident.

The following day the French crossed the mountains and finally made contact with the allied rear guard, the 2nd hussars, King's German Legion, who had only left the Escurial on the 3rd. In d'Espinchal's version, the hussars were put to flight with the loss of five men taken prisoner, although it seems more likely that a rather inconclusive skirmish took place. In fact, d'Espinchal soon found himself in a more serious situation. Near the Venta de San Raphaël he encountered a larger body of hussars, about a hundred strong. The Germans initially resisted the French charge but were then forced to give ground. The French pursued them for more than an hour, but had to stop when they came upon more squadrons of cavalry in echelon across the road. Although the allied cavalry was forced to retreat by the arrival of a French division, at the same time they continued firing, demonstrating the greatest sang-froid as they retired in good order. D'Espinchal launched two charges but was repulsed each time. By evening, though, the French infantry was at Espinar, the cavalry at Villacastin, and the King's Guard at Guadarrama. The pursuit was on, with the allies only about five leagues ahead.

The following day there was yet another encounter between the allied rear guard and the French advance guard. This time some confusion between the allied cavalry and infantry led to disorder which enabled the French to chase the allies from the field. Their spoils were a gun, an officer whom d'Espinchal described as a young brigadier of the 2nd hussars, King's German Legion, five dragoons and 130 infantrymen, as well as waggons intended for Salamanca. There is no confirmation of these losses in any allied account, however.

Hill now received the dispatch Wellington had sent from Rueda ordering him to change the direction of his march from Arevalo to Alba to Tormes by way of Belanjos and Peñaranda. This change of route required Hill to follow bad footpaths between Belanjos and Fontiveros. He also directed the Spanish troops, which were on their way to Arevalo, to change direction for Fontiveros. This was fortunate, because the first troops of the Army of the South reached Arevalo on 6 November, although the French forces remained strung out.

For one officer, at least, unaware of the change of route, Arevalo was the scene of a narrow escape. Captain Wood, who was suffering from a painful attack of rheumatism, had been travelling in a spring-waggon. When the army

> turned off and proceeded by a different route, I was taken out of the waggon, and again placed on my horse, which my servant had with him, and was desired to proceed to Arviola [sic], where I was informed there was a depôt: but, on arriving at that place, I did not meet with a single British soldier in the town; and so far from its being a depôt, it was entirely deserted, with the exception of a

Spanish regiment of dragoons, fully accoutred and in readiness to abandon it to the enemy, who were now very near. In this state of affairs, necessity compelled me to go to the Alcalde for billets. He told me that he was very much astonished at our application (for I had, on entering this town, overtaken an officer who was very ill, and who had also been misinformed); that the French were seen very distinctly from his balcony, advancing on this place; that they had set the fine town of Segovia on fire, and that the smoke was also visible from his window. However, strange as it may appear, he gave us billets, and we went in. I do not now recollect of what regiment this poor officer was, nor is it of much importance: he was, like myself, very ill; but necessity compelled us, even in the face of danger, to seek some refreshment, for nature was now literally sinking under the effects of famine, filth, and disease; therefore, while our servants were feeding the horses, we set about preparing some chocolate, and had just time to drink it, when we were informed that the French were entering the town. We instantly mounted our horses, and joined the cavalcade that were flying on the road, with what valuables they could bring off with them; we were now thrown out of the route of the British army, and pursued by a part of the French; and it was only by the greatest perseverance and diligence that we got out of their reach.[21]

Soult was engaged in searching for the Army of the North and left only his advance cavalry to pursue Hill and take up stragglers; 600 according to Soult, although 300 seems a more realistic figure. Nevertheless, the danger for Hill's forces was still real enough. Boutflower, former surgeon to the 40th, but just appointed staff surgeon, recorded in his diary that 'we halted at Fontiveros, four leagues; the enemy followed us, & remained two leagues from Sir R. Hill's HeadQuarters; a few shots in the course of the day were exchanged.'[22] Even without the close proximity of the French, the 5th was a particularly unpleasant day. Swabey wrote in his journal, 'In the morning joined the troop; marched all day in the rain. As we could not make the fire burn and had no wine, we had little food to eat.'[23]

The baggage had been sent ahead to Peñaranda, where Boutflower observed that

The numbers of Sick & the quantity of Baggage and Stores is so great that they appear to have no end. To cover these the Army has been obliged to make only a short march of only two leagues and a half to-day. This place is four Leagues from the Tormes, which River it is probable the Sick, Stores, & Baggage will cross to-morrow.

Boutflower could see only one outcome to the retreat.

Every one is ignorant of the intentions of his Lordship, but it is supposed, should Soult follow us with all his force, that his superiority in
numbers will be so great as to render the issue of a general Action too
hazardous to be risked; in which case nothing appears to remain for
us but to retire once more behind the Agueda; the mere possibility of
such an event is mortifying in the extreme.[24]

Hill established his headquarters at Peñaranda on the 6th, with the light
division and Morillo's Spaniards as his rear guard, covered by the cavalry
of Long and Victor Alten. Soult, meanwhile, was waiting for the Army of
the Centre to come up. He needed Joseph's army to hand in order to face
Wellington and Hill, whom he believed were about to combine their
forces, in which case they would outnumber him in his present position,
without either the Army of the Centre or the Army of Portugal. The king
now had to abandon Madrid for a second time, with the inevitable
consequence that the Empecinado and his guerrillas reoccupied the city,
while Elio moved into La Mancha and Bassecourt advanced to Cuenca.

*   *   *

By the 7th Hill's army was at Alba de Tormes, the objective Wellington
had given him. In Leach's opinion, this had been a successful retreat; they
had met with no adventures to disturb the five-day march, and the French
advance guard had not managed to overtake them. The only problem,
the violent rains that now set in, was beyond human power to amend. In
fact, their experience, he believed, had been very different from that of
Wellington's army, which had been much harassed throughout their
retreat.

Others, however, considered their situation rather differently. The light
division and Long's cavalry remained on the right bank of the Tormes for
the night in uncomfortable conditions, as Lieutenant John Cooke of the
43rd noted.

The country was perfectly open, without a house or tree to be seen. I
contemplated the dreary prospect, regretting the loss of my blanket,
placed under the saddle of my horse which I had sent to the rear, sick,
the previous morning. As the night closed on us, the rain began to
pour down in torrents. We were without food, or a particle of wood
to light fires.[25]

The light division was not alone in facing a hungry night. Sergeant
Robertson of the 92nd also commented that hunger was becoming a
most uncomfortable problem. The stores were exhausted and the French

controlled the road by which further provisions would have to be brought up, which suggested that they were about to face starvation.

Bell was more specific about the provisions they received.

When we got onto the plains on the other side [of the Guadarrama mountains], and crossed the Tormes, we expected some rest, a bit of sleep, and better rations, or some improvement in the foraging department, but things got worse and worse. I had been feasting the last few days on some bullocks liver without salt, and hard biscuit, abominable feeding until people come to know what hunger really is.[26]

Not surprisingly, the men blamed the incompetence of the commissariat for their hunger, although Burroughs suggested another reason.

The lands about Segovia, had been drained of their supplies, during the advance of the army to Madrid, and afterwards by the march of those troops destined to act against Burgos; and though the country is very fruitful, nothing could satisfy the inordinate devastation of soldiers, who wasted more than they generally consumed. When Sir Rowland Hill, therefore, commenced his retreat from the Tagus ... they suffered much from want of provisions.[27]

In a thinly populated country, it was impossible for the land to feed both the people that lived there and the armies that marched across.

Hill's forces, apart from the light division, crossed the bridge at Alba, which was to be mined, and then bivouacked on the left bank, about half a mile from the town. D'Urban, with his Portuguese cavalry, having arrived at the Tormes to find the whole army in position, was ordered to cross to the left bank and watch the fords, thought to be three in number, from the bridge upstream to Sieto Iglesias.

Swabey, at the rear of the army, had a rather different experience in Peñaranda. He had gone into a shop to buy some cloth because he was in desperate need of clothes;

whilst in the shop there was a cry raised that the French were coming and the Spanish cavalry galloped in disorder through the town. Sutton and I mounted our horses and rode our best till clear of the town. I then pulled up and with another officer tried to rally the Spaniards. We soon halted all the English, and discovered the cause of the false alarm had been some of the heavy dragoons galloping in by General Hill's order, to stop plunder, which had commenced. I then went back and completed my purchases, happy at having seen at a little expense the effect of the French entry into a Spanish town.

Whoever was in the street, man, woman, or child, took to their heels, many mounted their neighbours' mules which had thrown their riders, and much baggage was plundered and cut away so that people in charge might escape.[28]

On the 8th the light division and Long's cavalry joined the rest of Hill's army on the left bank. The light, 3rd and 4th divisions now moved towards Salamanca to join Wellington, while Howard's brigade of the 2nd division, comprising the 50th, 71st and 92nd, and Hamilton's Portuguese, crossed back to hold the town, with the bridge as a *tête de pont*. The bridge itself was being mined as the light division crossed; sappers and miners were noticed hard at work laying powder to blow up the centre arch, should it prove necessary. Even with this precaution, the position was not ideal because it was overlooked by higher ground a few hundred yards distant, but only heavy artillery could effectively threaten Alba. The bridgehead itself was protected by old fortifications which could be strengthened for the purpose of defence, although the fortress was in a very dilapidated condition. As for the walls, they rose only to knee-height, which meant the men had to work hard to strengthen them so that they would provide adequate defence.

While these defensive measures were put into place, Slade's cavalry, the 1st (Royal) dragoons and the 12th light dragoons, kept watch for the French. Further afield, Long's cavalry, Campbell's Portuguese and Penne Villemur's Spaniards patrolled the woods on the banks of the Tormes. D'Urban, with his brigade at Martinamor, continued to watch the fords or, more accurately, patrolled the river, having discovered that the true number of fords was twenty. The heavy rains, however, had swollen the river and made the fords impassable for the moment.

Webber, meanwhile, spent several hours on a wasted march, having received orders to march at 10.00am. Soaked to the skin after the wet, windy night, his troop had covered two leagues from their bivouac when they received orders to return to it. Unfortunately, in the meantime the heavy rain had caused the ground to become even muddier, so that by the time they reached their bivouac it was in a far worse condition than if they had never left it. As far as Webber could make out, these movements were in response to a French advance down river towards Salamanca.

While the allied forces, about 70,000 strong, held a line from San Christoval to Alba, waiting for the arrival of the French, Soult was still at Arevalo. Although he had finally located Souham and made contact with him, the Army of the Centre had advanced no further than Villacastin, held back by Joseph's concern that Ballesteros might have joined the allies in Avila. Since Soult's plan was a joint attack on Wellington by the three

French armies, he could not advance until Joseph's troops came up, as well as the rear divisions of his own Army of the South, which were still on the march between Villacastin and Arevalo. Bearing in mind how long it was taking the French forces to get into a position where they could threaten the whole allied army, it is probably no wonder that Souham had pursued Wellington so cautiously from Burgos.

It could be argued that Wellington now missed an opportunity to take out Soult, but Wellington preferred to adopt a more cautious approach. As he explained to Bathurst,

> It will still remain to be seen what number of troops can be brought to operate against our position; as, unless Madrid should again be abandoned to its fate by the King, arrangements must be made to resist the attacks which it must be expected that the Spanish troops under General Elio and the guerrillas will make on that city, even though General Ballesteros should not move forward in La Mancha. I propose, therefore, to wait at present on the Tormes till I shall ascertain more exactly the extent of the enemy's force; and if they should move forward I will either bring the contest to a crisis in the position of San Christoval, or fall back to the Agueda, according to what I shall consider at the time to be best for the cause.[29]

At least this pause in marching and manoeuvring was giving the Burgos troops a few days' rest, while conditions were also improving for most of Hill's army. Wellington could do nothing about the weather, but there were ample supplies in Salamanca which were finding their way to the troops. Cooke wrote that

> Continuing our march on the left of the river, we entered a dripping wood halfway to Salamanca and found our baggage waiting for us. The Division being dismissed, all the trees were filled with soldiers cutting and tearing down huge branches to build huts. In a short time great fires blazed up in every direction, while the soldiers encircled them with joyful countenances.
>
> Disencumbered of our drenched clothes, and rations having been served out, we set to work making dumplings. Before dark the canteens were laid with smoking tea, rum, hot puddings, and beef. This was a relishing and luxurious meal. The whole of the spirits having been exhausted, a heavy slumber under a tottering hut put an end to our carousel.[30]

Yet for some, unused to the conditions of a retreat, their recent experiences had been very uncomfortable. Robert Duffield Cooke, a seventeen or eighteen-year-old clerk in the paymaster general's office, was a civilian, and perhaps because of this, or on account of his youth and inexperience, he saw the retreat of Hill's army in very different terms from those expressed by a veteran like Leach, for example. In a letter to his father he summarized the discomforts he had suffered, undoubtedly for the first time.

> Our departure from Madrid was so sudden and unexpected that we knew of it only three or four hours before the entrance of the enemy. We were obliged of course immediately to pack and budge, exchanging good living conditions and good beds with *sheets to them* for barely sufficient to exist on, continual marching, and a wet muddy soil for our nightly *bivouacking*. We were then with General Hill's division and pushed so closely by the enemy that we could not make a halt for any length of time without previously taking up a position on some commanding eminence, by which means we kept our pursuers at bay. We were as near as I can recollect about eight days in this unpleasant situation during which time I never washed or undressed myself nor even took off my boots. We at length arrived at my favourite spot, Salamanca, and formed a junction with the noble Marquis.[31]

*Chapter 9*

# Stalemate

By 9 November the three French armies were finally in contact with each other; Soult had his headquarters at Peñaranda, Joseph at Flores de Avila and Souham at Villanueva. Wellington and Hill were also in close communication, Wellington at Salamanca and Hill at Alba de Tormes. As a result of this positioning it seemed inevitable that a crisis point had been reached. At 2.00am Wellington sent Hill a dispatch which summarized a report he had received from Lieutenant Bobers of the King's German Legion hussars. The lieutenant had discovered the previous evening that the French were moving in force on the fords of Huerte and Encinas. These were assumed to be Soult's forces since there was no sign of movement by Souham's troops north of Salamanca. Wellington instructed Hill to move to his left, to Machacón, leaving a brigade of the 2nd division and Hamilton's Portuguese in Alba, where they were already posted, with Long's cavalry as a covering screen. Should the French try to cross the Tormes at Huerta, they were to come under immediate attack. Wellington intended to keep his own troops at Calvarrasa de Arriba while he waited to see how the situation developed.

Three hours later, a further dispatch informed Hill that the army of Portugal was moving on Salamanca. Wellington had carried out his own reconnaissance, which confirmed that Souham's troops had been brought forward, and now occupied a line to the west of Salamanca from Pitiegua to Huerta as far forward as Moriscos. There had also been some skirmishing between French cavalry and Pack's Portuguese at Aldealengua. Wellington remained uncertain about the purpose of these French movements, though:

> All reports agree that the fords are not now practicable. Indeed there is a considerable increase of water in the river, and the best proof that they are not practicable is, that the people of the country have their cattle grazing on the left bank. I am certain that if the fords were practicable, the enemy would pass the river, rather than attack us on the heights of San Christoval, as it is I am doubtful. And as we have not on our position, or near to it, as many troops as we require, I

propose to move the troops now at Calvarrassa [sic] de Arriba into Salamanca early tomorrow morning.

Wellington further advised Hill to move his forces closer to Salamanca, but without abandoning Alba de Tormes. Never having visited the town, he was dependent on Hill's judgement when it came to holding the castle, but he assumed a garrison of about 200 men would be adequate.

If the river falls, so as to be fordable by all description of troops, all I shall wish is to put in a Spanish garrison, to prevent the enemy from using the bridge in case of an action, as they did before. As long as their movements are uncertain, it would be expedient to have a garrison of a better description. If you think it necessary to occupy the town of Alba, to prevent the enemy from crossing the bridge, what number should there be?

But he was confident

that the river is not fordable for troops, otherwise the cattle would not have been left on the banks; and all the peasants I saw of Huerta say it is not so, and not likely to become so. However, it is easy to have it marked this night, and you will know whether it will rise or fall before morning.

As an afterthought, which recognised the doubtful state of affairs, he now decided that only the light division, de España's Spaniards and Victor Alten's cavalry should be brought back to Salamanca.

The situation was fluid, however, and a third dispatch, written at 9.30pm, warned Hill that if the French were able to cross the Tormes at too many fords and in too great strength for him to resist, he should withdraw all his troops except a garrison in the castle to the Arapiles on the Salamanca battlefield, making sure that he immediately informed Wellington of this movement. As for the bridge at Alba, the consequences of blowing it up

under these circumstances would be the loss of the garrison in the castle, which would lose heart upon seeing all communication with them cut off; and nothing would be gained as to defence, if I am correct in the notion, that between the castle and the infantry on the left bank, the bridge cannot be carried, the river not being fordable for infantry.

The destruction of the bridge is a measure of great importance, in reference not only to the enemy's operations, but our own. I am not quite certain that if you were to lodge the powder in the mine, with the intention of exploding it only at the last moment, and that you should defend the left of the bridge, as I am convinced it would be defended, the enemy would not explode the mine for you, in order to be certain at least of your garrison in the castle.

Upon the whole, I am convinced that your situation depends upon the state of the fords and the use the enemy can make of them. If they are as I believe them to be, the enemy may make a desperate attack upon Alba de Tormes and the bridge, but must be defeated in that object; and they are liable to be attacked on this side.[1]

Although much of the information on which these instructions were based came from Wellington's own reconnaissance, others were also engaged in watching the French. Leith Hay was ordered by Hill to search out Soult's position.

When near to Babilafuente, a column appeared descending from the height on which the village is situated, directly towards the fords near to Huerta. Continuing in observation of this advance, to ascertain the description of force of which it was composed, upon perceiving that a brigade of cavalry was accompanied by infantry and artillery, I considered it important to proceed direct to Lord Wellington [who] immediately proceeded to the height above Aldealengua, commanding a view of the plains towards Alba, and from whence the enemy's movements towards the river were perceptible.[2]

This French advance drove in Long's cavalry and warned the troops in Alba to be in readiness for a vigorous defence, since Wellington's supposition that the French, unable to use the ford, would make a 'desperate attack' seemed about to be realized. Elsewhere, however, the situation was quiet. D'Urban bivouacked in the woods at Machacón. Webber, nearby, recorded his bivouac as the best since Zafra, many weeks before, particularly as they received rations from Salamanca. As for Larpent, having reached Salamanca after experiencing all the unfamiliar discomforts of a retreat, he now 'had a decent quarter and begun [sic] to be a little comfortable.'[3] Indeed, he also had time to look at the court martial papers Wellington had sent him, and continued to send him.

At 4.00pm on the 10th, however, Wellington was apologizing to Hill for not meeting him at Alba,

the more so, that I did not see the large force which Colonel Gordon tells me was collected in front of the town. However, the post is a good one, and held by good, determined troops; and it is my opinion that the enemy can do them no harm. Indeed, I should doubt their attacking them, and I think they are come to try the fords.[4]

This was a shift of opinion from his previous interpretation of French intentions, possibly based on the slow manoeuvring of the enemy forces, but it was soon challenged when the French acted as he had previously expected.

* * *

Soult was now at Alba with his cavalry and two infantry divisions, while the Army of Portugal, as Leith Hay had discovered, was at Babilafuente and the advanced guard of the Army of the Centre was at Macotera, west of Alba. Not that the French troops, particularly the Army of the South, were at their most efficient. They had been on the march since September, and many of them, having become acclimatized to the milder winters of Andalusia, were now suffering from the effects of a cold, wet autumn. To make matters worse, the roads were bad, and they were passing through a country where food was scarce. Not surprisingly, both men and horses were feeling the strain, and stragglers were falling by the wayside in large numbers.

Soult initially waited to see how Hill would react to his forward movement, recognizing that he would either blow up the bridge and retire or stand and hold the position at Alba. By 2.00pm, when there was no sign of an allied withdrawal, he ordered twelve guns and four mortars to be put into position on the heights above the town, ready to attack the allied entrenchment, while twelve companies of voltigeurs were also in position to march on the allied defences. On the heights the infantry was formed into attacking columns, while the cavalry manoeuvred on the plain to support the artillery. D'Espinchal conceded that for two hours

> The English made a lively response to the fire of our batteries; but, after two hours, having been forced to abandon their retrenchments, they defended themselves valiantly in the town, where our brave voltigeurs entered three times without being able to hold a position. Night, which brought an end to the combat, left the infantry in their positions, while the cavalry, bordering the Tormes, liaised with the Army of Portugal. The next day the attack recommenced at five in the morning, but the arrival of King Joseph stopped the combat ...[5]

D'Espinchal does not mention that the defenders were supported by four guns, which opened up from the opposite bank of the river and inevitably caused some French casualties, although not ideally placed to aid the defenders.

Robertson described what happened from the allied perspective when

> The several companies were told off to their respective posts on the walls, while some were stationed in the grand square, ready to give

assistance where it might be necessary. While this was going on, parties were employed in barricading the streets with stones, to serve as a covert in case we should be obligated to retreat; and the Miners stood ready to blow up the bridge. Every thing was bustle and confusion, and the thought of provisions had fled for the meantime, although we had not had any for the two preceding days. About twelve o'clock the main body of the enemy came in sight, having with it twenty-two pieces of cannon and two mortars, which they placed opposite the ground occupied by the 71st and the 92nd. All our cannon being taken to the opposite side of the river, we had none to oppose to those of the enemy's. We discharged a few rounds of musketry, but without any effect on account of the distance; while the French appeared at a loss how to place their cannon so as to bring them to bear upon us, as the ground that we occupied was below the range of their shot. At last, about two o'clock, they got them brought so near that every shot told with deadly effect, and their batteries poured showers of ball upon us.[6]

Leith Hay was struck by the violence of this cannonade, which he ascribed to twenty guns:

shells descending, crashed through the roofs of the houses, showers of balls swept along the streets, while occasional parties of voltigeurs, rushing forward, endeavoured to avail themselves of the consternation they supposed must have resulted from the bombardment to which this town had been subjected. They were invariably met, and bayoneted back. General Howard, and the brave regiments of his brigade, were neither to be intimidated by noise, nor forced from their post by the desultory attacks of French voltigeurs; and the enemy's general, spectator to this violent assault on the open and unsheltered quarters of three British regiments, ordered back the troops employed, and desisted from the hopeless attempt of gaining possession of the place without bringing on a much more serious affair.[7]

Hope noticed how the French infantry, 8,000 strong, repeatedly formed for an assault but 'the bold and determined manner in which the soldiers performed their duty, and the intrepidity and firmness of officers commanding regiments, completely deterred them from making the attempt.'[8]

The 1/71st was one of the battalions in Howard's brigade, along with the 1/50th and 1/92nd, which had been entrusted with the defence of Alba.

A part of us here were lining a wall; the French in great strength in front. One of our lads having let his hat fall over, when taking cartridges from it, laid his musket against the wall, went over to the enemy's side, and came back unhurt. At this very time the button of my stock was shot off.[9]

Such was the insouciance of the British soldier.

Although Soult withdrew his artillery, the French infantry remained on the heights and maintained their fire, so at dusk General Hamilton sent da Costa's Portuguese brigade across the bridge to strengthen the defence. At 5.00am Soult renewed his attempt to take Alba; the guns once again cannonaded the town, although the voltigeurs' attack lacked commitment and achieved nothing against the Portuguese, who were holding the point of attack. Nonetheless, da Costa's brigade took heavy casualties as they stood their ground. After several hours Soult abandoned the attempt, not necessarily because of the king's arrival, although he informed Joseph that he had fired 5,000 rounds into the town and that if they persisted in the attack they risked losing everything for no result. The French had lost two officers killed and six wounded, as well as 150 other casualties. Allied loses were twenty-one killed, eight of them Portuguese, and eighty-nine men wounded, including thirty-six Portuguese, which suggests that the second day had been no easier for the defenders than the first.

It is no wonder that Hamilton, in his report to Hill, wrote that 'from the cool and steady conduct of the 50th regt, Col. Stewart; 71st regt, Col. The Hon. H. Cadogan; the 92nd, Col. Cameron (General Howard's brigade), the enemy dared not attempt the town.' He acknowledged the considerable losses:

which I trust you will not deem great, when you consider the heavy and incessant fire of artillery for so many hours. The loss of the Portuguese was while on duty this morning, and I have real pleasure in reporting their steady and animated conduct.

I feel much indebted to Major-General Howard, who rendered me every possible assistance, as also to every officer and soldier of his excellent brigade, for their steady, zealous, and soldierlike conduct.[10]

Once again, an allied force had stubbornly held a bridge against French attack.

\* \* \*

Joseph's arrival brought about the union of the Armies of the South and of the Centre. He placed his army under Soult's command, despite his bitter resentment of so much of the marshal's conduct since Salamanca. He also replaced Souham with d'Erlon in command of the Army of Portugal, on account of what he regarded as Souham's tentative pursuit of Wellington from Burgos. Officially, though, the reason was the wound Souham had received at Salamanca, from which he was said not to be fully recovered. With the Army of Portugal in close contact, the French had about 90,000 men of all arms in the field. When they set about formulating their strategy, however, a clear difference of opinion emerged. The army could not be kept in one place for any length of time because of the permanent problem of supplies, which meant that Wellington needed to be dealt with quickly and effectively. Jourdan advocated forcing the line of the Tormes between Alba and Huerta, using the fords to make a frontal attack, an opinion based on his initial impression of the lie of the land and what he perceived as Wellington's weakness. This suggestion gained the support of most of the generals present, but Soult, who like Jourdan was not familiar with the ground, insisted that they should wait for the reconnaissance of the fords further upstream from Alba to be completed before making a decision. The reports when they arrived indicated that the passage of the high Tormes would now be easy, so Soult wrote to Joseph, suggesting that a better plan would be to use these easier crossing points to turn the allied right flank. Joseph recognized the risk of bringing Wellington to battle on ground of his own choosing and gave his support to Soult's suggestion, which would force the allies to retreat to Portugal.

When Wellington wrote to Hill during the evening of the 11th, he reiterated his conviction that the French would be deterred from trying to cross the Tormes by the present state of the river. Nevertheless, he kept the 3rd and 4th divisions at Calvarrasa de Arriba so that they could support Hill, should he need them. Earlier, he sent Major Josef de Miranda to Hill. This Spanish officer had volunteered to command a detachment of 300 Spaniards who would garrison the castle of Alba in place of the Anglo-Portuguese troops who were currently performing this duty.

> As it is determined to hold the town, if possible, as long as we can remain upon the Tormes at all, I think it would be desirable to put this gentleman in charge of his post with his garrison as soon as he shall arrive with his troops ... You will give him instructions to maintain himself in his post as long as the army shall remain in this neighbourhood; if possible, for the full extent of the ten days for which provisions shall be left for him.[11]

There were further instructions to cover an evacuation, should the allies be forced to leave their present position. Hill was also ordered to complete the mining of the bridge, which was to be fired when the allies were finally forced to evacuate Alba.

Wellington's reference to ten days is interesting because it suggests his intentions. As he had informed Bathurst shortly before, he was aware that his army needed a period of rest and recuperation. He thought the Salamanca position ideal for the purpose, particularly as the city was well stocked with supplies and there were several hospitals to accommodate the sick. He also knew (as did the French themselves) that the three armies assembled against him would quickly exhaust their supplies and have to separate; indeed, he seems to have been depending upon this factor to bring about their dispersal, and not without some justice. D'Espinchal commented on the discontent of the Army of the South, who were not only chafing at the inaction, but were short of forage, unable to procure supplies, and were suffering the mockery of the Portuguese, on the opposite bank of the river.

Not that all the allies were in a much better situation themselves, particularly those furthest from Salamanca who, as Robertson noted, were still not receiving provisions. Stealing food became a necessity against the pangs of hunger. A soldier of the 71st[12] related how some men of the battalion were helping themselves to flour from a mill beside the river when Colonel Cadogan

> rode down and forced them out, throwing a handful of flour on each man as he passed out of the mill. When we were drawn up on the heights, he rode along the column, looking for the millers, as we called them. At this moment, a hen put her head out of his coat-pocket, and looked first to one side, and then to another. We began to laugh, we could not restrain ourselves. He looked amazed and furious at us, and then around. At length the major rode up to him, and requested him to kill the fowl outright, and put it into his pocket. The Colonel, in his turn, laughed, called his servant, and the millers were no more looked after.[13]

Robertson was continuing to feel the discomfort of an empty stomach. As a result, when a quantity of wheat was discovered, it was dried and beaten into flour which 'afforded a kind of supper, without either salt or seasoning – hunger rendered it palatable enough.'[14]

D'Urban, meanwhile, was still watching the fords. On the 11th he noted that the enemy troops were in constant movement, and realised that they were making a thorough reconnaissance of the Tormes between Huerta and Ejeme, upstream from Alba, an activity which continued the following day. Webber, nearby, saw Joseph Bonaparte parading on the opposite bank of the river and observed two of his staff fording the river, although they soon returned to the French side. French intentions were becoming very much clearer.

During the 12th and 13th the French made a definite movement southwards: Soult to Anaya, six miles south of Alba, Joseph to Valdecarros to the marshal's right, while the advanced guard of the Army of Portugal occupied the heights above Alba, although d'Erlon kept his cavalry and infantry divisions at Huerta, except Maucune's, which was sent to Aldealengua. Here Maucune came into contact with what he thought was the allied advanced guard, although it was actually the rear guard. There was some skirmishing, but nothing came of this initial contact.

On the allied side, Leith Hay, still on exploring duties, was sent out with a patrol of the 13th light dragoons to reconnoitre as far as Salvatierra upstream and then back to Alba. The usual methods of gathering information were employed: questioning local peasants, using local guides, keeping concealed while watching enemy movements. On this occasion, although he came within two leagues of Alba, he found no obvious evidence of French movement, and no reason for the allies to change their position. At this point, Hill's troops were in the woods beyond Alba, the 3rd and 4th divisions were at Calvarrasa de Abajo, Long and D'Urban's cavalry still watched the Tormes, and Pack and Bradford's Portuguese were at Aldealengua and Cabrerizos. The remaining Anglo-Portugese divisions and the Galicians held the San Christoval position, fronted by Anson, Alten and Ponsonby's cavalry. Meanwhile, Wellington continued to reconnoitre, and Foy commented in his journal that it was strange to see him on horseback at the Tormes, at the moment when a superior force was ready to fall on him.

Although the allied position seemed secure as long as the French were on the right bank of the Tormes, there were some tense moments when action seemed inevitable. Cooke related how

> some musketry was distinctly heard in the direction of the position of San Christoval. Our Division had been dismissed as usual early in the morning, but was again formed and ordered to crown those heights, where we remained the whole day. The alarm had been occasioned by a few Spanish Guerrillas firing at French cavalry.[15]

As for Wellington, he was frustrated by his inability to interpret Soult's manoeuvres and by the continued French presence at Huerta, which prevented him from leaving San Christoval and reinforcing Hill.

This uncertainty continued throughout the 13th. Burroughs heard distant cannon fire in the morning and later saw smoke, which suggested action but was actually caused by Hill's men cooking their meat. Green believed that when his division was marched to the position they had occupied on 20 July, two days before Salamanca, it meant that a battle was imminent. No French appeared, however, and the 7th division returned to their quarters in a convent on the north side of Salamanca. D'Urban observed the French moving troops into the wood behind Ejeme, a manoeuvre which would enable them either to follow the high road to Avila or to cross the Tormes by the fords above Alba.

The French intended to adopt the latter course now the river had fallen, and by the end of the day the Army of the South was in position to cross. At 11.00pm the light cavalry and a brigade of dragoons silently established themselves on a hillock on the right bank, with orders to cross before daylight. This crossing was effected at dawn on the 14th, using the fords between Galisancho and Encinas. For d'Espinchal there was some personal satisfaction when 'a post of two hundred Portuguese, taken by surprise, was almost entirely sabred as a souvenir of the insults which they had lavished on us'[16] – although most of them survived to make their escape and give the alarm. Once the French dragoons were across the river they secured the left bank and the infantry were able to cross.

Leith Hay, who had been sent once again to observe the French, witnessed the crossing.

> Upon arriving at high ground, from whence what was passing in the valley below became distinctly observable, I perceived troops crossing over. From that time, the French army defiled without intermission. Apparently, the fords were of a description not admitting of very rapid passage. The infantry moved across temporary truckle bridges, in single files; while the cavalry and artillery forded the stream a short distance higher up its course.[17]

By the end of the day the Army of the South was across the river and in position from Mozárbez to Martinamor. They were followed by the Army of the Centre. At Alba, as the Army of Portugal approached the town, Hill withdrew Howard and da Costa's troops. The bridge was blown up, while Miranda in the castle first refused to surrender and then prevented the French from repairing the bridge. D'Erlon, therefore, had to make a more protracted crossing at Torrejon, four miles south of Alba. (Miranda, sometime later when there was no further need to hold Alba, escaped by making a sudden and successful sally.)

Wellington was kept informed of the French movements, and initially responded aggressively by taking the 8,000 strong 2nd division and the cavalry of Slade, Long, D'Urban and Penne Villemur, which had been stationed on the middle Tormes, into position to contain or even attack Soult. He instructed Hill to watch the roads from Alba with the 4th division and Hamilton's Portuguese, while the divisions on the heights of San Christoval were brought down, closer to the rest of the army. At noon, when D'Urban first became aware of Wellington's intention, he was convinced that an attack on the French troops which had already crossed the river was certain of success, since it neither risked anything nor committed the allies to an all-out attack. At the same time it would have frustrated the French in their attempt to manoeuvre.

Soult might be stronger with his 90,000 men, against the allies' 60,000, but by this time there was a strong suspicion on the allied side that his intention was to force the allies to retire, rather than to attack. Hope ascribed this intention to the events of 22 July when Marmont's fine army had been destroyed, a fear which he believed still haunted the French. Aitchison, however, was more complimentary to Soult, believing that the manoeuvre demonstrated 'that judgement of spirit of enterprise which has distinguished him above all other French Generals.'[18] If forcing the allies back to Portugal was the best policy for the French to adopt, then Soult's tactics are difficult to fault.

The day was passing. There was still no sign that a battle was about to be fought. The mood of the men in the ranks became increasingly obstreperous. The weather was as bad as ever, which did nothing to improve their mood. 'The wind blew strong; it rained fast, and murky fogs occasionally enveloped the ground, so as to render any object at a hundred yards distance, perfectly invisible.' When the order was given to cook,

> it was obeyed without cheerfulness or alacrity ... For the soldier is aware, if the route should come, while he is engaged in cooking, the most valuable and essential part of his meal, (the soup) will be thrown away, and he is not willing to sacrifice to chance the comforts of a dinner. Upon these occasions, our soldiers in their conversation with one another, frequently indulge their spleen, in loading the French with an immoderate share of invective, as if they had done them the greatest personal injury.[19]

Part of the frustration was caused by the sense that the allies stood on the verge of victory. Wellington had

> assumed his former position on the Arapiles, but here he had everything to hope – the ground was already consecrated by the blood of Heroes on 22 July, he still fought in the same righteous cause – the troops who that day had signalised themselves were still with him – *impatient* to repeat their former deeds – their brethren from the Alemtejo glowed with emulation, and the newly raised Spaniards

were desirous of equalling their allies and rivals the Portuguese – the army was confident of Victory.[20]

Yet so far there had been nothing but inaction.

By the end of the day, though, in the light division at least, the mood was improved by the optimistic expectation

that a great action would be fought on the following day. The country was illuminated for miles around from the quantity of fire that illuminated our bivouac. All hands caroused until nearly midnight, fully determined to make themselves happy before the supposed approaching struggle. Then stretching themselves under the trees or around the fires, they tranquilly slept until an hour before daybreak, when we formally stood to arms and were again dismissed.[21]

Nevertheless, there was still time for events to develop into the battle that not only the light division, but the whole allied army, eagerly anticipated.

## Chapter 10

# The Game is Lost

Wellington was as ready for battle as his troops, but he was also aware that a withdrawal might well become his only option in the face of Soult's manoeuvres. As he later explained to Bathurst,

> In the course of the night [of the 14th] and the following morning I moved the greatest part of the troops through Salamanca, and placed Lieut. General Sir Edward Paget with the first division of infantry on the right of Aldeatejada, in order to secure that passage for the troops over the Zurguen, in case the movements of the enemy on the right flank should render it necessary for me to make choice either of giving up my communication with Ciudad Rodrigo or Salamanca.[1]

By daybreak the allied forces were in battle order, from Calvarrasa de Arriba on the left to Miranda de Azan on the right. In the first line the 4th division on the extreme left held the heights of Calvarrasa de Arriba, including the village. The centre ground, which extended to include the two Arapiles heights and the village of Arapiles, was occupied by the 2nd division and Hamilton's Portuguese, while the 3rd division were to the right of them with Morillo's Spaniards, close to the position they had occupied in July. The second line, from left to right, comprised the light division, Pack and Bradford's Portuguese, the Galicians, and the 5th, 6th and 7th divisions, although the exact sequence of these three divisions is uncertain. As already noted, the first division, which was at Aldeatejada on the Ciudad Rodrigo road, was acting as a flank cover for the allied army. Most of the cavalry was also on the right to cover the infantry, but D'Urban, Campbell, Penne Villemur and Long were behind Calvarrasa de Arriba on the left. The extreme right was held by Bock's brigade, at a point popularly known as Packenham's Hill, the point where the 3rd division, having advanced from Miranda de Azan, descended on Thomière's division on 22 July. The German heavy dragoons were supported by Ponsonby, Alten, Anson and Slade.

The baggage had already been sent half a mile to the west and Wellington had given orders on the 14th for Salamanca to be evacuated, which involved in the first instance removing such stores for which there was carriage and destroying the rest. Not surprisingly, as in Madrid, this was not popular with the local population, although Salamanca had seen so many arrivals and departures by both French and allies that the population was familiar with the process. At this point

> A general expectation prevailed in the camp that another battle of Salamanca would, before night, be enrolled in the annals of these campaigns. Everything seemed to justify the opinion: the hills were literally filled with troops; Salamanca was left open as in July; and all our forces withdrawn from that side of the river were assembled upon the hills around it. Lord Wellington was upon the Arapiles with the [2nd] division, observing the movement of the enemy.[2]

What Wellington observed, however, convinced him that Soult had no intention of offering battle to the allies.

> On the morning of the 15th, I found the enemy fortifying their position at Mozárbez, which they had taken up the night before, at the same time they were moving bodies of cavalry and infantry towards their own left, and to our communications with Ciudad Rodrigo. It was obvious that it was the enemy's intention to act upon our communications: and as they were too strong, and too strongly posted for me to think of attacking them, I determined to move upon Ciudad Rodrigo. I therefore put the army in march in three columns, and crossed the Zurguen, and then passed the enemy's left flank, and encamped that night on the Valmuza.[3]

Wellington finally decided upon a retreat to Portugal at about 2.00pm, thus playing the role Soult's strategy required of him. Joseph Donaldson of the 94th remembered the reaction of the men in the ranks.

> We had been so much harassed in retreating from Madrid in severe weather, that we felt much more inclined to fight than go farther, but we were disappointed, and after performing some evolutions, we filed off on the road leading to Rodrigo, and commenced retreating as night was setting in. I never saw the troops in such bad humour.[4]

Leith Hay, however, focused on the skill with which Wellington extricated his army from its vulnerable situation.

> It is impossible to conceive more unfavourable weather for the commencement of a retreat, the roads had become extremely deep from the effects of the great quantity of rain that had fallen; nor did there appear the slightest prospect of alteration in the cold, damp, boisterous season that had set in. Notwithstanding, the army retired

without confusion. That the change of circumstances, so rapidly produced by the French general's manoeuvring to cut off the communication of the allies with Ciudad Rodrigo, did not occasion great difficulty, where the encumbrance of so large an army, and an extensive depôt, had to be withdrawn from such a town as Salamanca, and put in immediate march, proved the excellent arrangement of its commander. When afterwards with the French army, I was questioned by its officers, whether the removal from Salamanca, and suddenly decided upon retreat, had not been attended with confusion and inconvenience, and when replied to in the negative, they were loud in praise of Lord Wellington's qualities as a general.[5]

In contrast, Robertson described

such confusion as I never saw. The four divisions came on the road all at one time, pushing forward, so that the best part of it fell to the lot of the strongest. All the waggons and ammunition that could be dispensed with were destroyed. The rain now began to fall again in torrents, so that the roads were rendered nearly impassable. At the same time the French dragoons were close on our rear, and all that fell out of the ranks were taken prisoners. The retreat to Corunna never presented any thing to equal this, for all was uproar and confusion.[6]

However, he was looking at a detail of the withdrawal while Leith Hay was evaluating the whole picture.

As Robertson noted, the weather, bad enough beforehand, seemed to deteriorate the moment the retreat was decided upon. There had been steady drizzle all morning, creating a mist which had made observation difficult, but now, with the rain becoming torrential, the ground quickly became a quagmire which seriously hindered the movements of the allies. Nevertheless, the infantry marched off in fighting order. The cavalry on the left stayed to cover the withdrawal, while the other cavalry units followed the infantry to act as a rear guard.

The routes allocated to the three columns all led to Ciudad Rodrigo, the first by way of Matilla, the second by San Muñoz, and the third by Aldehuela de la Boveda, along the road known as the Calzada de Don Diego. The first column comprising the 2nd, 3rd and 4th divisions was commanded by Sir Rowland Hill; the centre, made up of the 1st, 5th, 6th, 7th and light divisions, by Sir Edward Paget; and the third, the Spanish army,

who in case of an action would have formed a corps of reserve. Salamanca was thus abandoned; we left it behind on our right, and in

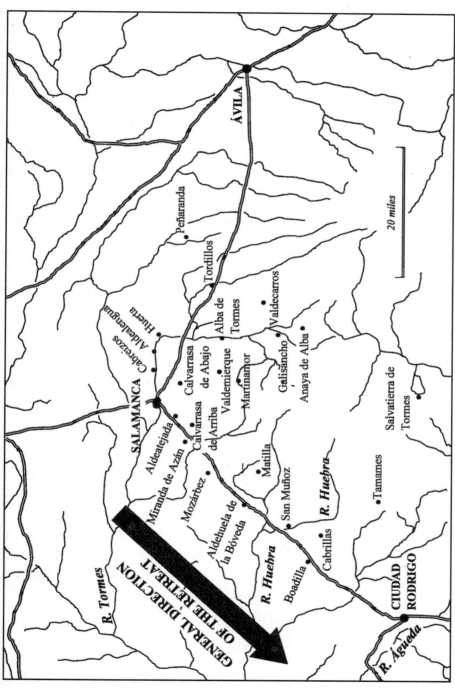

Map showing the general direction of the retreat from Salamanca to Ciudad Rodrigo, 15–18 November 1812 (from a map of 1796).

the course of the day, passed the French forces at Mozarbes [sic], on our left. We made roads for ourselves, for we did not observe or follow any; sometimes ascending hills upon stony and ploughed grounds and then into plains inundated with water, and intersected with swamps. We continued our march for about five leagues, and arrived at seven o'clock in the evening, (it being dark and raining fast) on the Valmusa; and encamped near Rozadas under Olive [sic] trees.[7]

Burroughs was right to comment on the lack of roads. Although the Galicians were following the main route from Salamanca to Ciudad Rodrigo, the other two columns had nothing better than tracks to guide them. Consequently, the artillery faced their usual difficulties: 'the final part of the road was through cornfields which were so soft that that wheels of our gun carriages sank up to the naves in mud.' Webber quickly became aware of a further problem.

Those men who were weak or sickly were fast dropping in the rear, certain of falling into the hands of the enemy unless we would mount them on our carriages, which feelings of humanity in opposition to a sense of our duty almost tempted us to do as far as we could – but from the number of our sick we only brought on three.[8]

Even when the troops reached their bivouacs there was no improvement. Thanks to the inefficiency of the quarter-master general, Colonel Willoughby Gordon, the supply train had been sent to Ciudad Rodrigo on the road through San Felices, twenty miles from the routes the army was following. This would have been a problem in itself, but Gordon appears not to have informed Wellington of the route he had chosen. Consequently, lack of food was now added to the other miseries of the troops.

We were in a very uncomfortable plight, our clothes being soaked with wet. We managed, however, to light a fire of green branches, which afforded us but little warmth, until we got some of the large trees kindled, which was by far the best method of raising heat that we had hitherto tried.[9]

Nor were things any better in the light division. According to Costello,

When we reached our halting-ground for the night, our prospect was most desolate for we were wet to the skin, and without fire or shelter. The first thing I did was to take off my jacket and shirt and wring about half a gallon of water. I placed them upon my back to dry as they might. Most of our men cut down boughs of trees to keep themselves out of the mud, but it was some hours before we could obtain that greatest of luxuries, a good fire. It had been a fatiguing day, and although possessed of a ravenous appetite, we had nothing to satisfy it. We had not a morsel to eat, no rations having been issued, so our men suffered from pangs of cold, and hunger.[10]

*       *       *

The day which had proved so miserable for the allied troops did not entirely satisfy their French opponents either. Although it had been obvious by 9.00am, when the allies were distantly observed through the rain mist in line of battle, that Wellington was waiting for an attack, Soult had no intention of satisfying him. A battle, though, was as much the desire of his troops as his opponent's. D'Espinchal, noting that they were in the same position occupied by Marmont with such disastrous consequences on 22 July, but with a superiority of numbers which Marmont had not enjoyed, believed that

> The idea of erasing this memorable defeat with a brilliant victory, the sight of this fatal field of battle, still covered with wreckage and remains of our brothers in arms, the sight of the Anglo-Portuguese seeking a refuge behind the Arapiles on which they had raised the trophies of their victory, all contributed to augment the energy of the soldier and nourish the impatient desire which we had to come to blows ...[11]

Soult was keeping his troops in close contact, slowly moving them westward, led by his own Army of the South who were on the French left. This movement was taking them towards the Ciudad Rodrigo road, but at the same time Soult had also ordered the entrenching and fortifying of Mozárbez in case Wellington launched a frontal attack against him, just as he had against Marmont in July. Towards noon Joseph, Soult, Jourdan and the senior French generals assembled on a small hill behind Mozárbez to decide on their next move. Foy was present and subsequently, when writing in his diary, created a picture of a relaxed command taking their time to make a decision. He even fell into conversation with the king, who wanted to hear his opinion on whether the enemy was retreating and whether the army wanted a battle. Then Marshal Jourdan suggested that the Army of Portugal should pivot towards the left, taking its right wing towards Salamanca. 'This absurd opinion, clearly expressed, gave me the measure of talent with which we were directed; from this moment I could predict what would happen.'[12] And that would not be the battle that he and his men desired. This was particularly disappointing for Foy because only the evening before he had been convinced that Wellington would not be able to retire on Ciudad Rodrigo without fighting.

As d'Erlon commenced this movement Foy heard cannonading. D'Espinchal later wrote that this was the discharge of twelve French guns from a position near the Arapiles, which took off many men and horses. He also described how the head of d'Erlon's troops attacked the first line of the allied army. No allied accounts refer to such an attack, but d'Espinchal was convinced the battle had been about to begin when the mist thickened, covering the allied movements and allowing them to escape.

By 4.00pm darkness had fallen. The conditions were now no better for the French than for the allies: 'the rain, falling in torrents, soon made the battlefield nothing but a vast, deep quagmire. The smallest ravines became dangerous precipices, the ever-increasing darkness did not fail to augment the horror of the scene ...'[13]

Joseph now took the Army of Portugal and his personal guard to Salamanca. The Army of Portugal received the order to retire at 6.00pm and Foy had to repeat it three times because neither officers nor men could understand how they could be turning their backs on a retreating enemy. The order was particularly galling when they knew that they had the initiative. They enjoyed the advantage of larger numbers of cavalry, the most useful arm for pursuing a retreating army, and the rain meant that neither allied artillery nor allied musketry could have functioned effectively. Nor was the withdrawal to Salamanca easy, as they crossed the inundated plain up to their knees in water. Supplies of rum and flour were found in Salamanca, however, courtesy of the inefficiency of the allied commissariat, and that offered some consolation to the French soldiers. Had they reached the city moments earlier they would have been able to take a half-troop of the 2nd hussars, King's German Legion, who were departing with a motley collection of stragglers, sutlers and refugees. Instead of becoming prisoners of war, the hussars safely escorted their charges to Ciudad Rodrigo via Ledesma, well away from the French pursuit.

This pursuit, under Soult's personal command, was initially conducted by 50,000 men. The cavalry of the Army of Portugal followed the Galician column on the third road, heading for Aldehuela de la Boveda, while Soult concentrated on the other two columns. D'Espinchal would be engaged in this pursuit, but he spent the night of the 15th sleeping on the field of battle, drenched by the rain and up to his knees in mud. The only consolation, as Soult pointed out, was that the appalling weather was as seriously inconvenient for the enemy as for themselves.

\*    \*    \*

The allies left their bivouacs at daybreak on the 16th to face another day's march in abominable conditions.

> The weather was severe, and the ground so heavy, that the horses at every step sunk to the fetlock, and the men to their ancles [sic]. The former suffered much last evening, not having any provender; whilst the bark of trees, and sprigs of wild briar, afforded but an indifferent substitute indeed, we felt for these invaluable animals, and well we might, for their existence was essentially necessary to our own ... The enemy did not press upon our rear, but contented himself with picking up those men, who from fatigue and indisposition, had fallen out from their regiments. Some baggage that had strayed or lost itself in the wood, we were marching through, likewise fell into their hands; and what between the weather and the empty state of our stomachs, a gloom was thrown over our march, which rendered us very indifferent companions for one another.[14]

Hunger was indeed an increasing discomfort, made worse by the knowledge, which quickly spread through the army, that the provisions, other than the half-starved oxen that accompanied the columns, were miles away on a different road. Finding food became a necessity. When the 2nd division reached Matilla, although there was no bread available some officers of the 34th were lucky enough to find some potatoes, which they bought and boiled over a small fire. Comfortably ensconced in a mean hovel, they were laughing over their good fortune – but Sherer and his fellow officers' meal was about to be interrupted.

Desperate men would eat anything, Lieutenant George Simmons of the 95th observed.

> Our poor fellows lit fires, and then, being nearly starved, went about in search of something to eat. Some lean and half-starved bullocks were here and there lying dead in the mud in the deep parts of the road, yoked to carts laden with baggage. From these, the hungry soldiers sliced off a delightful repast, which was grilled, half-smoked, and half-roasted, and as tough as a shoe sole, but severe hardship and hunger made this an agreeable substitute for better food. Other soldiers would be groping about on their hands and knees under a bastard description of oak and cork tree for acorns. These trees yield them in abundance, and at this time of year they are to be found in plenty. Although hard and bitter, still such food was found better than none.[15]

William Brown of the 45th certainly found the acorns unpalatable; although they 'served the turn with many ... they brought so vividly to my recollection the prodigal son and the husks, that they actually stuck in my throat and would not go down.' However, cabbages were more acceptable. These were found in a large garden and seemed

> as if by a miracle, to have been preserved from all the ravages that preceded us; but which now, as if by a counter miracle, were as suddenly plucked up by the roots, for every man seized a head that could, and shared with his comrades who had got none. As there was no time for cooking, the whole were eaten, or rather devoured, in a few minutes, rough and raw as we found them, and was, I daresay, considered the sweetest morsel they had ever tasted.[16]

Nor was it just the men who hunted for food. Burroughs and Kincaid both recorded how they joined the search for acorns, and they were definitely not alone in this respect.

Some men had found a different solution during the night of the 15th.

> It being customary in Spain to drive the swine into the woods, to feed on the acorns that fall from the trees, the forest where we then lay contained a great number of these animals. A hunt accordingly took place, and a good many of them were caught and killed. So keen was the hunger that prevailed, that little ceremony was used in the process of cooking, the carcasses being roasted skin and all. So scarce was every sort of eatables, that one of the officers offered a dollar for a pound of the pork in its rough state, which was refused him.[17]

This was marauding, which Wellington punished by hanging two men from the 4th division and issuing a general order 'that the Assistant Provosts may attend their Divisions on the march, and that they will do their duty, as well in respect of this as of other offences.'[18] Moreover, as Kincaid recalled, other units were disturbed by

> a continued firing of musketry, which led us to believe that our piquets were attacked, and, in momentary expectation of an order to stand to our arms, we kept ourselves awake the whole night, and were not a little provoked when we found next morning that it had been occasioned by numerous stragglers from the different regiments shooting at the pigs belonging to the peasantry, which were grazing in the wood.[19]

Edward Costello of the 95th, however, offered a different explanation for Kincaid's disturbed night. He and some of his fellow soldiers fortuitously came across some carts belonging to the Spanish commissariat, laden with biscuit and aguadente. Temptation was too great and they were helping themselves when they were discovered by the Spanish guards. Both sides fired and the riflemen had to retreat from their prize, but Costello was still satisfied with the thought that he had consumed enough liquor to keep himself alive.

Despite general orders, even officers might find the temptation of fresh pork too hard to resist. Browne

> was returning to Head Quarters thro' the wood with another Officer of the Adjutant General's department, when we saw a cavalry Soldier trotting off with half a pig before him, bleeding as he went along. The man looked round, & it was immediately evident that he knew he was acting in disobedience of orders as he increased his trot. We soon however came pretty close to him, when he set off in a canter with his half pig before him, & we after him with our swords drawn. The real fact was, we wanted his pig & he wished to keep it. Ours were the best horses & we gained upon him, calling out to him to stop instantly, which however he did not seem the least inclined to do. We got still closer to him, when he once more looked round, & seeing the case was desperate let drop the half pig which lightened his horse & he changed his canter into a gallop & was soon out of our sight. Our object being gained we immediately stopped, divided the half pig with our swords, each taking his portion on his pistol holsters covered with his cloak. I never eat [sic] better pork, the relish for it having been greatly increased by the chase after its original owner the cavalry man.[20]

The worst experience was that of Ross-Lewin, which he puts before the army reached Salamanca but which, with its reference to lack of food, seems to belong to the final stages of the retreat. His column (Hill's) was being followed by Spanish and Portuguese stragglers.

> One day, after a total abstinence from food for the forty-eight hours preceding, I bought a piece of what I supposed to be pork from one of these fellows, and broiled it on some embers; but, having neither bread nor salt, I became so unwell soon after I had finished my unsavoury meal, that I with difficulty kept up during the remainder of the march; and the discovery that those ruffians, when disappointed by not meeting pigs, had sometimes cut off the flesh of dead men and sold it for pork, had no tendency to diminish the nausea that I already felt.[21]

To return to Sherer and his boiling potatoes, the interruption of his meal was caused by one of several French incursions into allied bivouacs.

the sound of a few shots caused us to run out, and we found about two squadrons of our German Hussars retiring before a large body of the enemy's horse. As we had only piled arms in columns at quarter distance, we were instantly formed, and the enemy halted about musket shot from us. We stood, for about fifteen minutes, calmly looking at each other. They were about two thousand in number, all covered with large white cloaks, and looked remarkably well. It certainly was a sight, which, on any ordinary occasion, it would have been worth losing a dinner for; but hungry and exhausted as we were, the bustle they caused was very unseasonable.[22]

D'Espinchal had spent the 16th rounding up allied stragglers, men, women and children, and taking waggons, animals and three abandoned guns, although these last had to be left where they were because the horses were not fit to march. It was 4.00pm when he and his men reached Matilla and came upon the rear guard of Hill's column. His account lacks the insouciance of Sherer's, and suggests a livelier encounter. Having been ordered by General Pierre Soult to attack the enemy, d'Espinchal moved forward, supported by Colonel Vinot, and General Avy's brigade of Polish lancers.

Immediately the passage of the stream had been effected, the Polish lancers, supporting my tirailleurs, marched against the enemy; but, having received two discharges of shot, the effective fire of two battalions and the charge of three regiments of English dragoons, we were brought back in disorder onto the lines of Colonel Vinoy who, at the head of the 2nd Hussars and 5th Chasseurs, recovered the combat until two regiments of Hanoverian hussars debouched from the back of the wood. Then the chasseurs d'Aremberg and the 21st became engaged; the combat became very lively, the melee lasted some moments and was finished by the sudden disappearance of the English cavalry, who, on retiring, left us under the deadly fire of the infantry and artillery ...[23]

Webber had been ordered to the wood upon the first sighting of French cavalry, but could not initially use his guns because some allied cavalry were in his line of fire. Drawn up in front of him were the 92nd, who received a furious cavalry charge but

remained form as a rock, the front rank had kneeled down ready to give them a volley but some of the English cavalry being in the way prevented them. Another party of French hussars charged Captain Bradley's Company of the 28th, but were obliged to wheel about, exposed to a volley which annoyed them a great deal.

We were ordered to another part of the wood where there was an opening and we had an opportunity of opening fire, first at 1,000 yards and afterwards at 800 yards, which had great effect and prevented the enemy's attempting anything further. This was at half past four, and at five we returned to our bivouac for the night. We had one man wounded by a rifle ball.[24]

D'Espinchal reported a similar conclusion, which implicitly left the French as victors. In his version, once the French infantry and artillery appeared the allies retired in good order, having first fired some parting salvoes which he claimed did no harm. However, he conceded that the French took casualties during the engagement in which the 'English' displayed their customary courage. The Polish lancers lost an officer and four men with about fifteen wounded, while the 2nd hussars had five killed and twelve wounded, including three lieutenants. Colonel Vinoy's helmet was severed by a sabre cut while his horse was killed by a shell splinter. As for D'Espinchal himself, he came perilously close to being taken prisoner and had to be rescued by some of his own hussars. He later learnt from three allied prisoners that the enemy had lost three killed and fifteen wounded.

Interestingly, remembering the condition of their opponents, the French officers and men alike now found themselves dependent on a diet of acorns, having outrun their supplies. D'Espinchal consoled himself with the thought that Spanish acorns were tastier than French ones.

\* \* \*

After their encounter with the French at Matilla Hill's column bivouacked undisturbed on high wooded ground. Early on the 17th, however, 'a cannonade, directed against the right [Paget's] column, and very distant from us, caused us to stand to our arms, shivering for two hours, after which we broiled our ration and lay down in a swamp, nearly ancle-deep [sic] in water, to repose.'[25] Sherer did not say what his ration consisted of. Webber, who was attached to the 2nd division, timed the start of a four-league march to the Huebra by way of Villalba de los Llaños at 3.30am, which makes Sherer's two hours at arms somewhat problematic, except that Sherer was in the 2nd division, which was acting as Hill's rear guard, while the guns seem to have been leading the column. Webber was across the Huebra by 2.00pm, having found a ford above San Muñoz, where Paget's column was to cross. Before the artillery could establish their bivouac, though, they were ordered to protect their ford, because the French were making a move to cross the river.

Although the whole of Hill's column reached the Huebra unmolested, the conditions made for hard marching. As Donaldson remembered,

About the same hour as the preceding morning, we again fell in and marched off, but the effects of hunger and fatigue were now more visible. A savage sort of desperation had taken possession of every bosom. The streams which fell from the hills were swelled into rivers which we had to wade, and vast numbers fell out, among whom were officers, who having been subject to the same privation were reduced to the most abject misery.

One instance in particular stuck in Donaldson's memory.

The wife of a young man who had endeavoured to be present with her husband on every occasion, if possible, having kept up with us amidst all our sufferings, from Salamanca, was at length so overcome by fatigue and want, that she could go no further; for some distance, with the assistance of her husband's arm, she had managed to drag her weary limbs along, but at length she became so exhausted, that she stood still unable to move; her husband was allowed to fall out with her, for the purpose of getting her into one of the spring waggons, but when they came up, they were already loaded in such a manner that she could not be admitted, and numbers in the same predicament were left lying on the road side. The poor fellow was now in a dreadful dilemma, being necessitated either to leave her to the mercy of the French soldiers, or by remaining with her to be taken prisoner – even then perhaps to be unable to protect her; the alternative either way was heart-rending, but there was no time to lose, the French cavalry were close upon them. In despairing accents she begged him not to leave her, and at one time he had taken the resolution to remain, but the fear of being considered a deserter urged him to proceed, and with feelings easier imagined than de-scribed, he left her to her fate, and never saw her again; but many a time afterwards did he deprecate his conduct on that occasion, and the recollection of it embittered his life.[26]

Although this is obviously an embellished recollection, the soldier's dilemma was real enough. Charles Cadell of the 28th described how at the beginning of the combat at Matilla the Polish lancers callously cut down several unfortunate women, who had fallen behind, before attacking the battalion. It was no wonder, therefore, that the men brought the lancers down with a particularly well-directed volley.

Nevertheless, however vulnerable women might be in general, there were some who demonstrated fortitude and devotion of the highest order, none more so than that Irish termagant, Biddy Skiddy. Her husband was servant to Ensign Bell, and it was Bell who immortalized her. Biddy was complaining of her back on one occasion, which prompted Bell to ask,

'What's the matter with your back, Biddy?' 'O, yer honour knows how my back was bruck on the rethreat from Madrid down to Portugal in the short days of winter rains, when everybody was lost. But Dan made promise niver to tell anyone, and there he is forenenst me,' giving him a sly look for permission to tell her story.

'Yer honour minds how we were all kilt and destroyed on the long march last winter, and the French at our heels, an' all our men droppin' and dyin' on the roadside, waitin' to be killed over agin by them vagabonds comin' after us. Well, I don't know if you seed him, sir, but down drops poor Dan, to be murdered like all the rest. Says he, "Biddy dear, I can't go on furder one yard to save me life." "O, Dan jewel," sis I, "I'll help you on a bit; tak' a hould av me, an' throw away your knapsack." "I'll niver part wid my knapsack," says he, "nor my firelock, while I'm a soger." "Dogs then," sis I, "you 'ont live long, for the French are comin' up quick upon us." Thinkin', ye see, sir, to give him sperret to move, but the poor crather hadn't power to stir a lim. Now I heerd the firin' behind, and saw then killin' Dan, as it was! So I draws him up on the bank and coaxed him to get on my back, for, sis I, "the French will have ye in half an hour, an' me too, the pagans." In truth I was thinkin' they had hould av us both, when I draws him up on me back, knapsack an' all. "Throw away your gun," sis I. "I won't," says he. "Biddy, I'll shoot the first vagabone lays hould av your tail," says he. He always was a conthrary crather when any one invaded his firelock.

Well, sir, I went away wid him on me back, knapsack, firelock, and all, as strong as Sampson, for the fear I was in. An' fegs, I carried him half a league after the regiment into the bivwak.[27]

* * *

Paget's column, marching in the order 1st, 6th, 5th, 7th and light divisions, had a more difficult advance on the 17th, to San Muñoz on the Huebra. The light division, as the rear guard, had an early encounter with French cavalry, who sought to attack them wherever openings in the oak woods allowed. 'While the men were folding their blankets' Captain John Dobbs of the 52nd

happened to go to the rear, and on looking into the valley saw several French dragoons riding at their leisure. I lost no time in giving the alarm; it appeared that our cavalry pickets had retired without giving us notice. During the day the enemy's cavalry were in our rear and upon our flank, and we were obliged to march in column at quarters distance, and frequently to form squares.[28]

The 14th light dragoons and King's German Legion hussars were also required to skirmish with the French dragoons, to keep them at bay. Less seriously,

A German hussar went towards [a French dragoon] and challenged him to single combat, provided he would cross the water. The Frenchman laughed, and as he approached quite close to the edge of the water, made a similar proposal. Thereupon the German advanced, but instead of fighting they entered into a jocular conversation and parted very good friends.[29]

Even for the divisions ahead of the light division conditions were grim.

On the 17th, at six o'clock in the morning, the army which was well concentrated, left its encampment. Our brows lowered with the clouds, and occasionally heavy showers, drenching as they fell, rendered us no less penitent, than desirous of fair weather. Ploughed lands lay before us, with an extensive wood; – it was with difficulty we could march, the columns halting every four or five minutes ... The enemy closely followed our rear, and as the weather was misty accompanied with rain, so that objects were rendered indistinct even at a little distance, the light companies of the regiments were ordered to extend themselves through the wood, to protect our flanks and cover our baggage. We could not, however, prevent the great force of the enemy's cavalry from being felt, and they took every advantage to annoy us, which numbers and the state of the weather, afforded them. At this time, the baggage of the Earl of Dalhousie was reported to be taken, though it proceeded at the head of his division.[30]

It is no wonder that Dalhousie's baggage was lost to the French. (Swabey, within pistol shot of the French, witnessed fifty or sixty French cavalry subsequently plundering Dalhousie's baggage.) An appreciable interval had opened up between the 7th division, which he commanded, and the preceding 5th division. This gap caused a more serious loss when General Paget rode back to investigate the cause of the 7th division's delay, and was taken prisoner. He seems not to have been aware of the presence of French cavalry, probably because of the poor visibility coupled with his own short-sightedness. Nor was he able to defend himself effectively, on account of his loss of an arm at Oporto.

In d'Espinchal's account, he had been sent to the right to reconnoitre and came upon a strong infantry column (Paget's column) making for the Huebra. Having sent a message to this effect to General Soult, he then spotted an officer attended by a corporal and two hussars. Paget was taken so quickly, by three of d'Espinchal's men, that the 'English' continued their march without suspecting that the French were so close to them and had taken their leader. D'Espinchal seems to have initially assumed that the man he described as wrapped up in his cloak was Wellington. The principal prisoner, however, then introduced himself as General Arthur Paget, second-in-command of the English army. Paget commended the courage and audacity of d'Espinchal's men while d'Espinchal, in return, was at pains to treat Paget with due respect, and reclaimed his coat for him from a soldier who had taken it without permission. He then placed the prisoner under the safeguard of a corporal, and conducted him to General Soult.

It has to be said, there are strong reasons for distrusting d'Espinchal's account, not just because of the confusion of name. It is generally agreed that the three men who took Paget belonged to Vinot's light cavalry. Also, Paget was accompanied only by his Spanish servant. Furthermore, Paget initially denied his identity and refused to communicate with his captors. But d'Espinchal was undoubtedly near to hand, and may well have escorted the prisoner back to General Soult.

Wellington later wrote to Paget,

> I did not hear of your misfortune till more than an hour after it had occurred, nor was I certain of it till the enemy attacked our rear guard, and the firing had continued for some time, and I found you were not on the field; and you will judge of my concern by the sense which I hope you feel I entertain of the cordial assistance which I received from you during the short time you have been with us.
>
> I cannot account for your misfortune, excepting that you were alone, and could not see the approach of the enemy's cavalry.
>
> That which must now be done is to endeavor [sic] to obtain your exchange. I have no French general officers in the Peninsula; but I beg you to make it known to the King and to the Duke of Dalmatia, that I will engage that any General Officer they will name shall be sent from England to France in exchange for you. If you should find that there is any prospect of your being exchanged, I recommend you to endeavor to prevail upon the King not to send you to France. It is not necessary to enter into the reason for giving you this advice. If the King, or the Duke of Dalmatia will not name an officer to be exchanged for you, the sooner you are sent to France the better.

I send you some money – 200l. I will take care of your friend Marley. You cannot conceive how much I regret your loss. This is the second time that I have been deprived of your assistance, at an early period after you had joined us, and I am almost afraid to wish to have you again; but God knows with what pleasure I shall hear of your being liberated, and shall see you with us.[31]

The column continued to march to the Huebra. Even when Paget's absence was discovered, there was nothing that could be done to rescue him. So close was the attendance of the French column on the San Muñoz column that when Wellington joined the light division

and continued riding on the left flank, quite close to our column; he could not well join the main body of his army as the enemy's horse scoured the road, and all our cavalry had retired ... Amongst the trees, the French heavy horse continued to accompany us on each flank, and frequently spoke to the soldiers in the ranks.[32]

The light division approached the Huebra at about 4.00pm, by which time the French had brought up a considerable force of infantry and artillery, while the cavalry still hovered nearby. As the infantry and cavalry came up close, Cooke was struck by the reverberation of sound in the wood and the dense atmosphere, making each musket shot sound like a 3-pound mountain gun. Skirmishers were now sent out to deter the cavalry while Wellington scanned the landscape for the best fighting position.

The 7th division had already crossed by the San Muñoz fords and were formed in close columns on the opposite bank. This made them vulnerable to the French guns posted on the high ground across the river. At this point

Whinyates took part of his Troop of Horse Artillery and kept up a well directed fire with round-shot and now and then common case on their Cavalry, who at times were within 200 yards and endeavouring to keep the ford. He completely kept them in check till they brought (as it is said) nearly 20 pieces of Artillery to the opposite heights, one near the village of Buena Madre, which was masked and commenced firing on Whinyates' guns. They dismounted one, carried away the wheel of another, killed two horses, wounded 2 men and knocked down Lieut Bent.[33]

Swabey was also present and suffered the same fire as Whinyates during the combat. Return fire was impossible, on account of the heights above us ... Almost the first shot wounded poor [Major] Macdonald and three men at my gun; Macdonald being so close to me that we touched, I supported him till he was carried off. We remained four hours calmly receiving the enemy's fire, and occasionally checking their infantry and keeping the passage of the river; Lord Wellington gave no orders but to reserve our fire for formed bodies, none of which appeared. Many were the hair-breadth escapes of men and horses; the wet state of the ground, which kept the shot from rising, and the mercy of Providence, alone saved us from certain destruction. At 11 o'clock we got to a camp in the rain and broiled some beef.[34]

Dyneley was also with the guns. He happened to enquire casually after Macdonald's whereabouts and was told that he had been taken, severely wounded, to the rear. About half an hour later he was presented with a piece of shell, which had been taken from the wound, and asked if he would like to keep it. Not surprisingly, Dyneley declined the offer, reflecting that he was likely to have something similar to take care of before the day was over.

For we remained on the spot from that time till dark with five guns playing from a hill on our right flank and four on our front ploughing the ground up in beautiful style, the troops standing counting the shot on their fingers ... we only expended 140 rounds the whole day and our loss was very trifling, only four men wounded. The poor infantry, who were immediately in front and directly behind us, suffered dreadfully.[35]

For the infantry, the combat of San Muñoz was particularly uncomfortable. The 7th division had already been under fire when they 'got clear of the wood', where they had been attacked,

and began to descend a steep hill, from which we had a cheering view of the British cavalry drawn up on the opposite hill: the sight was grand and encouraging to us. Having descended into the valley, we crossed a deep river, the water being as cold as ice: in a few minutes we had to cross another river, deeper than the former; and, to augment our distresses, the enemy posted themselves, with twelve pieces of cannon, on the hill from which we had just descended, and immediately commenced a desperate cannonading on our regiment and the 51st. We formed line, and stood for six hours up to the ancles [sic] in mud and water, and during that period were completely exposed, having nothing to shelter us from their fire; not a man, however, of our regiment was either killed or wounded. When the enemy's shots came near to us, we advanced two or three hundred yards, and the balls went over our heads a considerable distance; and when they shortened their quantity of powder, and the shots fell near us again, we retreated four or five hundred yards: by these means many lives were saved.[36]

However, Wheeler reported that in the 51st Captain McCabe was killed and many men were wounded.

Burroughs, a non-combatant given to flights of verbal fancy, became aware of a change of mood as soon as there was the promise of action.

Now the army was formed for battle, and every one forgot his fatigues in anticipation of victory. The meagre soldier in our ranks, whose furrowed cheeks bespoke an age of service, felt the fire of youth kindling in his veins, as the roar of the cannon played upon his ears; while the youth, who chiefly composed the strength of our battalions, had their memories too recently impressed with the brilliant achievements of Rodrigo, Badajos, and Salamanca, to have been readily forgotten.

Above all there was the effect of Wellington's presence:

The spirit of enthusiasm was however raised to the highest pitch by the electric effect of the words, – 'Here he comes,' which spread from mouth to mouth, with the rapidity of lightning. The noble commander passed our columns in review, as usual, unaccompanied with any mark of distinction or splendour; his long horse cloak, concealed his under garments, – his cocked hat soaked and disfigured with the rain.[37]

The French had been checked for the last time, although they were not yet ready to abandon the chase completely. Nevertheless, although separated from the enemy only by the Huebra, the allies settled down to enjoy what food they could find. For Burroughs it was some fresh-killed pork, bought from the Spanish. Toasted over a fire, it satisfied his hunger even without the useful additions of salt and bread. Leach and his fellow officers of the rifles were less fortunate. Although a fire was lit to cook their scanty rations, it was soon extinguished by the rain falling from the trees and they found themselves once again rooting for acorns.

About 1.00am on the 18th the orderlies circulated a general order to march, and between 3.00am and 4.00am the column began to move. There was some delay while a branch of the Huebra, about a mile further on, was forded. This held up the light division, still acting as rear guard. When they eventually marched, they left behind the dead and dying, the latter imploring their comrades not to leave them. No help could be given, however, because those who still had the strength to drag themselves forward were in no condition to assist their comrades. It was now very much every man for himself.

The French may have been held at the Huebra, but d'Espinchal believed the 17th had been a successful day for them. San Muñoz had been pillaged because its inhabitants had supported the allies during the combat. He had been informed by Captain Braun of the 2nd hussars, who had been on the spot, that they had taken three allied guns and 800 prisoners, although these claims are not supported by any allied accounts and seem to be a flight of fancy. Overall, according to d'Espinchal, the French had taken 2,000 allied prisoners and twelve guns during the retreat, as well as a great amount of abandoned provisions. This last detail is also suspect, since the allies had no provisions to lose.

As far as Soult was concerned there was no point in continuing the pursuit with infantry since the allies were heading for the Agueda, and then, presumably, on to Portugal, which had been his objective. Even Napoleon had finally accepted that Wellington and his army would not easily be removed from Portugal; but the Marshal had met the Emperor's wishes and driven them out of Spain, the first step to restoring French power in Spain. Furthermore, his own troops were in need of food and rest. The Army of the South had marched long and hard from Andalusia, and in the final stages of the campaign supplies had become scarce. Leaving the cavalry to harass the enemy back to Ciudad Rodrigo, Soult finally retired upon the Upper Tormes after he had kept the infantry under arms for two hours at the Huebra, until he was sure the allies were continuing their retreat.

\*    \*    \*

On the allied side the misery continued. The terrain was still challenging and made marching difficult. The country ahead of them was covered in gum cistus shrubs and dwarf oaks, while the track was narrow and deeply muddy so that men could only march in single file. According to Cadell, their progress was further hindered by the stupidity of the guides, who caused them to ford one river after another, and all of them swollen by rain. At one point the light division had to cross a narrow but deep stream in single file, using a fallen tree as a precarious bridge.

Nor were the cavalry any better off. According to the *Journal* of the 1st (Royal) dragoons, horses were dying from exhaustion and lack of forage, or had to be shot when they could go no further, so that

> Before long the dismounted far exceeded the mounted men in number, and these were sent off every morning under a subaltern an

hour before the rest of the regiment. Further, although the army marched no more than four leagues a day, yet night had always fallen before the cavalry reached their allotted bivouacs ... At each bivouac there was little to be done but tie each poor horse to some tree, and lie down in the mud, while the melancholy sky continued to discharge its rain. The men hardly had heart to light fires and, when they did, the glow of the still smouldering embers in the early morning would reveal the pale faces of comrades who had died during the night.[38]

Hunger was a continuing problem. Webber recorded in his diary that many of the troops had been without food for four or five days, while the Portuguese brigade in the 2nd division had received no provisions for six or seven days. When food became available it was more than welcome, however doubtful its quality. Kincaid was sent to General Charles Alten, in command of the light division, for orders.

While I was toasting myself at his fire, so sharply set that I could have eaten one of my boots, I observed his German orderly dragoon at an adjoining fire stirring up the contents of a camp-kettle that once more revived my departing hopes, and I presently had the satisfaction of seeing him dipping in some basins, presenting one to the general, one to the aide-de-camp and a third to myself. The meat which it contained I found, after swallowing the whole at a draught, was neither more nor less than the produce of a piece of beef boiled in plain water; and, though it would have been enough to have physicked a dromedary at any other time, yet, as I then could have made a good hole in the dromedary himself, it sufficiently satisfied my cravings to make me equal to anything for the rest of the day.[39]

Matters were made worse for some of the troops by the refusal of three divisional commanders in the central column to follow the route they had been given. In d'Urban's opinion, it was most fortunate that

the Enemy was either not up in force to-day, or did not choose to press – for the greatest confusion prevailed throughout. The principal column of the Army went astray without any Cavalry to cover it, and 'tis difficult to imagine the extent of the Evil that might, and probably would, have ensued from a vigorous and well-directed attack.[40]

Some weeks later Wellington wrote to Colonel Torrens, the Duke of York's military secretary, requiring that General W. Stewart should be placed under Hill's command.

I had placed him under Sir Edward Paget, in the 1st division; and on the night after poor Paget was taken, he and certain other General officers commanding divisions (new comers) held a council of war to decide whether they should obey my orders to march by a particular road. He, at the head, decided he would not: they marched by a road leading they did not know where, and when I found them in the morning they were in the utmost confusion, not knowing where to go or what to do. This with the enemy close to them, and with the knowledge that, owing to the state of the roads and the weather, I felt the greatest anxiety respecting the movement.[41]

As well as the 1st division under Stewart, Leach identified Dalhousie's 7th division and some other divisions which he saw floundering their way through a muddy defile not a mile from the light division. According to Oman the third division to have gone astray was the 5th division, since Oswald, like Dalhousie, had only recently joined the army in the Peninsula. Fortescue has Clinton, commanding the 6th division, as the offender, possibly because Clinton had shown inadequacies as a commander on several occasions since Salamanca in July. The generals' chosen route took them towards a bridge over the Yeltes, where the Galicians were crossing. There Wellington first treated them to the sharpness of his tongue, and then made them wait until all the Spanish had crossed.

Meanwhile, d'Espinchal was in command of the French cavalry unit, comprising 100 Polish lancers and 100 hussars, which went furthest in pursuit of the allies. For eight hours they followed a road made difficult by rain damage, passing abandoned baggage and waggons. At 2.00pm they reached the village of Sancti-Spiritus. D'Espinchal was convinced the enemy had now retired behind his lines and decided to turn back, taking with him the stragglers they had picked up along the way. They rode back to Rinconada, which they reached at 11.00pm, and were finally able to feed themselves and their horses. D'Espinchal was convinced that had they not discovered a waggon loaded with barley and beef they would have dropped dead from starvation and fatigue. It is obvious that d'Espinchal had spent three days every bit as gruelling as those experienced by the allies.

*   *   *

By the 19th the weather had changed, from wet to dry but very cold. However, it was only a short march to the Agueda. Provisions were waiting for the troops, but so desperate were the starving men to receive their rations that in some regiments sentries had to be posted with bayonets fixed to allow orderly distribution.

Some men hobbled rather than marched in. Green had been crippled on the 18th by sand which had got into his shoes as he crossed a river. On the 19th he was so exceedingly lame that I could not keep up with the regiment, but I followed, and did not arrive in Alla Madilla until the evening. Indeed, I walked with the greatest pain and trouble to myself, having frequently to take off my shoes and walk bare-foot.[42]

Kincaid, who had not taken his boots off for six days, found it necessary to cut them off, so swollen were his feet. As for Simmons, who had been wearing the same clothes, including the same shirt, for too long for comfort, he and some other officers waited only a day before plunging into the Agueda to rid themselves of infestation.

The final word goes to Burroughs, the first historian of the retreat.

This retreat was conducted over nearly one hundred and sixty miles of ground, in winter, when the aspect of nature is most wretched and forlorn, and at a season particularly severe. The country for the most part was champaign, and admirably calculated for the operations of cavalry, of which our force was small. Supplies fell short, for though the inhabitants sowed and reaped, the contending armies consumed, so that wherever the soldier came, famine followed. Hence arose the backwardness of the people to assist us, for as the oxen were embargoed for the use of the army, the plough necessarily stood still, and the sudden transition to indigence, was followed by indifference and despair. This was only a small share of their suffering, compared to the destruction of their houses and property; I have seen whole villages unroofed and pillaged by the French army, for the purpose of getting fuel to cook their provisions. Under these circumstances then, our situation would have been trying, even if we had not an enemy to contend with. But we had an enemy, whose armies were numerous and well commanded – an enemy, who by a rapid series of successes, during a course of twenty years, had awakened feelings of terror and admiration in every man's bosom; yet the British army retired with ranks unbroken and troops undismayed; they felt not the hardships attending a retreat, except that of hunger; the severity of the weather it was not in human power to controul [sic], and even the want of provisions has not infrequently been sustained by pursuing and victorious armies. Wherever the country allowed us to take a position, the army halted for battle. Positions were once considered equivalent to otherwise overwhelming numbers; but a new mode of warfare has shown that the best position cannot withstand the manœuvring of superior forces, when determined on its flanks, they threaten its communications with the rear. Every attempt to bring the enemy to action on the Tormes, was rendered abortive, by their outflanking or turning our position on the river, and even then, the hope was not destroyed, until it was ascertained the enemy was so strongly posted at Mozarbes, as to be inaccessible to attack.[43]

* * *

Although many of the accounts of the retreat were written retrospectively, sometimes several decades later, it is interesting that as a story it did not grow much in the telling, and contemporaneous accounts contain the same sense of suffering as the later versions. On 22 November Bingham wrote to his mother,

the weather being very unfavourable, raining as hard as it could pour, the soil being clay, and the roads at the best of times not very good, the marches were very distressing. Add to this on a retreat it is seldom prudent to have baggage with you, so that after being drench'd all day with rain, we had but the wet ground to sleep on at night. Neither ourselves nor our horses had much to eat, and both men and officers three days without bread. Our loss has been very severe, many men exhausted by fatigue, and want, died on the road; others were left with their legs in a state of mortification from cold and wet.[44]

The next day Dyneley told his sister,

To give you an impression of the miseries of our retreat would be impossible unless I had you here to talk it over. Suffice to say that nothing could have been worse conducted. We commenced our march on the 14th November and it never ceased raining until our arrival at Alamandilla on the 21st, therefore you may suppose the state the country was in for the poor men and horses. I am un-acquainted with the number of each we have lost, but it must be prodigiously great. You can easily imagine this when I tell you that the enemy were pushing us hard the whole way and that I saw some hundreds of men, women, and children stuck in the mud, and unable to move from hunger and sickness. In a great many instances our poor wounded men had only the alternative either of being left behind and falling into the hands of the enemy, or being dragged along by two men of their regiment. You may judge of my feelings on being obliged to refuse applications to carry these unfortunate beings on our gun-carriages. Many of them, to excite compassion, would pull their clothes aside to shew their wounds, but we were obliged to turn a deaf ear to them or risk the loss of our guns by overloading the horses.[45]

When Hope wrote to a fellow officer on 21 November, he was succinct in his summary of the retreat and its miseries.

> It is almost impossible to give you any idea of our sufferings during the last ten days. Without money, without clothes, and often not well supplied with provisions our situation, as you may conceive, was not an enviable one.
>
> For some days past, our men have subsisted chiefly on wheat, oak nuts, and tough beef, the very sight of which was often sufficient to satisfy the cravings of hunger. The countenances of the soldiers are sufficient to convince any person who sees them, that the miseries and hardships they have endured in this retreat have been of no ordinary kind.[46]

In 1833 Hope worked the letters he had written during his time in the Peninsula into a narrative account. In this version of the retreat, though, for all the extra details that he added, of ragged and lice-infested uniforms, the lack of shelter and the scantiness of provisions, the story remained essentially the same. Indeed he challenged the reader to answer the question,

> Placed in the field without tents to shelter them from the midnight blast, without a change of linen, or money either to purchase that luxury, or to add to their scanty stock of provisions, was it possible for them to be so long exposed, night and day, to the pelting of the pitiless storm, *without suffering severe privations?* Let those who doubt the fact make a trial on the first opportunity, and be convinced.[46]

Inevitably, comparisons were made with Sir John Moore's retreat to Corunna in the winter of 1808–09. Gomm was possibly one of the first to do so, in a letter to his sister, in which he commented that his recent experiences

> revived many recollections of the dreadful race to Corunna. In some respects the hardships were greater, for on that occasion the troops were generally under cover, such as it was, during the night; but here the only resting-place ... was a bleak, swampy plain, with more temptation in it to watch than sleep, and to look out with impatience for the break of the following day.[48]

Like Gomm, Captain John Patterson of the 50th had experienced both retreats. He later wrote:

> We certainly had a good specimen of retreating in Gallicia [sic]; but this, I mean from Salamanca, for the time it lasted, was allowed by

those concerned in both, to be equally as bad a business, and would make a very affecting sequel or episode to the other. True, we had not in the present case, quite so far to travel, nor was the route or country so indifferent; but being totally left without our baggage, the officers at least not having a cloak to cover them, it was felt with as much severity, and the casualties in proportion just as great.

I really think that the weather was even worse; for in the north of Spain, although there was excessive snow, still the rains were not so heavy; here it was one continuous downpour from the Tormes to the Agueda, at which, when we arrived, we were thoroughly soaked ...[49]

When Leith Hay converted his diary into a narrative of the Peninsular War, he added an extended evaluation of the two retreats, finding one significant difference that made Wellington's more perilous than Moore's.

The country through which Lord Wellington moved was incomparably more dangerous, more susceptible of affording scope for manœuvre and the harassment of a retreating force, than that from Astorga to Coruña; lateral roads branched off in every direction; cavalry could act in all parts of the country; there were no mountain positions to defend; nor were the flanks of the retiring columns ever secure.[50]

On the other hand, Wellington had an experienced army, used to the hardships of campaigning, an army furthermore that was no longer in awe of French invincibility.

According to Brown, after the 'unparalleled and unheard of hardships' they had suffered,

Many men who had been under General Moore, during the disastrous retreat to Corunna, avowed they had undergone more fatigue, and suffered greater privations on the retreat from Madrid, than they had ever done the whole of their lives.[51]

Naturally, from a perspective of two hundred years, it is impossible to debate the merits of these judgements. But they certainly convey the sense of suffering that was felt on all sides, and which lived on in men's minds. George Wood was fully convinced that 'the Corunna retreat, from what I experienced of it, and the opinion that I have heard given by those officers who were on both, will bear no comparison with this.'[52] Furthermore, he claimed that

The difficulties, privations, and hardships we encountered, were probably almost as severe as those endured in the retreat of the French from Moscow, with the exception of the distance; and, for myself, I certainly should prefer marching through frost and snow, to rain and mire. I do not think that I exaggerate greatly, in saying that we lost nearly as great a number of men, in proportion, as the ill-fated host of fugitives from Russia.

Although few might accept the validity of this comparison with the retreat from Moscow, that Wood draws such a parallel demonstrates how strongly the horror of his experiences had seeded itself in his memory.

# PART IV

# Aftermath

# Chapter 11

# The French Perspective

Once the allies had been forced back to the Portuguese border both sides could evaluate their successes and failures during a long year's campaigning, which had begun nearly eleven months earlier. From the French point of view, after the earlier disasters of Ciudad Rodrigo, Badajoz and Salamanca, a vital strategic objective had been achieved. To all intents and purposes Spain had been cleared of the allied presence, and those officers who wanted the war carried into Portugal had reason to believe their hopes would be realized. They could console themselves for the lack of a second battle of Salamanca with the belief that only the weather had saved Wellington and his army, even though Soult had never intended that such a battle should be fought. Looking at the overall picture, they could adopt the view that 'the year ended apparently less badly that its disastrous beginnings had promised.'[1]

D'Espinchal certainly ascribed to this view. Soult had achieved his goal by forcing Wellington back to the border and inflicting heavy losses, 4,000 killed, 6,000 prisoners of war and an immense amount of baggage, grain and animals, plus fifteen guns.

> our worthy commander ... gave the king his capital back, repossessed the two Castiles and La Mancha, where the army could occupy good winter quarters; the thing he missed to crown this campaign, victory in battle, would undoubtedly have been achieved had the rains not come as an insurmountable obstacle to the ardent desire of the army.[2]

For Lieutenant William Grattan of the 88th, the mystery was not that Soult had failed to offer battle. His successful threat to the allied right flank made clear what his intentions were. But why did he not press the pursuit in order to inflict heavier casualties and greater disruption on the allied army?

> It is not possible for me to say what his motives were for discontinuing a pursuit which had been productive of so great a disorganization of our army. His own, perhaps, were nearly as ill off; but it is

most certain, that, had he followed our footsteps for three days longer with the same energy he had done on the preceding ones (for the country was still open), our artillery and cavalry must have suffered serious loss.[3]

Soult himself gave a possible answer to this question in the advice he is supposed to have left for his successor after he was summoned to Germany at the beginning of 1813.

Whenever you find the British army in retreat, let them alone, and they will go to the devil their own way; but if you go near them, they will get into their places, and give you such a drubbing as you never had before.[4]

This is a useful reminder that men are not machines. Soult had experienced how the British could turn and fight at Corunna in 1809. On a lesser scale, the same point had been demonstrated at Puente Larga and Alba de Tormes. He had also, in his own mind, beaten the allied army at Albuera in 1811, but he was the one who had withdrawn from the battlefield when the allies refused to admit defeat. He knew that Wellington's army was still capable of standing their ground, even as they struggled back to Ciudad Rodrigo, just as he had known, if he were to offer battle on the 15th, he could possibly share Marmont's fate. Better to let them go than waste the (admittedly limited) success he had achieved.

Napier, generally an admirer of Soult, offered an extended examination of his failure to bring the allies to battle.

It has been said that the only drawback to the duke of Dalmatia's genius, is his want of promptness to strike at the decisive moment. It is certainly a great thing to fight a great battle; and against such a general as Wellington, and such troops as the British, a man may well be excused, if he thinks twice, ere he puts his life and fame, and the lives and fame of thousands of his countrymen, the weal or woe of nations, upon the hazard of an event, which may be decided by the existence of a ditch five feet wide, or the single blunder of a single fool, or the confusion of a coward, or by any other circumstance however trivial. To make such a throw for such a stake is no light matter. It is no mean consideration, that the praise or the hatred of nations, universal glory or universal, perhaps eternal contempt, waits on an action, the object of which may be gained by other means, for in war there is infinite variety. But in this case it is impossible not to perceive, that the French general vacillated after the passage of the river [Tormes], purposely perhaps to avoid an action, since, as I have before shown, he thought it unwise, in the disjointed state of the

French affairs and without any fixed base or reserves in case of defeat, to fight a decisive battle. Nor do I blame this prudence, for thought it be certain that he who would be great in war must be daring, to set all upon one throw belongs only to an irresponsible chief, not to a lieutenant whose task is but a portion of the general plan; neither is it wise, in monarch or general, to fight when all may be lost by defeat, unless all may be won by victory. However, the king, more unfettered than Soult, desired a battle, and with an army so good and numerous, the latter's prudence seems misplaced; he should have grappled with his enemy, and, once engaged at any point, Wellington could not have continued his retreat, especially with the Spaniards, who were incapable of dextrous movement.[5]

A modern biographer of Soult accepts that

It was for the French a disappointing end to what had been a successful campaign. They had indeed lost their last chance of winning the Peninsular War ... Soult was entitled to feel that an all-out attack mounted from Andalusia might have had a quite different result. Now, because of the king's timidity and obstinacy, the whole of southern Spain had been lost. However, short of winning a complete victory, Soult had achieved something. All the territory – and more – lost by Marmont had been regained. In their rapid retreat British casualties, killed, wounded and prisoners, numbered some 5,000 in addition to their sharp losses in the abortive attack on Burgos. A mass of arms and equipment had been captured and once again the British had been cleared out of central Spain. They would not return for another six months. By then the responsibility of fighting them was no longer Soult's.[6]

These views can be conceded, although they somewhat disingenuously ignore French losses, which were certainly considerable.

Wellington had a clear opinion of Soult: 'He did not quite understand a field of battle: he knew very well how to bring his troops on to the field, but not so well how to use them when he had brought them up.'[7] Significantly, men who served under Soult had an explanation for what might be termed his caution. According to one officer,

If I say that he loved vigorous enterprises I must add that he loved them provided they did not involve too much personal danger, for he was far from possessing the brilliant courage of Ney or Lannes. It might even be said that he was the very reverse of rash – that he was a little too careful of himself.[8]

Another French officer identified his weakness as an inability to respond to the ebb and flow of battle. If what he had planned should happen did not happen, he could not cope effectively with developing circumstances. Fortunately for Soult, his intentions at Salamanca were realized.

Whatever the truth of these various judgements, Foy had no doubt about who was the victor in November 1812.

> The campaign is over. Lord Wellington retires undefeated, with the glory of the laurels of the Arapiles, subsequently having returned to the Spanish the country to the south of the Tagus, after we had to destroy our magazines, our materiel, our fortifications, in a word everything which was a product of our conquest and could assure its continuation.[9]

On the 19th Soult had withdrawn to Salvatierra, by way of Tamames. He then established his headquarters at Salamanca, before passing the winter at Toledo, while Joseph returned to Madrid, and the Army of Portugal was dispersed around Toro and Valladolid. There was no attempt to regain Andalusia. As for Soult himself, he returned to France in March 1813, when relations between him and Joseph became intolerable for both men, and then served with Napoleon in Germany. When he next returned to Spain, he would be trying to hold a line at the Pyrenees.

*    *    *

An interesting view of the campaign from the French perspective is contained in a letter Joseph Bonaparte sent to his brother on 21 November, and which was intercepted and delivered to Wellington. The letter starts with a resumé of the situation which pertained when the king wrote to Napoleon on 22 September. He then explained what had subsequently happened.

> On the 1st October the Army of the South joined with the Army of the Centre. I met the marshal, Duke of Dalmatia, at Fuente la Higueda on the 3rd. I detached 6,000 men from his army who were ordered to unite with the Army of the Centre at Cuenca, the command of which I gave to Count d'Erlon. I made for Cuenca with my Guard and the Army of the Centre; the Duke of Dalmatia marched by the Royal Road with the Army of the South. The fort of Chinchilla was taken in passing by Count d'Erlon. The enemy troops which infested these provinces were thrown back before us as far as the Tagus, which they passed at Fuente Dueña [sic], and on the 28th the two armies united on the left of the river from Fuente Dueña as far as Lillo.
>
> Eighteen days before leaving Valencia I sent Lucotte, my aide-de-camp, post haste to the headquarters of the Army of Portugal to repeat my order to contain Lord Wellington, and to follow him with-

out engaging until our movements on the Tagus forced him [i.e. Wellington] to leave the north. Six officers later carried the same orders at different times.

I was still unsure whether all the enemy's forces were united on the Tagus. The first reconnaissance, made to Aranjuez, confirmed that they were, but during the night of the 31st the enemy abandoned the bridge of Xarama and retired. We followed him and on the 2nd November the armies found themselves at the gates of Madrid. I stayed there in person on the 3rd while the Army of the South reached the foot of the Guadarrama [mountains] in pursuit of the enemy. I joined them the following day.

Hill's corps had been ordered to march to join with Lord Wellington at Arevalo; or to try to join him there. We did not give him time: we were at Arevalo the 5th and 6th November; the Army of the Centre was ordered to follow this movement. I still had no news of the Army of Portugal, so the English avoided an impending battle.

Not until the 8th was I informed by an aide-de-camp whom I had sent from Valencia to the Army of Portugal that this army had arrived at Simancas on the 30th October. On the 9th November I received reports from Count Souham. [At this point it is easy to understand why Joseph decided Souham would have to be replaced.]

On the 11th I came to Alba, which was occupied by the enemy. I descended on the Tormes at Huerta to observe the fords and reconnoitre the English army. It had taken up a position which extended from Alba to San Christoval, General Hill on the right, and Lord Wellington on the left. The enemy appeared ready to accept battle, I ordered all the necessary preparations for crossing the river, and I made dispositions for the 14th.

I added the two divisions of infantry and two divisions of cavalry in the Army of the Centre to the Duke of Dalmatia's command.

I gave command of the Army of Portugal to Count d'Erlon, and reserved the command of my Guard and the Spanish troops to General Merlin.

The enemy occupied a strong position. He had considered it for a long time. It was that of the Arapiles. I first intended to make a frontal attack; if broken in the centre, the enemy would perhaps separate into two and lose most of his army. But I was struck by the observations of the generals who knew the area, and I decided to operate on the right of the enemy by passing the Tormes at Galisancho.

The Armies of the South and the Centre effected a crossing on the 14th in the morning; that of Portugal made a demonstration at the fords of Huerta opposite Alba de Tormes as if to take the town so that it would be evacuated by the effect of our movement to the right, and to take its place in line with the other armies. If Alba was not abandoned, it was to cross the river at the same place where the Armies of the North [presumably the South] and Centre had passed.

Bridges were thrown across the Tormes, but the ardour of the soldiers would not allow them to wait until they were in place, and the crossing was easily effected during the morning of the 14th. The enemy's outposts were taken, the 8,000 men who were defending Alba were evacuated; during the night of the 14th and 15th the armies were on the left bank of the Tormes, the Army of the South held the right at Mozarbas. The Army of Portugal was ordered on the 15th to take position on the right, on the plateau of Nuestra Señora de Utiera; those of the South and Centre were to make a movement to their left in order to put themselves on the right of the enemy and cut his line of operations.

This same day, the Army of Portugal occupied the plateau, and the troops of the Armies of the South and the Centre the heights of the chapel de N.S. de Valbuena; but the movements of the enemy were hidden by a thick mist, succeeded by continual rain, which rendered all our efforts fruitless. The smaller ravines became torrents, disrupting all movements.

However, many explosions in the direction of Salamanca announced the retreat of the enemy. The cavalry disrupted communications with Ciudad Rodrigo. The enemy army was in full retreat. The cavalry pursued them the next day, the 16th. Thousands of prisoners, including many officers, among them General Paget, second-in-command of the English army, were taken by the cavalry of the Armies of the South, Portugal and the Centre, as well as baggage and many vehicles.

The hopes conceived by the enemy since the 22nd July have now evaporated, and the people have been disabused of the puissance of their army.

The armies of your Imperial Majesty are full of ardour; Generals, officers, soldiers are animated by the best spirit.[9]

Joseph makes the campaign sound all too easy, as well as putting himself very much at the centre of operations while relegating Soult to a minor role. Joseph was to be the hero of the hour, victor in Spain, possibly in contrast to the younger brother whose Russian adventure had come to a disastrous conclusion. Yet, unlike Foy, one of the most perspicacious of French generals, he had failed to recognize that to scotch the snake is not to kill it. Seven months later he would pay the price for this mistake.

## Chapter 12

# Victory or Defeat

Having brought his army to Ciudad Rodrigo, Wellington could now address the question of what the French would do next. As he wrote to Bathurst on the 19th, he was uncertain of the enemy's intentions. Having received an intercepted letter which Soult had sent to the king, he knew that the marshal wished to take the war into Portugal, but not when he might judge the moment right for such a move. Wellington was confident, however, that it would not happen in the immediate future. Although the result of the campaign was

> not so favourable as I at one moment expected, or as it would have been, if I could have succeeded in the attack of the Castle of Burgos, or if General Ballesteros had made the movement into La Mancha which was suggested, is still so favourable, that this operation appears out of the question.[1]

In a much longer dispatch, written to Lord Liverpool four days later, he developed this point.

> When one army is so inferior in numbers to another as ours is to the French army now assembled in Castille [sic], its operations must depend in a great degree upon those of its opponent. It is impossible therefore for me at this period to point out what line I shall follow. The enemy having abandoned Madrid, and having given up all their communications with the north, solely with a view to collect a still larger force against us, there is no diversion would answer at present to effect an alteration in our relative numbers, even if I could depend upon the Spaniards to do anything ... Then there is another circumstance which must be attended to, and that is the situation of our own army. It has been actively employed since the beginning of last January, and requires rest. The horses of the cavalry and artillery in particular require both that and good food and care during the winter; and the discipline of the infantry requires to be attended to as is usual in all armies after so long a campaign, and one of so much activity.

I believe that the enemy require repose as much if not more than we do; and that their immense numbers are rather embarrassing to them in a country already exhausted. But I am not quite certain that they do not propose to penetrate Portugal this winter. I hope the enterprise will end fatally for them; but our troops will suffer a good deal if they are to have a winter campaign, and if the weather should continue as severe as it has been since the 15th of this month.

He then considered the strength of the French armies and the general situation before expressing the hope that by spring, when green forage would be available, he would be able to take the field with a large Anglo-Portuguese army, stronger in cavalry and artillery than at present, which was a less than subtle hint to Liverpool that the government should do more to support him.

Another issue that concerned Welllington was the public perception of the campaign, so he was careful to point out what had been achieved.

We have taken by siege Ciudad Rodrigo, Badajoz, and Salamanca; and the Retiro surrendered. In the mean time the allies have taken Astorga, Guadalaxara and Consuegra, besides other places taken by Duran and Sir H. Popham. In the months elapsed since January this army has sent to England little short of 20,000 prisoners, and they have taken and destroyed or have themselves the use of the enemy's arsenals in Ciudad Rodrigo, Badajoz, Salamanca, Valladolid, Madrid, Astorga, Seville, the lines before Cadiz, etc.; and upon the whole we have taken and destroyed, or we now possess, little short of 3,000 pieces of cannon. The siege of Cadiz has been raised, and all the countries south of the Tagus have been cleared of the enemy.

He next turned to the subject of Burgos, and his failure there.

The fault of which I was guilty in the expedition to Burgos was, not that I undertook the operation with inadequate means, but that I took there the most inexperienced instead of the best troops. I left at Madrid the 3rd, 4th and Light divisions, who had been with myself always before; and I brought with me that were good the 1st division, and they were inexperienced. In fact, the troops ought to have carried the exterior line by escalade on the first trial on the 22nd of September, and if they had we had sufficient means to take the place. They did not take the line because [Major Laurie, as already noted], the field officer who commanded, did that which is too common in our army. He paid no attention to his orders, notwithstanding the pains I took in writing them, and in reading and explaining them to him twice over. He made none of the dispositions ordered; and instead of regulating the attack as he ought, he rushed as if he had been the leader of a forlorn hope, and fell, together with many of those who went with him. He had my instructions in his pocket; and as the French got possession of his body, and were made acquainted with the plan, the attack could never be repeated. When he fell, nobody having received orders what to do, nobody could give any to the troops. I was in the trenches, however, and ordered them to withdraw. Our time and ammunition were then expended, and our guns destroyed in taking this line; than which at former sieges we had taken many stronger by assault.

I see that the disposition already exists to blame the Government for the failure of the siege of Burgos. The Government had nothing to say to the siege. It was entirely my own act. In regard to means, there were ample means both at Madrid and at Santander for the siege of the strongest fortress. That which was wanting at both places was means of transporting ordnance and military stores to the place where it was desirable to use them.

To emphasize this final point, he finished the dispatch with the pertinent reminder to the people of England, living in a richly resourced country with excellent roads, that they had no idea 'that important results here frequently depend upon 50 or 60 mules more or less, or a few bundles of straw to feed them; but the fact is so, notwithstanding their incredulity.[2]

A third dispatch, to General Cooke in Cadiz, recognized there would be a general sense of disappointment, but acknowledged that 'what has happened, and was expected and foretold by me when I thought it probably that Soult would raise the siege of Cadiz, and would evacuate Andalusia.' There was also a realization that, as far as the war in Spain was concerned, hopes could never be more than wishes. More significantly, Wellington speculated on what might have been if he had taken Burgos.

I might have driven the Army of Portugal, whose reinforcements were not then organised, beyond the Ebro, and I might have left there or at Burgos an army of 20,000 English and Portuguese (by the by, the worst of that description I have yet had, having nearly all the German troops among them), and from 12,000 to 16,000 Spaniards, against what turned out to be 45,000 French. If I could have stayed with them myself, this might have done; but there is nobody else on whom I could have imposed the task, or who would have liked to undertake it.

I reckon that the King and Soult brought out of Valencia about 45,000 men, of which from 5,000 to 7,000 were cavalry. Hill had on the Tagus about 30,000 of the best we have, and about 10,000 Spaniards of sorts. My plan was to bring Ballesteros upon the left flank and rear of Soult's march out of Valencia, by placing him at Alcaraz, in the Sierra, where he would have been safe, at the same time that nobody could move on the great road from Valencia to attack Hill upon the Tagus.

If this game had been well played, it would have remained my purpose. Soult and the King could not have remained in Valencia, and they must have crossed the Ebro, where I should have assembled all the allies, and should have worked upon their right flank.

Wellington was sufficiently realistic to acknowledge that the answer to the question, had he any reason to believe it would be well played, was

Certainly not. I have never yet known the Spaniards do anything, much less do anything well. Ballesteros has sometimes drawn the attention of a division or two for a moment, but that is all. Everything else you see and read is false and rotten. A few rascals called guerrillas attack one quarter of their numbers, and sometimes succeed, and sometimes not; but as for any regular operations, I have not known such a thing, and successful, in the whole course of the war.

Under these circumstances, probably I ought not to have remained so long at Burgos, and ought to have withdrawn Hill at an earlier period from Madrid, and to have taken earlier measures to retire to the Agueda. The way in which matters stood are as follows: I was deceived respecting the numbers in my front in the North. I had no reason to believe that the enemy were so strong till I saw them. Fortunately, they did not attack me: if they had, I must have been destroyed.

When I saw the enemy in my front, it was clear that I was less able to contend with them than Hill was with those in his front, and that the danger threatened him, the apprehension of which as coming from his quarter had induced me to move from Burgos. I therefore ordered him to move; and I fairly bullied the French into remaining quiet upon the Douro for seven days in order to give him time to make his march. Afterwards our situation on the Tormes depended in some degree on the weather. If the rain which fell on the 15th had fallen on the 13th, the French must have attacked me at St. Christoval, or we must have remained in the cantonments on the Tormes; and after all I don't know that we have sustained any great loss or inconvenience by remaining so long as we could in our positions at Madrid and the Tormes.

In short, I played a game which might succeed (the only one which could succeed), and pushed it to the last; and the parts having failed, as I admit was to be expected, I have at last made a handsome retreat to the Agueda, with some labour and inconvenience, but without material loss. I believe I have done right.[3]

If this attempt to play down the effects of the siege of Burgos and the subsequent retreat has a strong hint of self-justification, itself possibly suggestive of self-doubt, a dispatch written by the Duke of York on 26 November must have strengthened Wellington's belief that he had only done what was necessary. The commander-in-chief accepted that

> although I felt with others the regret which we must all experience at the imperious necessity which caused the siege of Burgos to be raised, and Madrid to be evacuated, yet I assure your Lordship I was fully sensible that, considering the reinforcements which the enemy had received from France, and the disappointment you experienced on the failure of the Spanish army in the south to operate on the rear of Marshal Soult and divert him from his progress to Madrid, you had no other line to pursue then the one you adopted; and that in this, as in all former instances, your conducted has been the best calc-ulated to meet and overcome the difficulties in which you were placed.[4]

In one respect, Wellington's conduct received approbation among those writing at the time, and that was in extricating his army from its position on the Arapiles and bringing it safely back to the Portuguese border. Gomm, for example, although critical of Wellington's obstinacy at Burgos, praised his demeanour during the final days of the retreat.

> I have seen something of him during these proceedings, and more to admire in him than ever. His temper, naturally hasty, seemed to grow more calm as that of the weather rose, but it was a calmness that indicated elevation rather than depression of spirit. He is eminently gifted with all sorts of qualities. His retreat has been masterly; he has withdrawn the army upwards, I believe, of 200 miles, the greater part of the time before a superior force, which has never once found him in a situation to attempt anything serious, except upon the Carrion, where they failed; and he has reached the point upon which, from the beginning, he directed himself, with his army unbroken, except by the elements and their own indiscipline.[5]

Patterson remembered a particular moment, when Wellington exhibited unequalled coolness.

> He was mounted on his 'dapple steed,' with his blue cloak thrown loosely across his shoulders; the triangular chapeau right fore and aft, and the white cravat. Raising his telescope to his eye, while peering with his sharp and penetrating glance towards the enemy's position, his attitude and whole demeanour were expressive of the collectedness and self-possession for which he is so eminently remarkable. The balls, somewhat in a random way, whizzed past us pretty smartly; and one would think, from the peppering direction to where he stood, that they were trying to administer a settler to his Grace, who, when the men were posted, and his reconnaissance concluded, rode off *deliberately*, followed by a shower of musketry.

Wellington did not have the common touch, but there could be no doubt that a sight of him was always welcomed by the troops. On this occasion, as they waited for the battle which would not happen, 'The soldiers were highly pleased by this immediate interview with their chief; and in their remarks about his astonishing "sang-froid," they displayed a considerable degree of humour, and not a little judgement.'[6]

There were bound to be some reservations about the conduct of the retreat, though, particularly remembering the sharp criticisms expressed in letters and diaries at Burgos. Years later Bell commented on what he interpreted as a certain inevitable short-sightedness in Wellington, particularly in relation to the shooting of pigs.

> The Great Commander, on whom we had the firmest reliance, was unrivalled in skill, vigour, and genius, but could not see at once into the wants and necessities of 70,000 men. The pursuing enemy captured much of our stores and baggage, and our loss of seasoned British soldiers on this retreat, in killed and wounded, and prisoners, according to the returns, came to 8,000 men. War tries the strength of military framework and hunger will not resist a pork-chop fried on the top of a ramrod. 'The pigs,' men said, 'had no right poaching on our grounds, and we had a right to our ration of acorn.'[7]

Most, however, were of d'Urban's mind, when he wrote:

> Thus concluded a retreat exceeding one hundred and fifty miles, made in face of a superior enemy, with the deliberation of an ordinary march, in which consequently the troops suffered nothing from fatigue [although that might have been challenged] and the casualties from the sword under 850. The casualties during the previous siege exceeded two thousand.

This retreat was conducted with singular coolness and ability. Lord Wellington was always master of his movements; he marched when (and only when) he thought proper, and halted to rest the troops whenever he found it expedient.[8]

Grattan, as we shall see, had much to say against Wellington. Having described the ordeals of men and officers alike, lack of food, extreme fatigue, long halts under torrential rain, he conceded, nonetheless, that 'under any other general except Lord Wellington, it would be hard to say what the result might have been.'[9]

Perhaps it is surprising that Aitchison, who was so often critical of Wellington, and in a letter to his father written in December was still blaming him for persevering at Burgos when failure was inevitable, could yet continue, 'On the whole I am still of the opinion that the campaign was as brilliant as ever made . . .' Indeed, in his opinion, the real culprits were the government, who had not provided the resources needed for victory. With such means, 'we might now have been in possession of Madrid with our left on the Ebro.'[10]

Despite his own attempts to present the retreat as inevitable in the wider context of the situation in Spain, there can be little doubt that Wellington shared the frustration of his troops that the campaign had ended so disappointingly for the allies. In such a mood he was prompted to express his irritation in a memorandum 'To Officers Commanding Divisions and Brigades', written on 28 November. In order to understand the reaction this provoked when it became public, it is necessary to consider the whole document, which opened with his decision to put the army into cantonments, and then continued,

But besides these objects I must draw your attention in a very particular manner to the state of discipline of the troops. The discipline of every army, after a long and active campaign, becomes in some degree relaxed, and requires the utmost attention on the part of the general and other officers to bring it back to the state in which it ought to be for service; but I am concerned to have to observe that the army under my command has fallen off in this respect in the late campaign to a greater degree than any army with which I have ever served, or of which I have ever read. Yet this army has met with no disaster; it has suffered no privations which but trifling attention on the part of the officers could not have prevented, and for which there existed no reason whatever in the nature of the service; nor has it suffered any hardships excepting those resulting from the necessity of being exposed to the inclemencies of the weather at a moment when they were most secure.

It must be obvious however to every officer, that from the moment the troops commenced their retreat from the neighbourhood of Burgos on the one hand, and from Madrid on the other, the officers lost all command over their men. Irregularities and outrages of all descriptions were committed with impunity, and losses have been sustained which ought never to have occurred. Yet the necessity for retreat existing, none was ever made on which the troops had such short marches; none on which they made such long and repeated halts; and none on which the retreating armies were so little pressed on their rear by the enemy.

We must look therefore for the existing evils, and for the situation in which we now find the army, to some cause besides those resulting from the operations in which we have been engaged.

I have no hesitation in attributing these evils to the habitual inattention of the Officers of the regiments to their duty, as prescribed by the standing regulations of the Service, and by the orders of this army.

I am far from questioning the zeal, still less the gallantry and spirit of the Officers of the army; and I am quite certain that if their minds can be convinced of the necessity of minute and constant attention to understand, recollect, and carry into execution the orders which have been issued for the performance of their duty, and that the strict performance of this duty is necessary to enable the army to serve the country as it ought to be served, they will in future give their attention to these points.

Unfortunately the inexperience of the Officers of the army has induced many to consider that the period during which an army is on service is one of relaxation from all rule, instead of being, as it is, the period during which of all others every rule for the regulation and control of the conduct of the soldier, for the inspection and care of his arms, ammunition, accoutrements, necessaries, and field equipments, and his horse and horse appointments; for the receipt and issue and care of his provisions; and the regulation of all that belongs to his food and forage for his horse, must be most strictly attended to by the officers of his company or troop, if it is intended that an army, a British army in particular, shall be brought into the field of battle in a state of efficiency to meet the enemy on the day of trial.

These are the points then to which I most earnestly intreat [sic] you to turn your attention, and the attention of the officers of the regiments under your command, Portuguese as well as English, during the period which it may be in my power to leave the troops in their cantonments. The Commanding Officers of regiments must enforce the orders of the army regarding the constant inspection and super-intendence of the officers over the conduct of the men of their com-panies in their cantonments; and they must endeavor [sic] to inspire the non-commissioned officers with a sense of their situation and authority; and the non-commissioned officers must be forced to do their duty by being constantly under the view and superintendence of the officers. By these means the frequent and discreditable recourse to the authority of the provost, and to punishment by the sentence of courts martial, will be prevented, and the soldiers will not dare to commit the offences and outrages of which there are too many com-plaints when they well know that their officers and non-commis-sioned officers have their eyes and attention turned towards them.

The commanding Officers of regiments must likewise enforce the orders of the army regarding the constant, real inspection of the soldiers' arms, ammunition, accoutrements, and necessaries, in order to prevent at all times the shameful waste of ammunition, and the sale of that article and of the soldiers' necessaries. With this view both should be inspected daily.

In regard to the food of the soldier, I have frequently observed and lamented in the late campaign, the facility and celerity with which the French soldiers cooked in comparison with those of our army.

The cause of this disadvantage is the same with that of every other description, the want of attention of the officers to the orders of the army, and the conduct of their men, and the constant want of authority over their conduct. Certain men of each company should be appointed to cut and bring in wood, others to fetch water, and others to get the meat, &c. to be cooked; and it would soon be found that if this practice were daily enforced, and a particular hour for seeing the dinners, and for the men dining, named, as it ought to be, equally as for parade, that cooking would no longer require the inconvenient length of time which it has lately been found to take, and that the soldiers would not be exposed to the privation of their food at the moment at which the army may be engaged in operations with the enemy.

You will of course give your attention to the field exercise and discipline of the troops. It is very desirable that the soldiers should not lose the habits of marching, and the division should march 10 or 12 miles twice in each week, if the weather should permit, and the roads in the neighbourhood of the cantonments of the division should be dry.

But I repeat that the great object of the attention of the General and Field Officers must be to get the Captains and Subalterns of the regiments to understand and perform the duties required from them, as the only mode by which the discipline and efficiency of the army can be restored and maintained during the next campaign.[11]

Not surprisingly, once this memorandum became public, when it was inserted into some of the regimental books, there was a storm of protest, although at least one officer wrote in his diary:

His Lordship's remark [on the want of discipline] is only too just. The cause originates in the officers who certainly have not exhibited, except in the moment of action, the necessary energy in the execution of their duties, and have neglected to enforce discipline amongst their men. This falling off has not, I am proud to say, reached the officers of the artillery, who are doubtless more soldiers by profession than any other part of the army.[12]

Swabey, like most artillery officers, took pride in his superior status as a trained officer, a factor which possibly influenced his judgement of other officers. He also seemed unaware of the misbehaviour that Dickson described, although Dickson certainly enforced discipline on the miscreants.

A more common response was that expressed by Robertson, that he was sure

those who know any thing of the seat of war, or have the least feelings of humanity, considering the sufferings and privations which were endured by the army under his own immediate command, and that under Sir R. Hill, would never have thought that such an order was called for. The opinion of every one was, that as he had committed a blunder in the Burgos affair, he wished to throw the blame of his failure on the army; when it is an indubitable truth that the army did not deserve the imputation thus cast upon it.' Robertson also assumed that Wellington had caused the memorandum to be published in the newspapers 'to divert from himself the censures which he was afraid might be passed on his conduct, on account of his own mismanagement.[13]

This last assertion is questionable, of course, because Wellington had not intended the memorandum for general consumption, and certainly not to appear in the newspapers. Indeed,

Colonel Ponsonby stated that it was not intended to have been made public. This he said as wishing to make the best of an imprudent letter, being written in a hasty moment when vexed with the result of the Campaign.[14]

Hope agreed that the memorandum was composed in a moment of spleen, and if Wellington had waited a few days before sitting down to write, it would never have been written.

As far as the specifics of the memorandum were concerned, many officers took issue with Wellington's claim that the army had suffered no privation except inclement weather. To be in constant rain, night and day, without tents, was no small hardship, as Tomkinson noted when he annotated the copy of the letter which he made in his journal. However, as Gomm remarked, even before Wellington had made his criticisms, 'he did not sleep out at night,'[15] while Sherer wondered whether the commander was even aware of his men's sufferings. This may have been the case, because, as already noted, there is no evidence to suggest that the quarter master general informed Wellington of the route he had chosen for the supplies. Tomkinson also commented on the deficiency of supplies, a point picked up by Aitchison, who asked rhetorically, 'Is it no privation to be without food – absolutely for 24 to 36 hours? ... Is it no hardship to march fourteen hours without food, on the worst of roads in bad weather?'[16] Furthermore, this was a hardship suffered by men and officers alike. Aitchison even defended the drunkenness at Torquemada, the only occasion of widespread drunkenness in the Burgos army, by comparing it with the order that had been given in 1810 to destroy everything on the retreat to the Lines of Torres Vedras, to prevent it falling into enemy hands. Put simply, what was the difference between retreating in Portugal and retreating in Spain?

As for the inefficiencies of the men cooking their food, in comparison with the French, both Tomkinson and Sherer remarked that if the British soldier could help himself to whatever wood was available, including doors and window frames, he would be able to cook as quickly as the French. But 'our orders, on this head, were properly, but particularly strict.'[17] Sherer also pointed out that the French used small kettles, designed to feed two or three men, while the allies had large iron camp kettles for a mess of ten men, so that the actual cooking inevitably took longer. Interestingly, on the next campaign, not only were these replaced by smaller, lighter kettles in the French fashion, but the men were also provided with tents, a recognition, perhaps, that Wellington did indeed appreciate some of the difficulties and privations under which his troops laboured.

The greatest outrage, however, was the general nature of the criticism. As Kincaid wrote,

in consequence of some disgraceful irregularities which took place during the retreat, he immediately after issued an order conveying a sweeping censure of the whole army.[18]

Certainly, in the light division, which prided itself on its profession-alism, it was this general censure which was so bitterly resented. Kincaid pointed out that Wellington could have brought about the dismissal of officers who failed to do their duty, and shot the most disorderly soldiers, but he would also have been obliged to hang the commissary for failing to issue regular rations. Hope added to this point by suggestion that Wellington could have instanced lack of tents, lack of baggage, lack of money and *'the partial failure of the objects of the campaign'*,[19] which were equally the causes of such disorder as there was.

In both his original letter and in his later account, Hope maintained that every officer in his battalion had performed his duty, and every NCO and private had obeyed the officers' commands. Sherer similarly defended his own corps and the many others which had also maintained discipline and where all losses could be satisfactorily accounted for. Aitchison was more specific, claiming that in the 3rd foot guards, including the battalion that was with Hill, order was never lost, and only one man had a complaint made against him. Similarly, the 2/30th, to instance a line regiment, had no man court martialled between May and the end of the year.

As for indiscipline, Donaldson believed that during the worst moments of the retreat

> we had now arrived at that pitch of misery which levels all distinc-tion of rank, and I believe no order would have been obeyed unless that which was prompted by regard to the common safety.[20]

The most impassioned response to the memorandum was written years later by Grattan; and every word conveys his sense of outrage as he sought to convey the realities of the campaign.

> The men who composed this fine army – which at Rodrigo, Badajoz, and Salamanca, carried all before them – were now greatly changed for the worse. Scarcely a man had shoes; not that they were not amply supplied with them before the retreat commenced, but the state of the roads, if roads they could be called, was such, as soon as a shoe fell off or stuck in the mud, in place of picking it up again, the man who had thus lost one kicked its fellow-companion after it. Yet the infantry was efficient, and able to do any duty. No excesses were committed, for Lord Wellington having taken the precaution of keeping the army away from the different villages, no man had an opportunity of obtaining wine or spirits, and thus drunkenness and insubordination were not added to the list of our misfortunes.
>
> But the cavalry and artillery were in a wretched state indeed. The artillery of the third, sixth, and seventh divisions, the heavy cavalry,

together with the 7th [a mistake] and 12th light dragoons, were nearly a wreck; and the artillery of the third division lost seventy horses between Salamanca and Rodrigo. It was next to impossible that the artillery and cavalry could have made, if vigorously pursued, three marches beyond the latter place. What force, then, was to arrest the enemy in his pursuit? – The infantry, and the infantry alone; yet this main-prop of the army was, by mismanagement, left without the means of nourishment! Had not the infantry, by their firmness in bearing up against all the evils they had to surmount – such as bad clothing, no tents to shelter them from the heavy rains that fell, and no means of dressing their food – presented the front they did, the army must have been lost before it could have reached Gallegos; and, if equal zeal had been exhibited by the general officers in providing for the wants of their troops, as was shown by the subordinate officers in the maintenance of discipline amongst them, the letter of Lord Wellington would never have been written.

Blame and praise, if properly employed, make a great change in the actions of a young man – so they do if improperly employed; and this letter of Lord Wellington, directed chiefly against the junior officers of his army, had a bad effect. Those officers asked each other, and asked themselves, how or in what manner they were to blame for the privations the army endured on the retreat? The answer uniformly was, in no way at all. Their business was to keep the men together, and, if possible, to keep up with their men on the march, and this was the most difficult duty they had to perform; for many, very many, of these officers were young lads, badly clothed, with scarcely a shoe or boot to their feet – some, attacked with dysentery, others with ague, and more with a burning fever raging through their system, had scarcely strength left to hobble on in company with their more hardy comrades, the soldiers. Nothing but a high sense of honour could have borne them on; and there were many who would have remained behind, and run all risks as to the manner in which they would be treated as prisoners, were it not for this feeling.[21]

\* \* \*

It would be easy to leave Grattan's defence of the army, particularly the infantry, as a final thought on the Burgos campaign and the subsequent retreat, but as the troops recovered in their cantonments, sheltered, rested and regularly fed, a different mood emerged. A full understanding of what had been achieved in 1812 was only possible retrospectively. Undoubtedly, though, some would have already glimpsed the truth of what Jones wrote in 1821, even before the start of the 1813 campaign, that

This was the most important campaign of the war, as it decidedly changed the relative feelings and strength of the contending parties. Duly to appreciate its merits, it must be recollected that the military means of Spain were never before or subsequently at so low an ebb. The French forces, including those that entered during the summer, exceeded 190,000, and were formidable beyond their actual numbers from the confidence and skill acquired in twenty years of general success. They were moreover in possession of all the fortresses on the line of operations, and commanded by officers of the highest reputation. The amount of the British and Portuguese, including every reinforcement, fell short of 75,000: a portion of which, acting against the general mass, and in actual collision, at various periods, with 130,000 of the French, captured and retained possession of two of the fortresses, and liberated all the southern provinces of Spain; being incontrovertible proof of superiority of tactic and combination, as well as of prowess ... whatever might have been the fate of the rest of continental Europe, the subjugation of the Peninsula was no longer to be apprehended after the operations of 1812.[22]

As 1813 was to prove, this was an army that could achieve great things. The failure at Burgos and the subsequent retreat proved to be temporary setbacks, but even with the withdrawal to Portugal as a seeming defeat, the initiative in the Peninsular War was definitely with Wellington and his army.

## Chapter 13

# The Cost of the Campaign

In this study references to losses sustained by the Anglo-Portuguese army have been included without comment, but the cost to Wellington's army of the siege and the subsequent retreat needs discussion. To start with French claims, it is fairly obvious that these are little more than guesswork. For example, Captain Marcel claimed that the allies lost 800 prisoners at Venta de Pozo, whereas Wellington's return for the period, which includes both that cavalry action, and the 5th division's stand at Villamuriel, gives only 243 'missing'. Nevertheless, such wild claims may still be found in more modern French works; in one such the allies are supposed to have lost 3,000 killed, wounded and missing at Celada del Camino, Villodrigo and Villamuriel[1], a figure with which neither Wellington's returns nor the casualty figures of the regiments involved come anywhere near to justifying. In a similar vein, Soult claimed to have taken between 1,700 and 1,900 prisoners on the three days from 16 to 18 November.

Several diarists made informed guesses as to the losses suffered. Browne, attached to the adjutant general's department, thought that 2,000 men had been lost at Burgos, killed, wounded and missing, and another 2,000 had been taken prisoner during the retreat. Boutflower also thought that the figure for the retreat was about 2,000, but he expected some of these men to return. Webber gave 700 as the figure for the losses taken by the 2nd division, with an estimate of 3,000 as the total loss in dead, wounded and missing. Oman looked at the morning state for 29 November, which covered the period from that date back to 23 October and gave as the figure for rank and file losses, missing or prisoners of war, 2,368 British and 2,374 Portuguese.[2]

However, the casualty returns, which were produced later, suggest that the true figures were somewhat lower, as men were brought in by the cavalry and Julian Sanchez's lancers or made their own way back to their regiments. These returns were produced later, time enough for the 800 men brought in by the cavalry and Julian Sanchez's lancers to return to their regiments. For example, the morning state suggested 357 men had gone missing from the two 'British' brigades in the 7th division (which actually included only two British battalions, the 51st and the 68th) during the period under consideration. The casualty returns, however, record 254. If deserters are added, then the figure does reach only one short of the morning state return. The problem here, though, is that the Brunswick Oels regiment had three companies detached to other divisions. Two were with the 5th division, so it is probable that the fifteen men returned as missing on 25 October were lost at Villamuriel. The 5th division suggests a definite discrepancy between the morning state return and the casualty returns: the former gives a figure of 453 (not including the probable fifteen Brunswick losses at Villamuriel); the latter is 360, even with the addition of ten deserters. This suggests that in two virtually all-British brigades the men made a greater effort to return to their regiments.

Of particular interest in this division are the returns of the first battalion of the 4th foot. Somewhat surprisingly, the casualty returns record only natural deaths. The musters, however, record a fuller story: four men killed, all at Villamuriel, one died of wounds, five missing and thirty-six returned as prisoners of war. What is more interesting, however, is the number whose whereabouts were subsequently established. The muster for 24 December lists seven who had rejoined the battalion, with another two added in the January 1813 muster. A further three had been located in general hospitals, at Vizeu and Celorico, while another two had made their way to Belem. Perhaps the most interesting are the six who reached the depot in England, having escaped from the French. Furthermore, the weak second battalion having returned to England at the beginning of 1813, six 'missing' men from that battalion joined the senior battalion during January. It must be assumed that the 4th was not the only regiment to regain men under these circumstances, further reducing the probable losses.

It is worth noting that the Portuguese troops appear to have suffered proportionately heavier losses than the British troops. This is particularly evident in Bradford's brigade where, according to Oman's figures, the loss between 23 October and 29 November was 764 men from an original strength of 1,645. This brigade, however, had come up from the south and seems to have suffered excessively from the weather and from fatigue. Also the Portuguese went several days longer without provisions than the British battalions. In the 5th division 359 Portuguese were returned as missing or prisoners of war between 23 October and 29 November, but it is possible this number, like the numbers in the two British brigades, would have fallen once all the stragglers had come in.

Obviously the 1,983 casualties enumerated in the official returns (see Appendix III) between 19 September and 21 October seem to justify

Browne's estimate. However, the number of wounded (1,484), which comprises about three-quarters of the total, is problematic since no distinction is made between those who subsequently died of their wounds, those who were sent on to a general hospital, and those who quickly recovered. The point can be made by looking at a group of officers who were at the subsequent action at Villamuriel. Captain Hitchens, Lieutenants Andrews and Brissac, and Ensigns Madden and Tincombe of the 2/30th were all returned wounded in the monthly return for October. Hitchen and Andrews, however, were back with the battalion before the next return in November, and the remaining four officers had rejoined before the December return. Consequently, the number of wounded, although of temporary significance, may not give a valid idea of total losses.

As well as looking at the morning state of 29 November in order to establish the number of men who had gone missing during the preceding thirty-six days, Oman also considered total losses for the same period: 45,003 against 48,124 were present under arms, a loss of over 3,000, while 200 were lost in the artillery, staff etc.[3] He made the point, however, that by 29 November the battalions Skerrett had brought up from Cadiz, the 1st battalion of the 1stt foot guards, both from England, and the 1/82nd from Gibraltar, had arrived as reinforcements. (He also includes the 1/91st, although as we shall see, they had not joined by 29 November.) Nevertheless, as Oman argues, these reinforcements would seem to mask an additional loss of over 5,000 men.

As already suggested, only by analysing the casualty returns is it possible to reach any conclusion on the actual losses, and even then there are problems. The first is the state of the returns. Ink has a tendency to fade and pages become torn, with the result that parts of some returns cannot be deciphered. The returns themselves, though, asked for specific information: a man's company, his name, trade, place of birth, date of enlistment, date when his service with the regiment ended and reason, and the identity of any beneficiaries if there was money owing. Regiments which had been at Walcheren also recorded this fact against a man's name. In theory, then, the casualty returns give all the information needed to identify how many were lost during the period under consideration, and the circumstances. Unfortunately, the reality is rather different. Whereas some battalions made a careful distinction between died a natural death, killed in action and died of wounds, others simply recorded that a man died on a particular date. Some indicated where a man died, in a general hospital for example, but this is only the minority. Nevertheless, in the early stages of the siege at least it was unlikely that a man who died in a general hospital, particularly one of those in Portugal, would have been at Burgos.

Further reasons for a man leaving a regiment were desertion, missing or being taken prisoner. To take just the last two categories, some regiments made a distinction, while others returned men as 'missing/prisoner of war'. As for deserters, these too create a problem, which is best illustrated by considering the two regiments notoriously most prone to desertion, the Chasseurs Britanniques and the Brunswick Oels. During the four days when the army was retreating from Salamanca to Ciudad Rodrigo, the Chasseurs Britanniques returned fifty-two men as deserters, forty-six as missing, and one as a prisoner. Obviously there is no way of establishing how they were able to differentiate between the deserters and the missing; possibly it was based on knowledge of the men themselves. The Brunswickers, who had twice earned Wellington's displeasure, actually returned a small number of casualties during the final stages of the retreat, three deserters and nineteen taken prisoner of war. This was one of the battalions that did not distinguish between missing and prisoners, returning them all in the latter category. The figures suggest an assumption, however, that men missing from the ranks had fallen into French hands with the exception of just three who, for whatever reason, could be confidently identified as deserters.

One set of statistics which can be established from the casualty returns is the total losses, for whatever reason, taken by the British battalions in each division between the beginning of September and 24 November. This covers the period of Wellington's campaign, including some days for the effects of the retreat to be felt. Not surprisingly, of the Burgos divisions the heaviest losses were in the 1st division, who bore the brunt of the siege (just over a thousand from all causes). The 5th and the 7th divisions had similar casualties, about 650 each, although in the 7th division this was as a result of the high desertion rate from the Chasseurs Britanniques and the Brunswickers (assuming that some of the men posted as prisoners in this unit were actually deserters), while the 5th division took heavy losses at Villamuriel. Also, both divisions seem to have suffered from the appalling weather conditions and lack of shelter during the siege. The 6th division, despite being involved in the siege, had only about 330 casualties, but they were not involved in any of the major assaults and had the shelter of the town. Furthermore, they experienced no action like Villamuriel, nor were the men prone to desertion. Obviously, the relative size of the divisions has some significance, although the raw statistics accurately reflect the different experiences of these divisions.

Hill's troops took generally lower casualties, as might be expected. The 3rd and light divisions both returned about 350 losses, while the

4th division was about a hundred less. The exception was the 2nd division. It was not only the largest division; it also did not have a Portuguese brigade. Instead, Hamilton's Portuguese division was attached to it. Nevertheless, the raw figure for the period is about 600 casualties, of which over half were taken after 24 October, thus demonstrating the effect of the actions at Alba de Tormes and Matilla.

Once the troops were safely in the border region around Ciudad Rodrigo, and then cantoned in Portugal, except the 2nd division at Coria, it might be expected that the casualty figures would drop dramatically. However, this is not the case, and suggests that the true cost of the campaign can only be established by looking at the subsequent losses, which were nearly all natural deaths or deaths from wounds, with just a few desertions across all eight divisions. Three divisions, the 2nd, 7th and light, took markedly fewer losses in this second period, two-thirds fewer in the case of the light division, just under half the number of their earlier losses in the 2nd, and about a fifth fewer in the 7th division. This last is easily explained. The returns for natural deaths indicate that the six battalions, particularly the two light divisions of the King's German Legion and the Brunswickers, were particularly healthy. With very low desertion rates for this second period, their losses dropped dramatically. The other divisions returned similar figures across the two periods; the 5th and 6th divisions recorded a drop of about fifty casualties, the 1st division, an increase of just over a hundred, and the 3rd and 4th division lay somewhere between.

One set of documents explains why there was such a limited decrease in casualties during the three months which followed the campaign. These are the (unpublished) papers of James McGrigor, who had arrived in the Peninsular at the beginning of 1812 to serve as surgeon-general to Wellington's army. His first task was to ascertain the state of the general hospitals, and to this end he required reports on a monthly basis. He also needed to establish a working relationship with Wellington so that he would enjoy the support of the commander-in-chief for his proposed improvements in the medical system. This latter objective was not immediately realized. McGrigor, like most able men with a sense of mission, did not always know when circumspection was required. In Madrid, on an occasion when Wellington was sitting for Goya, McGrigor arrived to report how he had dealt with the Salamanca casualties who needed transporting to general hospitals elsewhere. McGrigor's own version continues, 'But when I came to inform him that for their relief I had ordered up purveying and commissary officers, he started up and in a violent manner reprobated what I had done.' McGrigor tried to point out that the needs of the numerous wounded were critical,

But all was in vain. His Lordship was in a passion ... 'I shall be glad to know,' exclaimed his Lordship, 'who is to command the army? I or you? I establish one route for the army, you establish another, and order the commissariat and the supplies by that line. As long as you live, sir, never do so again; never do anything without my orders.'[4]

By the time of Burgos the relationship had changed and McGrigor enjoyed Wellington's trust. When it became obvious that the siege would have to be abandoned, one of Wellington's concerns was for the sick and wounded who could not be moved. McGrigor replied that the sick and wounded were not numerous;

that seeing how his mind was occupied with the siege, I had taken it upon me to get carts from the commissariat, and to employ them and the mules which brought up provisions in removing the sick and wounded to Valladolid. 'Very well indeed,' was his reply; 'but how many have we in Burgos?' 'Not more than sixty, and these mostly too bad to move.' 'Admirable. I shall be off tonight. Let nobody know this from you, and make your own arrangements.'[5]

One of the surgeons who remained to care for those casualties that could not be moved was James Goodall Elkington, assistant surgeon in the 1/24th, who was promised a promotion as a reward for passing into French imprisonment, this being his inevitable fate. Elkington was a resourceful man, however, and once the prisoners were safely in the care of French surgeons, he made his escape. He also received the promised reward, and was promoted surgeon in the 30th foot.

To return to the reports which McGrigor received from the general hospitals, they present a clear picture of the prevalent diseases, the most common being continued, remittant and intermittent fevers, typhus, dysentery and hospital gangrene. Intermittent fever was malaria, while the other two forms comprised a range of fevers, such as typhoid-type diseases, but overall surgeons had only a limited means of identifying different fevers. Typhus was an inevitable result of lice-infested clothing, while dysentery often proved 'fatal to patients recovering from other diseases and to those who from wounds had been a long time in hospital and perhaps to not being able to treat it actively at its onset, from the subjects being too much debilitated by former diseases.' These comments help to explain the high mortality rate even after the campaign was over, but they also demonstrate that some of the losses recorded during the campaign could have been men still recovering from their Salamanca wounds. As for hospital gangrene, a parcel of highly infectious agents, it was first recorded at Coimbra in the autumn of 1812, this being the first incidence McGrigor had heard of in the Peninsula.

McGrigor himself had no doubt what was contributing to the mortality rates.

> During the progress to Ciudad, to Celorico and other places the sick were exposed to severe weather, heavy rain, this in their protracted journeys occasioned Simple Continued Fever and Intermittents, to degenerate into Typhus and Dysenteries and to assume so malignant a character as to baffle the skill of the medical officer, the case frequently proving fatal within a few days sometimes after being committed to his care.

The staff surgeon at Celorico made the same point: 'The heavy rain and bad weather which the sick met with in their progress from Ciudad greatly aggravated the diseases.'

At Ciudad Rodrigo in October there were thirty-four deaths from fevers, three from typhus, twenty from dysentery and eleven from wounds, in each case from hospital gangrene, which was obviously spreading through the general hospitals. At the 'St Bartholomew' hospital in Salamanca during the same month, however, there were sixty-eight deaths from dysentery, while most of the others were from fevers of one kind or another. McGrigor was still at Burgos, where he was concerned by the state of health of the 1st division, noting that

> The violence of many of these attacks seems to have depended and is only to be accounted for, by the increased morbid effects of miasma at the advanced period of the autumnal season, combined with alteration of heat and wet and coldness during the nights which prevailed during the month.

The staff surgeon with the fourth division, at the Escurial, and then at Valdemoro, reported that intermittent fevers and diarrhoeas were the most common complaints, although there were also cases of typhus and dysentery. He identified the 82nd and the 29th as the most unhealthy regiments in the division. Both had been at Walcheren, a reminder of how that ill-fated expedition had undermined the health of those involved.

By November McGrigor was identifying a further problem, the long lines of communication from the front to the general hospitals, and the great distress these caused to the sick and wounded, while also contributing to the heavy mortality. Dysentery continued to be a problem in the general hospitals, causing fifty-seven of the 163 deaths at Lisbon, Castello Branco, Coimbra and Ciudad Rodrigo (forty-six of 108 at Ciudad

Rodrigo). There were also twenty-nine deaths from wounds at Cuidad Rodrigo.

By December the situation might have been expected to improve but, as we have seen from the casualty returns, it did not for most of the divisions. In the 4th division the 82nd continued to be very sickly as they 'recovered from the effects of cold, fatigue, bivouacs on marshy ground, want of clothing, great coats and blankets . . .' This, of course, was not only a Walcheren regiment, but had come up from Gibraltar, so that the change of climate may well have been a factor in their poor health. At Coimbra, 'Dysentery, the scourge of all large armies, came in great numbers and in the most hopeless state from the front,' while at Celorico 'all the cases of this disease suffered much by removal in wet and cold weather.' At the same hospital, 'The fevers were mostly of the typhoid character.' Another problem was the premature removal of amputatees, which led to slough-ing of the wounds and often proved fatal. There was also an implicit criticism of the lack of medical resources. 'The men had been many days without being dressed, exhausted by wet and cold, suffering many severe privations.' The medical establishment was in such straitened circum-stances that there were rarely the three required surgeons per battalion, and there was no spare manpower to accompany the sick to the general hospitals and dress wounds. Like the weather, this was a situation which was out of Wellington's control and which undoubtedly contributed to the casualty figures.

At Vizeu the situation was no better. Fevers tended to develop into typhus of the worst kind, most of which proved fatal, and which the staff surgeon ascribed to 'the fatigue and privations and exposure [the men] underwent during the retrograde movement of the army . . .' McGrigor commented that 'The effects of the retreat began to show . . .'

The reports for January introduced a further factor. Boutflower, who was now staff surgeon with the 4th division, thought that 'the fatigues of the retreat and the want of clothing are the predisposing, and drunken-ness the exciting causes of disease in this division.' A similar comment was made about the 61st regiment in the 6th division; 'excess in the use of new country wine' was linked to a disease showing typhoid symptoms. In the 36th regiment, though, which was in the same division, 'the Con-tinued Fever which prevails has been induced by excessive fatigue and privations during the retreat, the greater part of the men being destitute of shoes and stockings.' To take two more battalions as examples of high sickness rates, the men of the 79th, in the 1st division were suffering from 'fever occasioned by the hardships of the retreat and those which the men suffered before the retreat at the siege of Burgos', while in the 32nd there were several cases of gangrene in the toes which the surgeon had previously associated with the retreat to Corunna.

The corps giving the most concern, however, was the 1st battalion of the 1st foot guards. They had joined Wellington's troops on 25 October after a hard march from Corunna. In the days following dysentery quickly made its appearance, and after the retreat there were many cases of typhus. Many of the subsequent fatalities were ascribed to total exhaustion as well as to the actual diseases. Nor did the situation improve the following month. '... so completely has the 1st Guards been cut by the Fever that [the surgeon] has not yet (three months) seen any individual fairly recovered who had the fever.' At this point the brigade of guards had 400 men in the hospital at Vizeu. Wellington strongly believed that smaller units of acclimatized men were of more use to him than larger units of newcomers who immediately upon their arrival sent large numbers into the hospitals, as was happening with the 1st foot guards. For this reason he fought a determined battle with the Duke of York during the next few months to keep the depleted units that he had formed into provisional battalions.

A comment about the 6th division indicates another reason for high rates of sickness and mortality. As well as instancing the familiar factors of exposure, fatigue, lack of food, and the cold and wet conditions, the staff surgeon included 'debility of body and depression of mind' as causes of illness ... Unfortunately, the means of intoxication were everywhere at hand.'

By February the situation was beginning to improve. Although many men were still in the general hospitals, the mortality rate was falling fast. Hospital gangrene had virtually disappeared, possibly due to the strict hygiene conditions that McGrigor was enforcing, and typhus had adopted a milder form. At Santarem, despite 200 cases of intermittent fever and seventy of dysentery, there were only twenty deaths. Of the seventy-eight fever patients at Abrantes, only eight died while at Alter de Chão there were three deaths among seventy-two dysentery and fever cases. These low death rates were repeated in the other general hospitals, although soldiers were still dying of wounds at Ciudad Rodrigo and the 1st foot guards continued to cause great concern. There were 140 deaths in this battalion and of the hundred men who rejoined the battalion, forty subsequently died. Also, a further disease made its appearance, pneumonia, which was described as 'very much the disease of soldiers'. But the worst was over.

Furthermore, there were some generals who had taken their own measures to deal with the problem. General Frederick Robinson took command of the 2nd brigade of the 5th division in the spring of 1813. He wrote to his sister:

The Army has been dreadfully sickly until within the last fortnight, the men are now recovering fast – One battalion of Guards that joined the Army in October last in front of Salamanca, has buried near 700 men in the course of the winter – my old regt [38th] buried 150 in this town [Lamego], yet in no place are the Officers sickly, on the contrary they are very healthy, and therefore as young and old underwent the same hardships and privations as the men during the retreat, the cause of such a difference must be a striking one; I ventured my opinion on it to Lord W. – and I think I clearly proved to him, that Kitchin physick was what the men wanted to restore their constitutions, that the ration was not enough with men who required every possible means to recruit their strength, and who had not money to purchase little comforts – That all the cases were declared by the Medical Staff to arise from poverty of blood and debilitation, for which reason every patient died of a putrid fever of the most fatal kind. – The first thing I did on joining my Brigade was to examine the state of the Mens Messes, and the Hospitals; and oblige the reluctant Commissary to issue good Wine, instead of bad Rum, Bread instead of Biscuit, and Two Ounces of Rice per man each day to put in their soup – which makes it as *smooth* as Mollys – I tasted one kettlefull so often the other day that the men began to look D-sh sulky, but my putting down a twelve sous piece to buy some *salt* restored their smiles – I have been reaping the benefit of these regulations for ten days at least – 150 men have been restored to the ranks, and no more new cases have occurred than would have happened in any other country – This will prove to you, that good feeding has been all along wanting.[6]

To sum up, when considering the cost of the campaign, not only is it necessary to acknowledge Wellington's miscalculation in laying siege to Burgos, but also the effects of the unseasonal weather, the failings of the commissariat, and more specifically the quarter master general, and the inadequate provision for the sick and the wounded. Since Colonel Willoughby Gordon had been foisted on him thanks to his connections in high places, none of these three factors can be directly ascribed to Wellington himself.

The point has been made that men returned as 'missing' might later rejoin. The same applied to supposed deserters, and there are several cases of this happening. The following example, from the artillery who had gone missing, however, represents an extreme illustration of the point.

On 24 October Alexander Dickson signed a 'Return of Non Commissioned Officers & Gunners of the Royal Artillery belonging to the Reserve that have been missing since the night of the 21st inst. There were two sergeants, six gunners and a driver on the list. The driver, who was in charge of three horses, was supposed to have deserted to the enemy. The whereabouts of the other men was unknown. Eventually, Dickson received a letter explaining the mystery, and written at Braganza on 16 November.

Sir,

I wrote you from Sagun [Sahagun]. Mentioned how I marcht. I will give you the undermentioned stages. The night before I left the camp before Burgus [Burgos] 21st October, to march for Valladelid [Valladolid] I went two much to my right, following the different baggage of the army.

I marcht to Oremellas Commo [Hornillos del Camino] 22nd October. At a leat hour I applyed to the General Commanding the 5th division for his directions, how to march. He ordered me to march for Belevester [Benavente] without delay which I accordingly did.

Being 23rd on my march to Bellvesto [Benavente]. On the same day the enemy being close upon me I was ordered, both by British and Spanish Officers Commanding the rear guard of the 3rd Dragoons to strick into the mountains and keep to my right till I could make Valledolid. If I did not thy told me I should certainly fall into the hands of the enemy as there advance guard was two or three miles in our front.

I accordingly tooke there drections, and by the best information I could get both from Spainsh Officers and the Alcaldys of the different villageses in the mountains, I keept to my right. I reach Sagun being unwilling that any of the stores in my charge should fall into there hands.

Statement of my different stages:-

October 23.  St Maria Delmarro Dano
    24.  Santoyo
    25.  Amayas de Arieben [Amayuelas de Arriba]
    26.  Carrion
    27.  Le Dioyes [Ledigos]
    28.  Sagun, this being the place I was drected to make on leaveing the high road on the 23rd of October.

I was then ordered by the Commadant to make for Resack [Rioseco] that being the place of rendezvous for all Spanish stranglers and likewise British from Burgus. I accordinly received my drections, being my dirict road for Valledolid. On the 29th reacht Soreata. I had one Government oxen dieyed.

30th reached Billy Lone [Villalón] 3 legues from Reosack, the place of rendevoues.

At a late hour a Spainsh officer arived with intillegance that the French would be in Reosack that evening, and gave orders for all British, Spainsh, & Portuguese soldiers to leave the town immedantly. It being the place of my distenation, I did not no how to acte. I emmedantly called on the Alcaldeys for his directions, where to make for. He then gave me stages for León, saying I could make for no other place, or fall into the enemys hands.

I accordinly marcht for León in compy with a number of other cars belonging to different regiments, that was forced to take the mountains the same day as me.

| October | 31. | Reached Mandistortes. One horse & one oxen deyed. |
| November | 1. | Santer Martes |
| | 2. | Le Mansilla |
| | 3. | Leon |
| | 4. | Wating for a pass port which I recived on the evening of the 4th instant. |
| | 5. | Marched by a rout recived from the Commadant for Puble de Senabria [Puebla de Sanabria] where he told me I shoueld meet with English Officers and than I shoueld be abble to get every information I could wish for. Reached Birgen de Camina [La Virgen del Camino] |
| | 6. | La Baneza |
| | 7. | Pimela. One oxen deyed |
| | 8. | Cubo [Cubo de Benavente]. One oxen deyed |
| | 9. | Bumbo [Mombuey] |
| | 10. | Asterianos [Asturianos] |
| | 11. | Bubla de Senabrica [Puebla de Sanabria]. 2 oxen deyed. |
| | 12. | Peteralva |
| | 13. | Bassall [Baçal, Portugal] |
| | 14. | Brganza where I meet with Colonel Meade commding, 91st first regiment of foot which he have detained me until further orders, allso all the detachments of British that is come this road. |

Sir, I will thank you to sende a rout to joine my Compy with the stores, as I am very uneasy to joine it and you.

Return of the ammunition and stores in my charge.

Round shot   18 pounder      121
Do. Do.          9 pounder       60
Cartridges filled with      9 pounder 93 at 3lbs each.
  powder                  24 Pr. for howitzers – 28 at 2 lbs each.
Tin funnels   Large 3
              Small 2
Beams and scales with weights – sets 2
Tin powder measures   One of three lbs. two of 2 lbs.
Spare Washers 6.   Linchpins 6.
Copper powder measures   11
Cork Scru    1

|                    |                          |     |
|--------------------|--------------------------|-----|
|                    | (Parchment 18 Pounders   | 75  |
|                    | (Flannel do.             | 20  |
| Empty Cartridges   | (9 pounders              | 34  |
|                    | (24 pounders for 2 lbs.  | 196 |
|                    | (For a French howitzer   | 76  |

Primming irons   8
One pair of large Bellessoes [bellows]
Harness for 2 horses – sets 2
Round tent of Captain Powers
Government oxen 17 Do. one horse & 9 cars.
Serjeant Parkington and Gunner Holder have been very ill during the march. They are at present very wake.

A List of the Detachment

| Serjeants | David McLeran       | Captain Glubbs Compy., 5th battn.   |
|-----------|---------------------|-------------------------------------|
|           | John Parkington     |                                     |
| Gunners   | Thomas Gosselin     |                                     |
|           | Samuel Holder       |                                     |
|           | Ronald Miller       |                                     |
| Gunners   | J. Thompson         | Lt Colonel Mays Campy., 1st battn.  |
|           | David Doncaster     |                                     |

I am Sir, your hunbel servant,
(sd) David McLeran
Serjt. Royal Artillery

On the back of the letter was a further note, written at Villa Nova del Foscoa on 2 December, which explains that he was unable to send the letter because he could not find an officer to take or post it. He is now on the march to Coimbra with the 91st on Lieutenant Colonel Meade's orders, even though he explained that he needed to march to Almeida. He finishes: 'I ame exciding sorey that I cane not joine the Compy. I hope you cause me to joine it. Excues this as I had no time to write a nuther.' [7] He also adds that another gunner of Mays' company joined them at Braganza.

One assumes that Sergeant McLeran and his party eventually joined Dickson. But they were not alone in having become seriously detached from the main army during the retreat, as McLeran makes clear in his reference to other detachments, and this explains why morning states, monthly returns and even the musters may give a very inaccurate picture of how many men were actually lost during the campaign.

*Appendix I*

# Engineers' and Artillery Means for the Attack

**Engineers' means for the attack**

### OFFICERS

Lieutenant-Colonel Burgoyne, commanding.
_____ John T. Jones (severely wounded)
Captain J. A. Williams (killed)
Lieutenant Pitts
_____ Reid

Ten officers, volunteers, to act as engineers, and 81 soldiers of the line, being either miners, carpenters, or masons, or volunteers, joined the department on the day of the investment; and there were present eight rank and file of the corps of Royal military artificers.

A party of 200 men was also at the same time selected from the troops, to make fascines and gabions.

### PARK

The engineers' park was formed under the shelter of the heights between Villa Toro and the castle, and contained

| | |
|---|---|
| Picks and shovels . . . . . . . . . . . . . . . . | 600 |
| Felling axes . . . . . . . . . . . . . . . . . . . . . | 100 |
| Bill-hooks . . . . . . . . . . . . . . . . . . . . . . . | 200 |

With a few small tools and stores, being a proportion carried on fifty mules, with the head-quarters of the army.

A few days subsequently to the investment, a depot of French tools and sand-bags was found in the town of Burgos, and moved to the park. A portion of the artificers were employed constantly in the park, throughout the siege, in superintending the making of fascines and gabions, and cutting plank for platforms. The remainder went on duty in the trenches with the officers.

**Artillery means for the Attack**

### OFFICERS

Lieutenant-Colonel Robe, commanding
_____ Dickson, in charge of the reserve
Captain Power
Lieutenant Robe
_____ Pascoe
_____ Elgee
_____ Haugh
Captain C. Blatchley, joined 1st October
_____ Gardiner )
_____ Dansey  )Alternate days from
_____ Greene  )the field-brigades
Lieutenant Monro)
Major Ariga, and 5 subalterns, Portuguese artillery

### NON-COMMISSIONED OFFICERS AND GUNNERS

British . . . . . . . . . . . . . . . . . . . . . . . . . . 90
Portuguese  . . . . . . . . . . . . . . . . . . . . . . 57

### ORDNANCE AND AMMUNITION

The park was formed near Villa Toro, and contained-

18-pounder guns . . . . . . . . . . . . . . . .      3
24-pounder iron howitzers . . . . . . . . .      5
24-pounder round shot  . . . . . . . . . . .    900
24-pounder common shells  . . . . . . . .    208
24-pounder spherical case  . . . . . . . . .    236
18-pounder round shot  . . . . . . . . . . . 1,306
Do. Spherical case . . . . . . . . . . . . . .    100

(From Sir T. Jones' Journal of the Sieges in Spain, 272–4)

# Wellington's Memoranda for the Siege of Burgos

**Plan for the attack of the exterior line of the Castle of Burgos**
22nd Sept. 1812

1. Lieut. Colonel Brown to take possession of the houses along the south front as soon as it is dark.
2. He is to be supplied with 12 axes, which are to be sent to him by a person who will certainly find him this night.
3. The 400 men of the 1st division ordered to be in readiness, are to move as soon as the moon rises, and to proceed to the fleche immediately on the right, looking from the camp, of the horn work. Lieut. Colonel Burgoyne will take care that there is an officer to conduct them to the spot.
4. They are then to take up the ladders and 12 axes, and are to proceed and place themselves under cover of the banks opposite the exterior line of the castle.
5. At 11 p.m. 200 men of this party are to move forward to storm the wall of the exterior line at the place pointed out by officers to be named by Lieut. Colonel Burgoyne. The remaining 200 men are to be formed behind the bank, and are to protect by their fire the advance of the party to storm. The storming party are to consist of 30 men, to carry five long ladders, 12 men with axes, and then one officer and 20 men, who are to mount the ladders, to be followed immediately by 50 more as soon as the ladders are planted, and then by the remainder of the party of 200 appointed to storm.
6. At ten minutes before eleven, Colonel Brown is to order 130 men of the troops under his command to move out from the houses on the south front of the castle. They are to pass the small ditch, etc., and are to move up to the palisade, which they are to cut down, and open a communication with the storming party, which will move to the front of the line.
7. These men are to protect the right of the storming party, being themselves covered by the palisade; and Colonel Brown will direct that

a heavy fire may be kept up from the houses to be occupied his troops on the enemy's interior line.

8. As soon as the enemy are driven from the interior line, and the storming party are established in the guard house, and a communication established with Colonel Brown's detachments, the 200 men in reserve behind the bank are to be employed at work in laying open the wall, and securing the storming party on the ground before morning.

### Memorandum

Villa Toro, 29th Sept., 1812

The mine to be exploded this night at twelve o'clock.

The covering party in the trenches, which is ordered to be augmented in the evening to 300 men, and the working party must be moved into the village before the mine is sprung, excepting 100 men of the covering party, who are to remain in the parallel to the right and left.

As soon as the mine shall be exploded, the breach which it will have made must be stormed.

The 100 men who are to remain in the parallel while the mine shall explode, are to be the storming party.

An officer and twenty men are to advance immediately from the right of the parallel to the breach; keeping on their left the trench leading to the breach of the mine.

The 20 are to be supported by 50 more of the 100, which 50 are to advance as soon as the leaders of the first party shall have ascended the breach.

That part of the covering party which shall have been sent to the village before the mine shall be exploded are to return, and form in the parallel as soon as the explosion shall take place, and the storming party must be supported on the breach.

The working party must be in readiness to establish the party on the breach.

The Field Officer will take care to tell off his parties according to these orders; and that the officers commanding each party understand clearly what he is to do; where he is to go; and at what time.

In case the enemy should commence a fire from the parapet on the leaders of the storming party, the 80 men which are to remain in the parallel till they shall mount the breach, are to fire upon the parapet so as to keep down the fire of the enemy.

The field officer of the day, on the hill of San Miguel, is to move a detachment of 50 men into the hollow way between the horn work and the castle, at about eleven at night. This detachment will move up and make a false attack on the gate leading from the exterior line to the esplanade in front of the castle, as soon as the mine shall explode. Lieut. Colonel Brown shall likewise keep up a fire from the houses on the enemy's left of the exterior line; and will make a false attack on the church, etc., at the moment of the explosion; and if he can, he will get possession of the house still held by the enemy.

He will keep up a fire on the palisades in front of the gateway of the interior line.

### Memorandum for Lieut. Colonel Burgoyne, Royal Engineers
Villa Toro, 4th October, 1812

The mine in the exterior line is to be exploded this evening at [blank] o'clock.

The 24th regiment is to be employed to storm the breaches made in the exterior line by the explosion of the mine, and by the fire of the artillery.

The storming party for each breach is to be formed of one officer and 20 men; who are to rush forward to the breaches as soon as the mine shall explode. These are to be supported by 50 men for each breach; who are not to move out of the parallel till they shall see the leading men of the storming parties ascend the breaches. The remainder of the regiment to remain in the parallel, in readiness to support those who shall be in the breach.

The covering party in the parallel of the exterior line must keep up a fire on the parapet, so as to keep down the fire of the enemy. The breaching and other batteries are to enfilade the exterior line, and the second and other lines, so as to support the attack.

Lieut. Colonel Brown will fire on the rear of the enemy's new palisade, and will make a false attack from the village; and if possible, get along the wall inside either palisade, which he will break through.

As soon as the storming party shall have entered the breach made by the mine, they are to turn to the left, and break through the palisade, and communicate with the storming party of the old breach.The working party and engineers will be prepared to establish the parties in the breaches.

Colonel Kelly will tell off the parties for these several services; and they will be ready to rush forward the moment the mine shall explode.

## Memorandum

To Lieut. Colonel Burgoyne, for the attack of the enemy's second line.
Villa Toro, 18th October, 1812

1. The enemy's second line is to be attacked this afternoon at half past four.
2. The mine under the church of San Roman is to be exploded at that hour; and Colonel Brown will immediately order an officer and 20 men of the troops under his command to rush forward, and establish themselves on the breach which the mine shall have made. An officer and 50 men will be in readiness to support these.
3. Colonel Brown will have the effects of the mine well reconnoitred; and if he should find that it is practicable to enter the second line after his troops shall have been established on the emplacement of the church, he shall order them to do so; and establish them within the second line, communicating by his left with the troops which shall attack the second line from the piles of shot.
4. If Colonel Brown should find that he cannot enter the second line, he will keep a fire on it from the emplacement of the church.
5. Six ladders of 18 feet long must be sent to Colonel Brown.
6. The troops of the 6th division, cantoned in Burgos, must be under arms to support the attack upon the second line, if it should be necessary.
7. When the mine shall explode at half past four, a camp colour will be displayed on the hill to the west of the castle; which is to be the signal for the attack on the other parts of the line. At four o'clock, the parallel along the parapet of the 1st line must be fully occupied.
8. When the signal shall be made, an officer and 20 men, who must previously be placed in the sap leading to the palisade in front of the gate of the second line, are to rush forward and drive the enemy from behind that palisade; and follow them into the covered way.
9. The sap must be immediately reoccupied by an officer and 30 men, who are to protect the rear and right flank of the detachment which shall have entered the covert way.
10. At the same time, an officer and 40 men, 18 of them carrying ladders, must rush forward from the left breach in the first line to the shot piles, where they will descend the ditch, which they shall pass, at the places where the palisades have been destroyed by our shot. They are then to scale the line at that point.
11. An officer and 50 men are to be in readiness at the trench in the first line, to rush forward to the shot piles as soon as the first party which shall have gone there shall have advanced from thence. These troops

are to support the storming party; and are to move on from the cover of the shot piles as soon as they shall find the head of the storming party established on the parapet of the second line. These men are to carry with them three ladders.

12. Fifty men must be in readiness to move up to the shot piles, as soon as the 50 ordered in paragraph 11 shall have moved forward to the escalade. These are likewise to carry three ladders.

13. As soon as the party shall have succeeded in the escalade, they are to turn to their left, and communicate with those who shall storm the breach in the second line.

14. As soon as the party shall have escaladed the line, the 30 men ordered into the sap are to endeavor [sic] to force the gate of the second line; and if they should succeed, to communicate by their left with the party which shall escalade.

15. Three hundred and fifty men of the relief for the trenches this evening must go down under the command of a field officer, so as to be in the trenches at three in the afternoon. As soon as they shall arrive, the whole of the covering party now in the trenches, which shall be on the left, are to go down to the right; and the left of the trenches and the horn work shall be occupied by the relieving party.

16. When the signal shall be made that the mine is sprung, an officer and 20 men are to rush forward from the advanced trench to storm the breach.

17. Fifty men are to be in readiness to follow these, and are to move out as soon as the head of the 1st detachment shall have ascended the breach.

18. One hundred men are to be in readiness in the advanced trench to support the storming party in the breach. But they are not to leave the trench till the storming party shall be established on the breach; and then only in case support should be wanted.

19. When the storming party shall enter the breach, they must turn along the parapet to the left, and drive the enemy from the stockade which he has established there.

20. The troops formed in the parallel along the parapet of the first line, and in the trenches under the horn work, must keep up a fire during the storm on the enemy's third line and the castle, so as to keep down the fire of the enemy.

21. Lieut. Colonel Burgoyne will convey these orders to the field officer in the trenches; and he will see that they are carried into execution according to the intentions of the Commander of the Forces on the right. Lieut. Colonel Sturgeon will convey these orders to the field officer commanding the relief for the trenches ordered by the 15th paragraph, to be there at three o'clock; and he will see that all the

arrangements ordered are made, and that the intentions of the Commander of the Forces are carried into execution on the left.

## Memorandum

For General Pack, for the Blockade of Burgos.
Villa Toro, 20th October, 1812

1. While the enemy shall be in force in front of the army, Brig. General Pack will take charge of the blockade of Burgos, keeping possession of the ground which has been acquired during the siege. He will have under his command, besides his own brigade, the 24th and 58th regiments, Colonel Brown's battalion of caçadores, the 11th, 53rd, and 61st regiments, and the Spanish battalions of Asturias and Guadalaxara [sic], which are in the town of Burgos.
2. The guns, howitzers, and ammunition now in the trenches, are to be brought down this night, for which purpose a working party of 200 men must be ordered for this evening at 5 p.m.
3. Orders will be sent to Colonel Robe regarding the disposal of the artillery and ammunition.
4. Orders will likewise be sent for the 11th, 53rd, and 61st regiments to go round and occupy the bivouac lately occupied by the brigade of Guards.
5. Brig. General Pack, and all the troops under his command, will be in readiness to march at a moment's notice, with the exception of 500 men, in their due proportions of English and Portuguese troops, to relief the trenches at the hour of the next relief, and Colonel Brown's battalion of caçadores, and the two battalions of Spanish infantry. The officer who shall take General Pack his orders will show him the road he is to march.
6. When General Pack shall move, he is to give charge of the blockade to Colonel Brown, who will concert measures with Lieut. Colonel Burgoyne to preserve all the ground gained.
7. General Pack will settle with the Commandant of the Spanish troops, to take some of the duties in the town, now taken by the caçadores.
8. All the avenues from the town to the castle should be barricaded.
9. One of the French guns and an howitzer might be left in the right hand battery, in order to give the enemy a shot occasionally, and to check sorties. An officer and artillerymen of the reserve must remain for this purpose.
10. The Engineer officer must load the mines in the horn work, and these mines must be sprung, if by any accident it should be necessary to withdraw from the trenches.

## Memorandum

For Colonel Robe for the removal of guns

1. The guns and howitzers now in the batteries are to be moved down this night, with the exception of a French gun and howitzer, to be left in the right hand battery, to give the enemy a shot occasionally, and to check sorties.
2. Those howitzers that are serviceable, with their ammunition, must be sent to Riobena.
3. The 18 pounder guns, with their ammunition, and the unserviceable howitzers, are to be sent, as soon as they shall be brought down, through Quintana-dueñas as far as the neighbourhood of Villalon. They are there to halt, 200 yards short of the village, where they will not be seen from the Castle of Burgos.
4. The reserve ammunition of the field train should be sent this evening to the same place; and to-morrow morning before daylight it should march by Tardajoz to Frantovinez.

*Appendix III*

# Official Return of Killed, Wounded and Missing

19 September to 19 November

|  | Killed | Wounded | Missing |
|---|---|---|---|
| 19 Sept | 71 | 333 | 16 |
| 20 to 26 Sept | 59 | 289 | – |
| 27 Sept to 5 Oct | 76 | 323 | 4 |
| 6 to 10 Oct | 127 | 292 | 18 |
| 11 to 17 Oct | 28 | 73 | – |
| 18 to 21 Oct | 96 | 174 | 4 |
| 22 to 29 Oct | 127 | 522 | 243 |
| 10 to 11 Nov | 21 | 92 | – |
| 15 to 19 Nov | 50 | 139 | 178 |
|  | 655 | 2,237 | 463 |

# Notes

## Chapter 1

1. Dispatches of the Duke of Wellington IX, 355.
2. Dispatches IX, 359.
3. The Letters of Private Wheeler, 94.
4. Leach, Captain of the 95th (Rifles), 177.
5. Dispatches IX, 254–5.
6. Dispatches IX, 256.
7. Dispatches IX, 256–7.
8. Despatches IX, 301–2.
9. Dispatches IX, 299.
10. Girod de l'Ain, Vie Militaire du Général Foy, 178.

## Chapter 2

1. Lachouque *et al.*, Napoleon's War in Spain, 145.
2. Girod de l'Ain, 192.
3. Lachouque, 145.

## Chapter 3

1. Lachouque *et al.*, Napoleon's War in Spain, 149.
2. Dispatches of the Duke of Wellington IX 318.
3. Joseph Bonaparte, Correspondence IX, 45–7.
4. Dispatches IX, 370.
5. Girod de l'Ain, Vie Militaire du Général Foy.
6. Dispatches IX, 375.
7. D'Espinchal, Souvenirs Militaire II, 39–41.
8. Dispatches IX, 320–1.
9. Gleig, The life of Arthur Duke of Wellington, 175–6.

## Chapter 4

1. Thompson, An Ensign in the Peninsular War, 190.
2. Thompson, 195.
3. Daniell, Journal of an Officer, 162.
4. Green, The Vicissitudes of a Soldier's Life, 111.
5. Dispatches of the Duke of Wellington IX, 393.
6. Dispatches IX, 394.
7. Thompson, 196.
8. The Letters of Colonel George Bingham.
9. Mills, For King and Country, 214.
10. Douglas, A Soldier's Tale, 50–1.

11. Thompson, 197–8.
12. Thompson, 197.
13. Mills, 218.
14. Thompson, 197.
15. Life of Sir William Maynard Gomm, 287.
16. Daniell, 164.
17. Dispatches IX, 397.
18. Dispatches IX, 398.
19. Page, Intelligence Officer in the Peninsula, 192–3.
20. Dispatches IX, 409.
21. Mills, 220.
22. Letters of George Ridout Bingham.
23. Letters of Private Wheeler, 98.
24. Douglas, 51.
25. Green, 111.
26. Tomkinson, Diary of a Cavalry Officer, 212–3.
27. Green, 112.
28. Dispatches IX, 423.
29. Supplementary Dispatches and Memoranda of Field Marshal Arthur, Duke of Wellington, 420–1.
30. Tomkinson, 203.
31. Tomkinson, 204.
32. Mills, 223.
33. Dispatches IX, 428.
34. Green, 112.
35. Dispatches, IX 430.
36. Tomkinson, 204.
37. The Napoleonic War Journal of Captain Thomas Henry Browne, 185.
38. Mills, 225.
39. Browne, 185–6.
40. Tomkinson, 204.
41. Daniell, 166.
42. D'Urban, The Peninsular Journal, 287.
43. Browne, 186.
44. Green, 113.
45. Browne, 186–7.
46. Jones, Account of the War in Spain and Portugal II, 125.
47. The Dickson Manuscripts IV, 134.

### Chapter 5

1. Jones, Journal of Sieges in Spain I, 278–9.
2. Page, Intelligence Officer in the Peninsula, 195.
3. Tomkinson, Diary of a Cavalry Officer, 206–7.
4. Jones, Journal I, 280.
5. Dispatches of the Duke of Wellington IX, 437.
6. Dispatches IX, 442.
7. Dispatches IX, 438–9.
8. Jones, Journal I, 284–5.
9. Mills, For King and Country, 229.
10. The Letters of Colonel George Bingham.

11. Jones, Journal I, 285.
12. Dispatches IX, 273–4.
13. Dispatches IX, 455.
14. Dyneley, Letters Written while on Active Service, 55.
15. D'Urban, The Peninsular Journal, 288.
16. Jones, Journal I, 290.
17. The Letters of 2nd Captain Charles Dansey R.A., 55.
18. Jones, Journal I, 290.
19. Jones, Journal I, 289.
20. Dispatches IX, 450.
21. Dispatches IX, 453.
22. Jones, Journal I, 294.
23. Jones, Journal I, 296.
24. Jones, Journal I, 297.
25. Thompson, An Ensign in the Peninsula, 203.
26. The Dickson Manuscripts IV, 750.
27. Jones, Journal I, 300–1.
28. Dickson IV, 751.
29. Dispatches IX, 464–5.
30. Tomkinson, 208–9.
31. Bingham.
32. Jones, Journal I, 307.
33. Mills, 238–9.
34. Bingham.
35. D'Urban, 290.
36. D'Urbam, 290–1.
37. Dispatches IX, 470.
38. Mills, 240.
39. Rous, A Guards Officer in the Peninsula, 37.
40. Tomkinson, 204.
41. Jones, Journal I, 313.
42. Tomkinson, 209–10.
43. Dispatches IX, 479–85.
44. Dispatches IX, 478–9.
45. Life of Sir William Maynard Gomm, 287.
46. Ross-Lewin, With the 32nd in the Peninsula, 144.
47. Supplementary Dispatches of the Duke of Wellington, 452.
48. Thompson, 207.
49. Dispatches IX, 487.
50. Green, The Vicissitudes of a Soldier's Life, 114.
51. Mills, 241.
52. Jones, Journal I, 326–7.
53. Mills, 243–4.
54. Dispatches IX, 512–3.
55. Dispatches IX, 513.
56. Letters of Private Wheeler, 99.
57. Gomm, 288.
58. Dispatches IX, 509.
59. Jones, Account of the War in Spain and Portugal II, 133.
60. Burroughs, Retreat from Burgos, 1–3.

61. Daniell, Journal of an Officer, 173.
62. Thompson, 208–9.
63. Jones, Account II, 129.
64. Jones, Journal I, 334–6.
65. Gleig, Life of Arthur Duke of Wellington, 179.
66. Gomm, 291.
67. Marcel, Campanes en Espagne et au Portugal, 145.
68. Dispatches IX, 515.
69. Jones, Journal I, ix.

**Chapter 6**

1. D'Espinchal, Souvenirs Militaire II, 42.
2. Lachouque *et al.*, Napolean's War in Spain, 149.
3. Webber, With the Guns in the Peninsula, 45.
4. Hope, Campaigns with Hill and Wellington, 103.
5. Webber, 46–9.
6. D'Espinchal II, 44.
7. Webber, 47–9.
8. Dispatches IX, 405.
9. Dispatches IX, 418.
10. Swabey, Diary of Campaigns in the Peninsular, 132.
11. D'Espinchal II, 45.
12. Webber, 58.
13. Sherer, Recollections of the Peninsula.
14. Webber, 64–5.
15. Swabey, 135.
16. Dispatches IX, 442.
17. D'Espinchal II, 46.
18. Hope, 105.
19. Swabey, 137.
20. Hope, 107.
21. Webber, 73.
22. Dispatches IX, 463–4.
23. D'Espinchal, 46–7.
24. Dispatches IX, 469.
25. Sherer, 211.
26. Dispatches, 480–1.
27. Supplementary Dispatches of the Duke of Wellington, 451–2.
28. Supplementary Dispatches, 459.
29. Webber, 92.

**Chapter 7**

1. Burroughs, Retreat from Burgos, 14–15.
2. Burroughs, 16.
3. The Napoleonic War Journal of Captain Thomas Henry Browne, 189.
4. The Letters of 2nd Captain Charles Dansey R.A., 58.
5. Supplementary Dispatches of the Duke of Wellington, 464–5.
6. Dispatches of the Duke of Wellington IX, 516.
7. Marcel, Campagnes en Espagne et au Portugal, 145–6.
8. Douglas, A Soldier's Tale, 55–6.

9. Letters of Private Wheeler, 106.
10. Mockler-Ferryman, Life of a Regimental Officer during the Great War, 220.
11. The Dickson Manuscripts IV, 712.
12. Letters of Colonel George Bingham.
13. Douglas, 56–7.
14. Burroughs, 17–18.
15. Daniell, An Officer's Journal, 74–5.
16. Girod de l'Ain, La Vie du Général Foy, 381.
17. Douglas, 57–8.
18. The Journal of James Hale, 98.
19. Napier, History of the War in the Peninsula V, 301.
20. Dispatches IX, 517.
21. Douglas, 59.
22. Hale, 99.
23. Supplementary Dispatches, 465.
24. Life of Sir William Maynard Gomm, 289.
25. Dickson IV, 712.
26. Burroughs, 25.
27. Napier V 304 – NB prone to exaggeration, but conditions were to deteriorate as the retreat continued. See also, Hill's retreat.
28. Burroughs, 27.
20. Dispatches IX, 518.
30. Daniell, 177.
31. Wheeler, 100.
32. Burroughs, 30.
33. Mills, 251.
34. Girod de l'Ain, 382.
35. Dispatches IX, 522.
36. Dispatches IX, 523–4.
37. Thompson, An Ensign in the Peninsula, 215.
38. Mockler-Ferryman, 217–8.
39. Gomm, 289–90.
40. Dansey 53.
41. Hay, Reminiscences 1808–1815 under Wellington, 76–7.
42. Dispatches IX, 532.
43. Leith Hay, A Narrative of the Peninsular War II, 93.
44. The Private Journal of F.S. Larpent I, 35–6.
45. Dispatches IX, 539.
46. Letters of Colonel George Bingham.
47. Dispatches IX, 544.

## Chapter 8

1. D'Urban, 293.
2. Wood, The Subaltern Officer, 144.
3. D'Espinchal, 63.
4. D'Espinchal, Souvenir Militaire II, 63.
5. Boutflower, The Journal of an Army Surgeon during the Peninsular War, 63.
6. Hope, Campaigns with Hill and Wellington, 111–2.
7. Kincaid, Adventures with the Rifle Brigade, 85.
8. Bell, Soldier's Glory, 51.

9. Dispatches of the Duke of Wellington IX, 519.
10. Journal of Sergeant D. Robertson, 85–6.
11. Bell, 52.
12. Hope, 113.
13. D'Espinchal II, 65.
14. Swabey, Dairy of Campaigns in the Peninsula, 151.
15. Webber, With the Guns in the Peninsula, 101.
16. Leach, Captain of the 95th Rifles, 177.
17. Swabey, 152–3.
18. Kincaid, 86.
19. Sherer, Recollections of the Peninsula, 215–6.
20. Swabey, 155.
21. Wood, 149–5.
22. Boutflower, 167.
23. Swabey, 155.
24. Boutflower, 167–8.
25. Cooke, A True Soldier Gentleman, 168.
26. Bell.
27. Burroughs, 44.
28. Swabey, 155–6.
29. Dispatches, 545.
30. Cooke, 169.
31. Duffield Cooke, At Wellington's Headquarters, 30.

**Chapter 9**
1. Dispatches of the Duke of Wellington IX, 548.
2. Leith Hay, A Narrative of the Peninsular War II, 96.
3. Larpent, 39.
4. Dispatches of the Duke of Wellington IX, 546–9.
5. D'Espinchal, Souvenirs Militaire II, 71.
6. Journal of Sergeant D. Robertson, 87–8.
7. Leith Hay, A Narrative of the Peninsular War II, 96–7.
8. Hope, Campaigns with Hill and Wellington, 114.
9. Memorials of the Late War I, 101
10. Dispatches IX, 558–9.
11. Dispatches IX, 551.
12. This man has been variously identified over the years.
13. Memorials I, 101-2.
14. Robertson, 88.
15. Cooke, A True Soldier Gentleman, 169.
16. D'Espinchal II, 72.
17. Leith Hay II, 101.
18. Thompson, An Ensign in the Peninsula, 218.
19. Burroughs, Retreat from Burgos, 55–6.
20. Thompson, 218.
21. Cooke, 170.

**Chapter 10**
1. Dispatches of the Duke of Wellington IX, 560.
2. Daniell, Journal of an officer, 181.

3. Dispatches IX, 560.
4. Journal of Sergeant D. Robertson, 279.
5. Leith Hay, A Narrative of the Peninsular War II, 104.
6. Robertson, 89.
7. Burroughs, Retreat from Burgos, 59.
8. Webber, With the Guns, 114.
9. Robertson, 89.
10. Hathaway, Costello – the True Story of a Peninsular War Rifleman, 200–1.
11. D'Espinchal, Souvenir Militaire II, 72–3.
12. Girod de l'Ain, La Vie du Général Foy.
13. D'Espinchal II, 73.
14. Burroughs, 61–2.
15. Simmons, A British Rifleman, 256.
16. Brown, Narrative of a Soldier, 190–1.
17. Robertson, 90.
18. General Orders, Vol. IV, Spain and Portugal, 209.
19. Kincaid, Adventures in the Rifle Brigade, 90.
20. The Napoleonic War Journal of Captain Thomas Henry Browne, 194–5.
21. Ross-Lewin, With the 32nd in the Peninsular and Other Campaigns, 147.
22. Sherer, Recollections of the Peninsular, 220.
23. D'Espinchal II, 75.
24. Webber, 115.
25. Sherer, 221.
26. Donaldson, Life of a Soldier, 282–4.
27. Bell, Soldier's Glory, 146–7.
28. Dobbs, Recollections of an Old 52nd Man, 45.
29. Cooke, A True Soldier Gentleman, 171–2.
30. Burroughs, 63–4.
31. Dispatches, 556–7.
32. Cooke, 172.
33. Webber, 116.
34. Swabey, 157.
35. Dyneley, Letters Written while on Active Service, 57–8.
36. Green, The Vicissitudes of a Soldier's Life, 127–8.
37. Burroughs, 68–9.
38. Clarke Kennedy, Attack the Colour, 66.
39. Kincaid, 92.
40. D'Urban, The Peninsular Journal, 300.
41. Supplementary Dispatches of the Duke of Wellington, 494.
42. Green, 130.
43. Burroughs, 77–9.
44. Letters of Colonel George Bingham.
45. Dyneley, 57.
46. Hope, The Iberian and Waterloo Campaigns, 118–9.
47. Hope, Campaigns with Hill and Wellington, 117.
48. The Life of Sir William Maynard Gomm.
49. Patterson, Camp and Quarters II, 170–1.
50. Leith Hay II, 108.
51. Brown, Narrative of a Soldier, 191.
52. Wood, The Subaltern Officer.

**Chapter 11**

1. Lachouque *et al.*, Napoleon's War in Spain, 152.
2. D'Espinchal, Souvenirs Militaire II, 85.
3. Grattan, Adventures with the Connaught Rangers II, 143.
4. Cadell, Slashers, 91.
5. Napier, History of the War in the Peninsula V, 328–9.
6. Hayman, Soult – Napoleon's Maligned Marshal, 183.
7. Stanhope, Conversations with the Duke of Wellington, 20.
8. Oman, History of the Peninsular War VI, 590.
9. Girod de l'Ain, 193.

**Chapter 12**

1. Dispatches of the Duke of Wellington IX, 562.
2. Dispatches IX, 570–4.
3. Supplementary Dispatches of the Duke of Wellington, 477–8.
4. Supplementary Dispatches, 479–80.
5. Life of Sir William Maynard Gomm, 290–1.
6. Patterson, Camp and Quarters II, 167–8.
7. Bell, Soldier's Glory, 59.
8. D'Urban, The Peninsular Journal, 301.
9. Grattan II, 141.
10. Thompson, An Ensign in the Peninsula, 223.
11. Dispatches IX, 582–5.
12. Swabey, Diary of Campaigns in the Peninsula, 166.
13. The Journal of Sergeant D. Robertson, 82.
14. Tomkinson, The Diary of a Cavalry Officer, 228.
15. Gomm, 290.
16. Thompson, 228.
17. Sherer, Recollections of the Peninsula, 224.
18. Kincaid, Adventures in the Rifle Brigade, 94.
19. Hope, Campaigns with Hill and Wellington, 118.
20. Donaldson, Life of a Soldier, 257.
21. Grattan II, 150–2.
22. Jones, Account of the War in Spain and Portugal II, 141–2.

**Chapter 13**

1. Lachouque *et al.*, Napoleon's War in Spain, 50.
2. Oman, History of the Peninsular war VI, 747.
3. Oman VI 746.
4. Blanco, Wellington's Surgeon-General, 130–1.
5. Gleig, Life of the Duke of Wellington, 181.
6. Robinson, J.S.A.H.R. 1956, 159.
7. Dickson, MS 774–7.

# Select Bibliography

**National Army Museum Sources**
6807/163 The Letters of Colonel George Ridout Bingham.

**The National Archives**
WO12 – Pay and Muster Lists.
WO17 – Monthly Returns.
WO25 – Casualty Returns.

**Aberdeen Medico-Chirurgical Society Library**
Sir James McGrigor Papers.

**Primary Sources**
*Dispatches of the Duke of Wellington, Vol. IX.*
*Supplementary Dispatches of Field Marshal Arthur, Duke of Wellington.*
*General Orders, Vol. IV, Spain and Portugal January–December 1812.*
*The Military Chronicle, Vols. I–V (1810–1813).*
Aitchison, John (W.F.K. Thompson ed.), *An Ensign in the Peninsula* (Michael Joseph 1981).
Anon, *British Cavalry on the Peninsula* (Mark Thompson Publishing 1996, reprint).
Beamish, N. Ludlow, *History of the King's German Legion, Vol. II* (Naval & Military Press 1997, reprint).
Bell, George, *Soldier's Glory* (Spellmount 1991 reprint).
Belmas, Jacques Vidal, *Précis des Campagnes et des Sieges d'Espagne et de Portugal,* (BiblioBazaar 2009 reprint).
Boutflower, Charles, *The Journal of an Army Surgeon during the Peninsular War,* (Spellmount 1997 reprint).
Brown, William, *The Narrative of a Soldier* (J. Paterson 1829).
Browne, Thomas Henry (Roger Norman Buckley ed.), *The Napoleonic War Journal of Thomas Henry Browne* (The Bodley Head for the Army Records Society 1987).
Burroughs, George Frederick, *A Narrative of the Retreat of the British Army from Burgos* (T. Egerton 1814).
Cadell, Charles, *The Slashers: the Campaigns of the 28th Regiment* (Leonaur 2008 reprint).
Daniell, T., *Journal of an Officer in the Commissariat Department* (London 1820).
Dansey, Charles (Gareth Glover ed.), *The Letters of 2nd Captain Charles Dansey R.A.* (Ken Trotman 2006).
D'Espinchal, Hippolyte, *Souvenirs Militaires, Vol. II* (Frédéric Masson et François Boyer 1901).
Dickson, Alexander (J.H. Leslie ed.), *The Dickson Manuscripts, Vol. IV,* (Ken Trotman 1987 Reprint).
Dobbs, John, *Recollections of an Old 52nd Man* (Spellmount 2000 reprint).
Donaldson, Joseph, *The Eventful Life of a Soldier* (William Tait 1827).

Douglas, John (Stanley Monick ed.), *Tale of the Peninsula and Waterloo* (Leo Cooper 1997 Reprint).

Duffield Cooke, Robert (Gareth Glover ed.), *At Wellington's Headquarters* (Ken Trotman 2009).

D'Urban, Benjamin, *The Peninsular Journal* (Greenhill Books 1998 reprint).

Dyneley, Thomas, *Letters Written by Lieutenant-General Thomas Dyneley C.B. R.A.* (Ken Trotman 1984 reprint).

Gomm, William Maynard (Francis Culling Carr-Gomm ed.), *Life of Field Marshal Sir William Maynard Gomm* (John Murray 1881).

Grattan, William, *Adventures of the Connaught Rangers, Vol. II* (Henry Colburn 1847).

Green, John, *The Vicissitudes of a Soldier's Life* (Ken Trotman 1996 reprint).

Hale, James (P. Catley ed.), *The Journal of James Hale* (IX Regiment 1998 reprint).

Hamilton, Anthony, *Hamilton's Campaign with Moore and Wellington* (Spellmount 1998 reprint).

Hay, William, *Reminiscences 1808–1815 under Wellington* (Ken Trotman 1992 reprint).

Hope, James Archibald, *Campaigns with Hill and Wellington* (Leonair 2010 reprint).

Hope, James Archibald (Stanley Monick ed.), *The Iberian & Waterloo Campaigns: the Letters of Lt James Hope* (Naval & Military Press 2000 reprint).

Jones, John T., *Account of the War in Spain, Portugal and the South of France, Vol. II* (T. Egerton 1821).

Jones, John T., *Journal of the Sieges Carried on by the Army under the Duke of Wellington in Spain, Vol. I* (Ken Trotman 1998 reprint).

Kincaid, John, *Adventures in the Rifle Brigade* (Leo Cooper 1997 reprint).

Larpent, F.S., *Private Journal of F.S. Larpent, Vol. I* (Richard Bentley 1853).

Leach, Jonathan, *Captain of the 95th Rifles* (Leonaur 2005 reprint).

Leith-Hay, Andrew, *A Narrative of the Peninsular War, Vol. II* (Henry Washbourne 1834).

Lowry Cole, Galbraith, *Memoirs of Sir Lowry Cole* (Ken Trotman 2003 reprint).

Marcel, Nicolas, *Campagnes en Espagnes et au Portugal* (Éditions du Grenadier 2001).

Mills, John, (Ian Fletcher ed.), *For King and Country* (Spellmount 1995).

Patterson, John, *Camp and Quarters, Scenes and Impressions of Military Life, Vol. II* (Saunders & Otley 1840).

Robertson, Duncan, *The Journal of Sergeant D. Robertson, late 92nd Foot* (Maggs 1982 reprint).

Robinson, Frederick, *The Letters of General Frederick Robinson from the Peninsula* (The Journal of the Society of Army Historical Research, 1956).

Ross-Lewin, Harry, *With the 'Thirty-Second' in the Peninsula and Other Campaigns* (Leonaur 2010 reprint).

Rous, John (Ian Fletcher ed.), *A Guards Officer in the Peninsula* (Spellmount 1992).

Sherer, Moyle, *Recollections of the Peninsula* (Spellmount 1996 reprint).

Simmons, George, *A British Rifleman* (Greenhill Books 1986 reprint).

Swabey, William, *Diary of Campaigns in the Peninsula* (Ken Trotman 1984).

Tomkinson, William, *Diary of a Cavalry Officer* (Swann Sonneschien & Co, 1894).

Webber, William (Richard Henry Wollocombe ed.), *With the Guns in the Peninsula* (Greenhill Books 1991).

Wheeler, William (B.H. Liddell Hart ed.), *The Letters of Private Wheeler* (The Windrush Press 1993 reprint).

Wood, George, *The Subaltern* (Ken Trotman 1986 reprint).

**Secondary Sources**

Blanco, Richard, *Wellington's Surgeon General* (Duke University Press 1974).

Butler, Lewis, *Wellington's Operations in the Peninsula, Vol. II* (T. Fisher Unwin 1904).

Chandler, David, *Napoleon's Marshals* (Weidenfeld & Nicholson 1987).

Clark-Kennedy, A.E., *Attack the Colour!* (The Research Publishing Company 1975).

Esdaile, Charles, *The Peninsular War* (Allen Lane 2002).

Esdaile, Charles, *Peninsular Eyewitnesses* (Pen & Sword 2008).

Fletcher, Ian, *Galloping at Everything* (Spellmount 1999).

Fletcher Ian (ed.), *The Peninsular War, Aspects of the Struggle for the Iberian Peninsula* (Spellmount 1998).

Fortescue, John, *A History of the British Army, Vol. VIII* (Naval & Military Press 2004 reprint).

Girod de l'Ain, Maurice, *Vie Militaire du Général Foy* (E. Plon, Nourrit et Cie 1900).

Gleig, George Robert, *Life of the Duke of Wellington* (Longman, Green, Reader & Dyer 1869).

Hall, John A., *A History of the Peninsular War, Vol. VIII: The Biographical Dictionary of British Officers Killed and Wounded* (Greenhill Books 1998).

Hathaway, Eileen, *A True Soldier Gentleman* (Shinglepicker 2000).

Hathaway, Eileen, *A True Story of a Peninsular Rifleman* (Shinglepicker 1997).

Hayman, Peter, *Soult, Napoleon's Maligned Marshal* (Arms and Armour 1990).

Hill, Joanna, *Wellington's Right Hand Man* (The History Press – no date).

Holmes, Richard, *Wellington, The Iron Duke* (Harper Collins 2002).

Humble, Richard, *Napoleon's Peninsular Marshals* (Macdonald & Jane's 1974).

James, Lawrence, *The Iron Duke, a Military Biography of Wellington* (George Weidenfeld & Nicholson 1992).

Lachouque, Henri, Tranie, Jean, Camigniani J.-C., (J.S. Mallender & J.R. Clements trans), *Napoleon's War in Spain* (Arms & Armour Press 1982).

Lipscombe, Nick, *The Peninsular War Atlas* (Osprey 2010).

Longford, Elizabeth, *Wellington, the Years of the Sword* (Weidenfeld & Nicholson 1962).

Lorblanchès, Jean-Claude, *Les Soldats de Napoleon en Espagne et au Portugal* (L'Harmattan 2007).

Myatt, Frederick, *British Sieges of the Peninsular War* (Spellmount 1987).

Napier, William, *History of the War in the Peninsular and in the South of France, Vol. V* (Constable 1993 reprint).

Oman, Charles, *A History of the Peninsular War, Vol. V and VI* (Greenhill Books 1995 reprint).

Page, Julia, *Intelligence Officer in the Peninsula* (Spellmount 1986).

Pivka, Otto von, Brunswick Troops 1809–1815 (Osprey 1985).

Mockler-Ferryman A.F., *The Life of a Regimental Officers during the Great War 1793–1815* (William Blackwood & Sons 1913).

# Index